BravO!

To Nancy Macdonald,
   A fellow opera enthusiast.
My best wishes,
   Rosemary Cunningham

BravO!

THE HISTORY OF OPERA IN BRITISH COLUMBIA

ROSEMARY CUNNINGHAM

HARBOUR PUBLISHING

IN MEMORIAM
John R. "Cut" Cunningham, Q.C.
1922–2002

Harbour Publishing Co. Ltd.
P.O. Box 219, Madeira Park, BC, V0N 2H0
www.harbourpublishing.com

Edited by Meg Taylor
Dust jacket and text design by Five Seventeen, PicaPica.ca
Dust jacket photograph by Tim Matheson: Sarastro, King of the Sun, played by Kevin Short, in
        Vancouver Opera's production of *The Magic Flute*, 2007.
Title page photograph by Tim Matheson: Hwang Sin Nyung plays the Queen of the Night
        in the Vancouver Opera's 2007 production of *The Magic Flute*. The costumes were designed by
        Christine Reimer and John Powell.
All Barry Glass photographs are courtesy of the Barry Glass Estate.

Printed on paper containing 10% PCW recycled stock using soy-based inks
Printed and bound in Canada

Harbour Publishing acknowledges financial support from the Government of Canada through the
Book Publishing Industry Development Program and the Canada Council for the Arts, and from
the Province of British Columbia through the BC Arts Council and the Book Publishing Tax Credit.

LIBRARY AND ARCHIVES CANADA CATALOGUING IN PUBLICATION

Cunningham, Rosemary, 1928–
        Bravo! : the history of opera in British Columbia / by Rosemary Cunningham.

Includes index.
ISBN 978-1-55017-486-1

        1. Opera—British Columbia—History. I. Title.

ML1713.7.B8C973 2009   782.10971'1   C2009-904038-7

Contents

Preface

the first full performance in Victoria took place in 1877 and in Vancouver in 1891. Since then, opera in BC has survived two world wars, the Great Depression and numerous financial setbacks. On the threshold of the fiftieth anniversary of Vancouver Opera and the thirtieth anniversary of Pacific Opera Victoria in 2010, opera lovers celebrate the success of this unique art form in the province. The popularity of BC's two major opera companies, as well as the proliferation of new operas and opera groups in the province, is a testament to this success.

I believe the reason for opera's enduring popularity lies in its inspired combination of theatre and music, which has the power to transport us to heights of imagination and emotion no other form of entertainment can match. When this happens, the memory of such an experience remains long after the performance is over. I first felt this when, as a girl barely into my teens, I was taken to a performance of *Aida* by the San Carlo Opera Company in the Strand Theatre in Vancouver. I have never forgotten that production and the intensity of the feelings it evoked in me.

Another reason for opera's enduring appeal can be found in the universal themes that operas are built on: from the earliest works to those written in this century, composers and librettists have taken as their subjects stories that revolve around the human condition, portraying the full spectrum of emotions—love, jealousy, joy, anger, grief, courage, greed and more. Many will recall a *La Bohème* or a *Rigoletto* that made them weep, a *Marriage of Figaro* or a *Barber of Seville* that delighted them with its wit and comic nonsense, a *Magic Flute* that transported them to an exotic and enchanted world or a *Macbeth* that revealed the twisted minds of those who lust for power. These works were written in the late-eighteenth and nineteenth centuries, but composers of twentieth-century opera

◄   The view of the stunning painted dome and opulent stage from the upper balcony of the Orpheum Theatre in Vancouver, restored to its original Spanish Baroque elegance in 1976. Between 1927 and 1959, the theatre was the venue for many early operas in the city.

continue with universal themes: for example, the struggle of the individual against the mob in Benjamin Britten's *Peter Grimes*, or the temptation of easy money in *The Rake's Progress* by Igor Stravinsky. Filmmakers have recognized the power of opera to evoke strong emotions and have used it effectively in movies such as *Moonstruck* (1987), *Philadelphia* (1993) and *Milk* (2008).

A number of years passed between my first live opera experience and the next, which proved to be equally memorable. In 1958, the first Vancouver International Festival staged Mozart's *Don Giovanni*, bringing Joan Sutherland from Covent Garden in London to make her North American debut in her first major role, Donna Anna, with big-name singers George London (the Don) and Léopold Simoneau (Don Ottavio). Few of us in the audience knew much about Sutherland, but by the end of her performance, no one was in any doubt about her great talent. During the late 1960s and 70s, while attending university as a mature student with three teenaged daughters at home, I had little time to indulge my passion; recordings and "Saturday Afternoon at the Opera" on CBC Radio had to suffice. When these demands eased, I began to attend live performances again, and over the years my enjoyment grew. Nevertheless, until I decided to write this book, I gave little thought to what went into the production of an opera.

Hillary Clinton popularized the African saying: "It takes a village to raise a child"; I have learned that it takes a small town to produce an opera. From the outset, before a company decides what to stage—planning from three to

▲ Audrey Stottler as Turandot poses her riddles to Renzo Zulian, who plays Calaf, her suitor, in this Act 2 scene from *Turandot*, VO, 2005. TIM MATHESON PHOTOGRAPH

five years into the future—a myriad of factors have already been considered at the board and administrative levels: the availability of singers, conductors and stage directors; opportunities for collaboration with other opera companies; the budget; and sponsors. Once the process begins, a production team and an army of backstage people with special talents go into high gear to ensure that sets, lighting, costumes, music for the orchestra and the conductor, and libretti are ready when rehearsals begin. And when newer imaging or sound techniques are used to enhance a production, a separate set of professionals is required. An opera to be sung in a difficult language, such as Czech or Russian, will require language coaches; no matter what language an opera is sung in, even English, surtitles must be prepared in-house or purchased.

The marketing people will be busy with promotional material, designing the opera's program and arranging community events beforehand. The loyal volunteers are vital, taking some of the workload on their shoulders. These are some of the unsung heroes of opera production that deserve our recognition and respect.

In the past few years, I have travelled to hear the productions of other companies. Only last year I sat for the first time in the Metropolitan Opera House at Lincoln Center in New York and heard a live Metropolitan Opera performance. I also attended my first production of the Canadian Opera Company in Toronto's new Four Seasons Centre for the Performing Arts. Thrilling as these productions were, I returned home full of pride in Vancouver Opera and Pacific Opera Victoria. As I write this, both

▲ Deception reigns in this ensemble scene which occurs late in Act 2 of VO's 2005 production of *Cosi Fan Tutte*. The singers are left to right John Tessier (Ferrando), Ute Selbig (Fiordiligi), Thomas Goerz (Don Alphonso), Kathleen Brett (Notary/Despina), and Kimberly Barber (Dorabella). TIM MATHESON PHOTOGRAPH

Bravo!

companies have announced their 2009–10 season. Pacific Opera Victoria, expanding to a four-opera season for the first time, will present *La Traviata*, *The Rake's Progress*, Richard Strauss's *Capriccio* (a one-act piece never before staged in BC) and *Così Fan Tutte*. Vancouver Opera's fiftieth anniversary season will include *Norma*, *Nixon in China*, *The Marriage of Figaro* and *Madama Butterfly*. The 2009–10 season promises to be a wonderful year for opera lovers. I hope to see you there.

Many have contributed to the creation of this book and deserve my gratitude. Those who made time for me to interview them willingly shared their memories and provided valuable historical perspective. Their names appear in the Selected Resources section, but I especially want to

single out Irving Guttman, whom I consider my muse and new-found friend. Irving has always shared his vast knowledge of opera, and he consented to read my manuscript. Similarly, Doug Tuck of Vancouver Opera has been so helpful in many ways, especially by giving me access to VO's archival photographs. I could not have completed this project without his support.

Brenda Glass Alexander, a singer in the VO Chorus, allowed me to delve into her late father's collection of photographs taken at early VO productions and has waived any copyright fee; for all her co-operation I thank her most sincerely. Bette Cosar, also a member of the VO Chorus, let me peruse her extensive collection of VO memorabilia. She loaned me several fine photographs from the 1993 production of *Dialogues of the Carmelites*, which I had

▲ Gregory Dahlas Ping, the Grand Chancellor, watches as the servant girl, Liù, played by Sally Diblee is captured by Turandot's guards The action occurs in Act 3 of VO's 2005 production of *Turandot*. TIM MATHESON PHOTOGRAPH

not seen elsewhere. Kate Hutchinson gave
me access to Modern Baroque Opera
photographs without charge. Yukiko
Onley offered her photos of MBO's
production of *120 Songs for the Marquis de
Sade*. Lech Janaszek photographed early
Pacific Opera Victoria productions and
has been most generous in sharing them
with me. Christine Reimer and John
Powell, costume designers who worked
together on the costumes for VO's *The
Magic Flute*, have kindly allowed me to
use their wonderful drawings. Nicolette
McIntosh donated her collection of
early Vancouver Opera programs and
memorabilia. VO volunteers Pat Hancock
and Susan LePage contributed to the
research for Appendix A.

Pacific Opera Victoria personnel have
been extremely willing to help. David
Shefsiek, the Executive Director, has
been a strong supporter and graciously
agreed to read the completed manuscript.
His comments were useful and much
appreciated. Barbara Foubister, POV's
Executive Secretary, has been goodness
itself, facilitating my visits to the office
in Victoria and answering my numerous
emails. Patrick Corrigan and Maureen
Woodall have been especially helpful with
archival images. Erika Kurth, Honorary
Life Member of Pacific Opera Victoria,
has unearthed some rare POV production
photographs, and Sandy Henderson at
the Victoria Conservatory of Music has
digitalized them for me; sincere thanks
to them.

Thanks to those who gave their consent
to quote from material for which they hold
copyright. Every effort has been made to
give credit to copyright owners for text and
image inclusions, but in the event of any
omissions, I would be glad to hear of them.

Thanks, also, to the staff of the City
of Vancouver Archives and the Vancouver
Public Library, who were always helpful.

Bouquets to Meg Taylor, my editor,
and Ruth Gaskill, my copy editor, who
have made my initiation into their area
of expertise such a pleasant, painless
experience.

Finally, I extend my loving
appreciation to my friends and family,
who have always been encouraging and
supportive.

ROSEMARY CUNNINGHAM
MAY 2009

▲ A scene from *Wozzeck*, POV, 2003 starring Theodore
Baerg in the title role and Jean Stilwell as Marie.
DAVID COOPER PHOTOGRAPH

Bravo!

Prologue
FROM MANTUA TO VICTORIA

OPERA ORIGINATED IN ITALY AT THE END OF THE SIXTEENTH CENTURY AS a new form of court entertainment for royalty and the nobility. Its antecedents were the dramatic music of the Greeks, liturgical drama and the Italian intermedio, a musical interlude comprising dancing, scenery and stage effects that took place between acts of a theatrical performance. Donald Jay Grout, the illustrious authority on all matters operatic, passes over Jacopo Peri, who wrote *Dafne* in 1597, and maintains that "Claudio Monteverdi's *Orfeo*, first performed in Mantua in 1607, has earned its composer the title of founder of opera . . . *Orfeo* represents the first attempt to apply the full resources of the art of music to drama, which is what opera is generally acknowledged to be."[1] *Orfeo* fell into the category of "opera seria," a term coined later that characterized most of the Italian operas written for the next one hundred years. Opera seria was typically of a "serious subject of heroic nature, treated in grandiose proportions and employing the utmost resources of singing, orchestral music, and staging."[2] Recitative as opposed to spoken dialogue was another distinction. Today opera seria has become commonly known as "grand opera."

As demand for opera arose from the ranks of the lower classes, works about commonplace people and situations, often comical, began to be written for public performances to appeal to the new Italian audiences, and the first public opera house opened in Venice in 1637. These works for ordinary folk became known as "opera buffa," a genre in which satire and parody, as well as comedy, were employed to engage the audience's sympathy for the easily recognizable frailties and idiosyncrasies of human nature; dialogue was usually spoken. From the Italian opera buffa, the French developed their own "opéra comique"; today we use "comic opera" to describe such works.

◄ A 1912 street scene showing the exterior of the Vancouver Opera House, 759 Granville Street.
CITY OF VANCOUVER ARCHIVES PHOTOGRAPH A24976

The popularity of Italian opera seria and opera buffa soon spread to other European countries, most notably France, Germany and England, during the second half of the seventeenth century, but in each country composers drew on their musical and theatrical traditions—the ballet in France, the singspiel in Germany and the masque in England—to put a unique national stamp on their works. The French were the most averse to wholehearted acceptance of Italian opera and were slow to create their own until Louis XIV extended his patronage to establish a national opera during the 1670s. French and German opera flourished while undergoing numerous transformations from the early forms, but English national opera, after the death of Henry Purcell in 1695, suffered a decline of almost two hundred years. English audiences had to be content with Italian, German and French operas until the appearance on the operatic scene of Dame Ethel Smyth, whose work *The Wreckers*, first performed in 1906, signalled an end to the drought.

Although opera was performed in most of the other European countries during the eighteenth century, most of those that produced famous composers of national opera—namely Russia, Czechoslovakia, Hungary and Austria—did not do so until the nineteenth century.

Opera in the United States during the colonial period, 1600 to 1775, and afterward was imported from Europe, but in 1845, William Henry Fry's *Leonora*, the

first operatic work by a composer born in America, was publicly performed in Philadelphia with modest success. Much later, Canadian impresarios with access to suitable theatres followed a similar pattern of relying on foreign opera. From 1839 onward, famous European singers and touring companies, mainly but not exclusively from the United States, expanded their US itineraries to give concerts and perform complete operas in Montreal, Quebec City, Ottawa and Toronto. Gradually, as transportation improved and opened up the country, more western cities—Winnipeg, Regina, Victoria and Vancouver—were added to the tours, but it was not until the middle of the twentieth century that Canada's human and financial resources were adequate to support professional opera companies and composers.

It may surprise many readers to learn that, despite the small population of Victoria and its remote island location, opera performances in British Columbia by professional touring companies took place there from 1867 on. The city was officially declared the capital of the Colony of British Columbia in January 1867, and remained so when BC joined Confederation in 1871; that year the city's population was 3,270 and by 1881 it had grown to 5,925. Situated on Vancouver Island, it could be reached only by sea, and, although cargo and passenger vessels were sailing between the mainland and Vancouver Island before the mid-1800s, most of the early British and

Scottish settlers who made up the core of the stable population had made the arduous sea journey via the Strait of Magellan or Cape Horn, or from San Francisco after an overland journey from New York. These people, augmented by the music-loving crew and officers of the naval station at Esquimalt, were the audiences that filled the old Royal Theatre at Government and View.

The Royal, opened in January 1860, was a two-storey frame building with an unpretentious entrance reached from a small platform raised above the wooden sidewalk and the unpaved street. A month after the opening, the theatre was closed for renovations, reopening in June 1860 as the Victoria Theatre. Prior to the opening, the following appeared in the *Colonist*, April 10, 1860: "The Theatre has been fitted up in elegant style, with Parquette and Pit, the Parquette enlarged, with cushioned seats; also New and Beautiful Scenery, Chandeliers, etc., etc. The Proprietor [Mr. Wilcox] also will ensure the patrons of the Royal that the theatre will be opened in a manner that the elite of Victoria may be induced to patronize and that on no consideration Indians will be admitted."[3] As well as Indians, "people of colour" were also refused admittance, which led to a violent riot at the theatre, reported in the press on November 6, 1860. During the early months of the following year, the theatre was gutted and refurbished, and reopened in June 1861. After further remodelling in 1867, it reopened and became known once more as the Royal Theatre. The Royal served the community until 1882, when, in serious disrepair, it was demolished. Although a new Victoria Theatre was erected in 1885 at Douglas and View streets, nothing really suitable as an opera house existed until a new Royal Theatre opened in 1913 at 805 Broughton Street.

The last half of the nineteenth century, particularly the 1870s and 1880s, was the golden age of the touring opera company. At least thirty such groups, of which "more than a third were led by determined and talented females," travelled the length and

▲ The cast and crew of an unidentified company's production of *Madama Butterfly* on the stage of the Victoria Theatre, c. 1890s. BRITISH COLUMBIA ARCHIVES PHOTOGRAPH E_01419

Bravo!

breadth of the United States and sometimes included Victoria in their itinerary when on the West Coast.[4] The first visiting opera company to play the Royal/Victoria was the Bianchi Italian Opera Company of San Francisco, who appeared in September 1867 for approximately two weeks performing selections from *L'Elisir d'Amore* (*The Elixir of Love*, Gaetano Donizetti) and *Il Trovatore* (*The Troubadour*, Giuseppe Verdi), *Norma* (Vincenzo Bellini), *La Sonnambula* (*The Sleepwalker*, Bellini), *Lucia di Lammermoor* (Donizetti), *Ernani* (Verdi), *La Traviata* (Verdi) and *The Barber of Seville* (*Il Barbiere di Siviglia*, Gioachino Rossini). In a review of one of the performances, the *Colonist*, on September 9, 1867, reported, "Of the orchestral accompaniment, candor compels us to say that it was far from good, and but for the efficiency and presence of mind of the vocalists, would have rendered the entertainment a partial failure." After an interval of nearly ten years, during which no other touring company visited Victoria, the Bianchi company returned to perform selections from *La Traviata*, *Il Trovatore*, *Don Pasquale* (Donizetti) and *L'Elisir d'Amore* on January 13, 14, 15 and 17, 1876. The performance on January 17 was described in the *Colonist*, January 19, 1876, as follows: "The farewell performance of the Marston-Bianchi Italian Opera Troupe . . . was more successful in point of singing if not in attendance, than others. The entertainment comprised the third act of Donizetti's 'L'Elisir d'Amore' and four acts of 'Il Trovatore' in which the company

appearing in appropriate costume, and apparently singing and acting with increased vigor and feeling, won rounds of hearty applause."

The distinction of being the first company to present a complete opera production in the province appears to belong to the English and Comic Opera Company, featuring the famous soprano, Miss Jennie Winston.[5] The company was in Victoria from April 16 to 23, 1877, and in its mixed repertoire were three operas: *La Sonnambula*, *Martha* (Friedrich von Flotow) and *La Fille du Régiment* (*The Daughter of the Regiment*, Donizetti). Victoria's enthusiastic welcome to Miss Winston was reported in the *Colonist*, April 17, 1877: "Theatre Royal was crowded by a fashionable audience, who had assembled to witness 'La Sonnambula' . . . the beautiful soprano entranced and held people spellbound." The next month saw the arrival of Mlle. Ilma De Murska and her Great Opera Company, who, on May 18 and 19, 1877, staged two performances of *Il Trovatore* at the Victoria Theatre. De Murska was nicknamed "the Croatian Nightingale" and was one of the most celebrated operatic singers in Europe.[6] Victorian audiences fell in love with her in the role of Leonora, as reviewed in the *Colonist*, May 19, 1877: "The wonderful sweetness of her voice, and the excellent control she exercised over it, established her a great favourite." Next to arrive in Victoria in 1877 was the Richings-Bernard Opera Company, who put on a mixed

program of opera and operetta between October 19 and November 1. Its opera repertoire, from the *Colonist*, October 2, 1887, comprised *Martha*, *Il Trovatore*, *Faust* (Charles Gounod), *La Traviata*, *Lucia di Lammermoor* and *The Marriage of Figaro* (*Le Nozze di Figaro*, Mozart). During subsequent years to 1899, most of the companies that visited Victoria performed operettas, but several notable troupes staged full-scale productions of grand opera. The *Colonist* of November 2, 1881, reported that the Inez Fabbri Grand English Opera Company would be in Victoria at the Royal from November 3 to 9, 1881, to stage *Il Trovatore*, *Faust*, *Martha*, *Lucrezia Borgia* (Donizetti), *Carmen* (Georges Bizet) and *Lucia di Lammermoor* with full chorus and orchestra. In February 1887, the Emma Abbott Grand English Opera Company was reported to arrive (*Colonist*, January 30, 1887) and, for three consecutive evenings at the Victoria Theatre, put on *La Traviata*, *Martha* and *Il Trovatore*. The company returned in 1888 to present a mixed program of opera and operetta. Although two operas were scheduled, only *Il Trovatore* was actually performed; *Faust* was cancelled and a Gilbert and Sullivan operetta was substituted, according to the *Colonist*, November 11, 1888. The newspaper reported on February 9, 1890, that the Emma Juch Grand Opera Company would appear in Victoria in early February to present *Faust*, *Der Freischütz* (*The Free-Shooter*, Carl Maria

von Weber), *The Bohemian Girl* (Michael Balfe) and *Carmen*.[7] The following year, Miss Juch and her company were reported to spend February 5, 6 and 7 in the city (*Colonist*, January 29, 1891), and to stage *Mignon* (Ambroise Thomas), *Rigoletto* (Verdi), *Carmen* and *Lohengrin* (Richard Wagner). The C.D. Hess Grand Opera Company was to stage *La Traviata*, *Faust* and *Lucia di Lammermoor* at the Victoria on March 21, 23 and 24, 1891 (*Colonist*, March 18, 1891). Four years passed before the next reported operatic event (*Colonist*, March 4, 1896): four operas by the Marie Tavary Grand Opera Company in March 1896—*Lucia di Lammermoor* and *Cavalleria Rusticana* (Pietro Mascagni) on March 9, *Mignon* on March 10 and *Carmen* and *Les Huguenots* (Giacomo Meyerbeer) on March 11. And on January 16, 1898, the *Colonist* reported the last operatic event of the century in Victoria, to take place on five nights between January 18 and February 16, 1898, featuring the Del Conte Italian Opera Company, whose repertoire comprised *La Bohème* (Giacomo Puccini), *Pagliacci* (Ruggero Leoncavallo), *Faust*, *Manon Lescaut* (Puccini) and *Un Ballo in Maschera* (*A Masked Ball*, Verdi).

After playing in Victoria in 1891, Emma Juch took her company directly

▲ Interior of the Vancouver Opera House showing the famous drop curtain, 1891. CITY OF VANCOUVER ARCHIVES PHOTOGRAPH A24560

Bravo!

to Vancouver to give Vancouverites their first professional opera performance on February 9, 1891. At that time, Vancouver was a small provincial town of fewer than 14,000 people, connected to the rest of the country only four years previously when the first Canadian Pacific Railway (CPR) transcontinental passenger train arrived on May 23, 1887. One year earlier, on June 13, 1886, the city's buildings and houses, which were mostly wood, had burned to the ground in what is referred to in civic history as "the Great Fire." During the feverish reconstruction that followed, Hart's Opera House, a building brought from Port Moody, BC, by Frank W. Hart and reassembled in Vancouver's Chinatown at the south end of Carrall Street, was one of the public structures erected in the year of the fire. According to archival records, it was 50 feet (15.2 m) wide, 130 feet (39.6 m) long, 12 feet (3.6 m) high, of board and batten construction, with benches for seating 400 to 500, and had flooring of rough boards, a wood stove for heat and oil lamps for light. Hart's Opera House was Vancouver's first stage to be built after the fire and indicates that, even during this trying period of rebuilding, there was demand for theatrical and musical performances, no

matter how primitive the venue. Although one source states that in 1887 the Pyke Opera Company presented a week of opera at Hart's, it is unlikely that these could have been full productions given the limitations of the theatre. Nevertheless, on October 8, 1888, the Juvenile Opera Company produced *H.M.S. Pinafore* (Gilbert and Sullivan) there, and during Hart's existence a number of visiting opera singers gave concerts on its simple stage.

Reconstruction and population growth were rapid in the ensuing years, mainly owing to the economic benefits of the CPR rail connection and the establishment of the company as a corporate entity in the city. Newcomers swelled the ranks of those interested in a cultural life, and very soon Hart's Opera House was inadequate. When the Imperial Opera House, a 600-seat theatre, opened its doors at 105 Pender Street in 1889, Hart's doors closed shortly after. But a new development was soon to eclipse the Imperial's short-lived prominence: the CPR announced its intention to build a much more substantial opera house at 759 Granville Street, a location obtained as part of an agreement that gave the company a huge portion—25 million acres (10 million ha)—of federal land in the city. With the new Vancouver Opera House completed, Vancouver was to become a destination for touring opera companies, giving its citizens their first opportunity to enjoy a complete opera.

Despite a snowfall of 5 inches (13 cm) on February 9, 1891, and although the

▲ J. J. Osborne's drawing of Hart's Opera House on Carrall Street in Vancouver as it was in 1886. CITY OF VANCOUVER ARCHIVES PHOTOGRAPH BU P691

carpets and permanent seats were not in place for the opening and formal dedication of the opera house at 8:30 that evening, an enthusiastic audience of 1,600 witnessed the inaugural performance of *Lohengrin*. The occasion was reported the next day as follows: "[*Lohengrin* was] sung with great effect by the Emma Juch Grand Opera Company . . . specially engaged for $10,000 to dedicate the opera house . . . Miss Juch was indescribably charming as Elsa . . . After the performance, Miss Juch stated that she had never sung in a more [acoustically] perfect building, and that in all respects it compares favourably with the finest opera houses in the world."[8]

To complete the opening festivities, Miss Juch and her company performed *Il Trovatore* at a matinee and *Carmen* the following evening. A retrospective article, "First Opera House Opened," in an unidentified publication from 1925 noted that "prices were rather high; . . . orchestra chairs $3; next two rows $3; rest of the lower floor $2.50; balcony, first two rows $2.50; rest of the balcony $2; gallery $1."

Built at a cost of over $200,000, the opera house was a splendid example of Victorian elegance and became famous for its drop curtain, which featured a full-width painting of the peaks of the Three Sisters Mountains at Canmore, Alberta. Apparently the attire of the audiences matched the grandeur of the house, as this report from the *Vancouver Sun Magazine Supplement* on October 1, 1955, confirms: "The theatregoer . . . attired himself to match the glory of his opera house. Evening dress was de rigeur in the stalls and dress circle, and the scene on a gala night . . . would have done credit to a West End London theatre. In the service of art, the late street cars waited on Granville for the crowd to pour out, tying up service elsewhere in the young city."

The opera house was booked for a number of concerts and other events during its first year, but few records exist to tell us which operas, if any, were on the program. The Boston Lyric Company and Pollard's Lilliputian Opera Company from Australia visited Vancouver in 1891

▲ The Pollard Lilliputian Opera Company photographed on the steps of the Badmington Hotel in Vancouver, 1905. CITY OF VANCOUVER ARCHIVES PHOTOGRAPH PORT P1375

Bravo!

and presumably played the opera house, but no details are extant. However, since Pollard's company had performed a program of operetta in Victoria in 1877, it likely did the same in Vancouver. One more reference to the Australian company appears in an article "Thirty years ago" from an unidentified 1939 publication: "The famous Pollard's Lilliputian Opera Co. will make their last appearance in Vancouver Opera House this week [last week of February 1909]. They are enroute to their native Australia." Although details of opera performances during the life of the Vancouver Opera House are meagre, a few have survived to substantiate the view that its productions were a regular part of Vancouver's cultural scene. Henry Savage's English Grand Opera Company frequently visited Vancouver: a program survives for a production of *Lohengrin* on February 15, 1906; another exists for *The Merry Widow* (Franz Lehár), which played on June 15, 1909. However, Ian Docherty (*Vancouver Province*, October 4, 1971) reported, "By 1909 regular visits by the Savage Opera Company were replaced by the Lombardi Grand Opera Company. Their repertoire included . . . *Thaïs*." Only one program, from 1911, exists in the archives for the Lombardi company's productions at the Vancouver Opera House. Although programs dated 1909 have been preserved for a production of *Thaïs* (Jules Massenet) performed on December 20, followed by *Faust* on December 21, *Lucia di Lammermoor* on December 22 and *Madama*

Butterfly (Puccini) on December 23, the name of the company is not mentioned.

Despite the excitement and fanfare that accompanied the opening of the opera house, both its prominence in the city and opera's initial popularity were relatively short-lived, probably because touring companies were experiencing increasingly high taxation and unionization. Vaudeville was replacing opera as the entertainment choice of many Vancouverites, and the CPR, wanting to get out of the theatre business, sold the building in 1912 to a Seattle firm who wanted it for a vaudeville house. An interesting anecdote from the notes of archivist Major J.S. Matthews about the sale bears repeating. The Seattle firm, Considine and Sullivan, was described as "aggressive" by Matthews; intending to frighten the CPR into selling cheaply, they began construction at Pender and Burrard streets on what was publicized as a new opera house. This had the desired effect, and as soon as the sale was complete, construction at the new site ceased and was never resumed. The original cost of the CPR opera house exceeded $200,000, and the sale price was $300,000. When the financial dust settled, the CPR had realized $50,000 for its twenty-two-year tenure.

The demise of the Vancouver Opera House did not mean the demise of opera in the city, however. Touring companies made do with other venues, such as the Avenue Theatre at 705 Main Street, the Orpheum Theatre at 761 Granville Street

"Carmen" Orpheum Theatre, April 18-19, 1927
National Grand Opera Co.

(no relation to the present Orpheum Theatre), the Vancouver Theatre at 765 Granville Street (later named the Lyric Theatre), the Strand Theatre at Georgia and Richards, the Capitol Theatre at its present location on Granville Street, and several auditoriums.

From 1919 until 1945, the San Carlo Opera Company from New York visited Vancouver annually, and, according to at least one source, the company's standards were very high: "The best-known and best-loved American touring company was the San Carlo, owned and operated by Fortune Gallo . . . The company toured by bus and train, muleback, wagon, and paddle-wheel steamer . . . on long annual tours . . . Gallo's performances were never shoddy. The singers were thoroughly rehearsed; each was adequate to his role. The orchestra played well . . . No one who heard the San Carlo ever forgot it."[9] The City of Vancouver Archives holds programs for several visits of the company: in 1920 the company performed *Rigoletto*, *Faust*, *Aïda* (Verdi), *Martha* and *Il Trovatore* at the

Avenue Theatre January 7 to 10; in 1934, *Aïda*, *Faust*, *Carmen*, *Cavalleria Rusticana*, *Pagliacci*, *Lohengrin*, *Madama Butterfly* and *Il Trovatore* were presented April 30 to May 5 at the Vancouver Theatre; in 1935, the same operas, except for a substitution of *La Bohème* for *Lohengrin* were seen at the Capitol Theatre between March 25 and 30; the following year at the Strand Theatre between March 23 and 28, a similar program with the addition of *Martha* and *Tannhäuser* (Wagner) in place of *Pagliacci* and *Lohengrin* was billed as the company's twenty-sixth annual transcontinental tour; during the week of March 28 to April 2, 1938, Vancouverites saw eight operas, including some of the old favourites mentioned above and *Hansel and Gretel* (*Hänsel und Gretel*, Engelbert Humperdinck) at the Strand; in 1940, between April 8 and 13, the company's repertoire included *The Barber of Seville* among its standard fare presented again at the Strand. The last program preserved is for the San Carlo Company at the Lyric Theatre, February 7 to 12, 1944, presenting its standard

▲ In 1927 the National Grand Opera Company brought *Carmen* to the Orpheum Theatre in Vancouver, where the cast was photographed onstage. CITY OF VANCOUVER ARCHIVES PHOTOGRAPH 403_1

Bravo!

repertoire. Although San Carlo's repertoire appears to have been relatively static over the years, the company could hardly have been expected to maintain any standard of excellence otherwise, given its gruelling schedule. Each visit comprised six evening and two matinee performances, ensuring that cities like Vancouver, without a resident professional opera company, at least had "a season" every year, albeit only a week.

In addition to the San Carlo, other touring companies came, mostly offering operetta or light opera. Programs exist at the City of Vancouver Archives for the D'Oyly Carte Opera Company in 1928–29, the Empire Opera Company and the Brandon Comic Opera Company in 1930, the English Light Opera Company in 1931, the Jin Wah Sing Opera Troupe in 1938, the American Savoy Gilbert and Sullivan Comic Opera Company in 1941, and the New York City Opera Company and the Baccaloni Opera in 1944. Stanley Bligh (*Vancouver Sun*, January 21, 1938) reported that the Saltzburg Opera Guild presented *Così Fan Tutte* (Mozart) on January 19, 1938, and *La Cambiale di Matrimonio* (*The Bill of Marriage*, Gioachino Rossini) and *Angélique* (Jacques Ibert) as a double bill on the following evening in the Empress Theatre, located at Hastings Street and Gore Avenue.

Although grand opera was a regular selection on the artistic menu in Vancouver between 1900 and 1950, it was on the decline in Victoria. The increasing expense of travel and the inconvenience of crossing the Strait of Georgia to perform to smaller audiences in Victoria were likely factors, as were, no doubt, the First World War and the Great Depression, but also the attraction of the touring professional opera companies for artists, both vocal and instrumental, was apparently waning. It is entirely possible that many chose to give up the hard tour life in favour of joining the increasing number of emerging professional companies and orchestras permanently based in the large cities of the United States. Between 1900 and 1946, only twelve touring companies visited Victoria. Familiar names such as the Lombardi Opera Company and Henry Savage's Opera Company disappeared from the Victoria scene after 1911, and only one company, the Quinlan Opera Company, performing in January 1914, appeared in the city until the San Carlo Opera Company made its first appearance in 1920. However, the San Carlo does not seem to have made annual visits to Victoria as it did to Vancouver. The records show it was not to appear after 1920 until 1936, and then not again until 1945 and 1946, after which no further appearances by any touring troupe are recorded.[10] Although no details of the repertoire offered to Victorians during these years are available, it is likely there were no deviations from the standard fare of the previous years. In a tie for top spot on the opera "hit parade" in Victoria were *Il Trovatore*, *La Traviata*, *Martha*, *Faust* and *Carmen*.

Despite being left out in the cold, as

it were, by professional companies after 1900, Victorians were too fond of opera not to do something about it. Even before the turn of the century amateur groups were active, but the tradition grew in strength to provide the city with a rich menu of operetta and opera productions over the lean years. Some of the most prominent groups were the Victoria Amateur Opera Company, the Victoria Dramatic and Operatic Society, the Playhouse Company, the Victoria Operatic Society, Victoria Civic Opera and the Victoria Grand Opera Association. The efforts of these enterprises to keep opera vital in their region were to bear fruit many years later, as will be seen in a later chapter.

The focus of this chapter has been on opera performances exclusively in Victoria and Vancouver in the early days, for the simple reason that no evidence has been uncovered that touring companies ever travelled to the smaller centres in the province, despite many having buildings euphemistically called opera houses—towns such as New Westminster, Nelson, Greenwood and Barkerville. These opera houses were really local centres for various forms of amateur and professional theatrical and musical entertainment, but seldom, if ever, for full-scale operas, as Ian Docherty (*Vancouver Province*, October 4, 1971) suggests: "Since few of these opera houses ever echoed to the arias of Verdi or Pwuccini, one must look to the social attitudes of those days to discover the reason such a high-flying name was chosen for what was, essentially, the local theatre and concert hall. The theatre and its professional practitioners were usually held in suspicion of immorality. Whatever the logic underlying this belief, it does not seem to have been extended to opera and opera singers."

Opera lovers in smaller communities, and most certainly those in remote places, would likely not have made the difficult journey to Vancouver or Victoria to attend live performances, given the limited transportation options in the province. Even for those who lived within practical travelling distance, attendance at an evening performance would have required an overnight stay; doubtless, matinees were a popular choice for out-of-towners.

However, one opportunity to hear live opera performances existed for everyone in the province who had access to radio: the Saturday afternoon broadcasts live from the Metropolitan Opera Company, which began on December 25, 1931. From then on, many opera fans, urban and rural, were glued to their radios every week to hear the mellifluous voice of host Milton Cross welcoming them to an afternoon of pleasure, "live from the stage of the Metropolitan Opera in New York City." Cross, who hosted the broadcasts until his death in 1975, described the scene, including what the singers were wearing, so vividly that with very little effort one could imagine being part of the audience; in fact, distance faded away as the glorious music began, and one *was* at the opera.

Overture

SETTING THE SCENE

IN 1945 THE END OF HOSTILITIES IN EUROPE AND THE PACIFIC ALLOWED
British Columbians to focus their attention beyond the war effort for
the first time in six years. Many cultured Europeans, particularly Jews,
had immigrated to British Columbia just before or during the Second
World War, seeking sanctuary from the Third Reich, and these people
were longing for the wide and varied cultural menu they had enjoyed in
their homelands. Among the newcomers were Paul and Edwina Heller,
who had escaped from Warsaw on the very day of the Nazi occupation,
going first to London, then to Montreal and finally settling in Vancouver
in 1942. Edwina Heller, a talented and well-known concert pianist in
her native Poland, described in an interview her dismay on discovering
the dearth of cultural groups, particularly for musicians, in Vancouver:
"I couldn't believe a city like this existed. [It was] a village — nothing,
culturally. In Warsaw we had seven symphony concerts a week, full-
time employment for musicians, twenty professional theatres, an opera
house . . . Vancouver was a small little town. I was at a loss [and] terribly
unhappy." However, the president of the Ladies' Morning Musical
Club in Montreal, who had befriended Heller and hired her for her first
professional engagement in Canada, suggested she contact two musically
prominent people in Vancouver: concert pianist Jan Cherniavsky and
Mrs. B.T. Rogers, a music lover and well-known patron of the arts, in
particular the Vancouver Symphony Orchestra. Mrs. Rogers invited
Heller and her husband to a musical party at her home where they
were introduced to Harry and Frances Adaskin, prominent musicians
and performers. Of the Adaskins, Heller said: "They were my mentors
. . . they changed my life . . . I got into a group of musicians . . . we met
sometimes until 2 a.m. . . . we discussed music [and] played together."

◀ The late Léopold Simoneau as Don Ottavio in a scene from *Don Giovanni*, the first Vancouver
International Festival's inaugural opera offering, at the Orpheum Theatre in 1958.
BARRY GLASS PHOTOGRAPH

This group of talented musicians was doubtless typical of those assembled throughout the province who had no other options for keeping their skills in top form during the early 1940s.[1] Although Vancouver and Victoria musicians played with the Vancouver Symphony and Victoria Symphony orchestras, founded in 1930 and 1941 respectively, Heller reported that all but six players in the Vancouver Symphony required day jobs and took students to make ends meet. Augmenting the scene was the formation in 1938 of the CBC Vancouver Orchestra, which provided an opportunity for approximately twenty-five musicians to play and be heard in radio broadcasts.

Similarly, singers had a difficult time finding opportunities. The Vancouver Bach Choir, giving concerts since December 1930, was the main group whose repertoire comprised serious music; but the singers were not, and are still not, paid. Under the auspices of the Vancouver Park Board, Theatre Under the Stars (TUTS) produced operettas and musicals from 1940 to 1963 on the outdoor stage of the Malkin Bowl in Stanley Park during the summer months. (The organization was revived in 1969 and continues to the present day.) TUTS gave part-time work and career advancement to many local singers, and was enjoyed by smaller communities when the company went on tour after 1944. During the winter months from 1944 to 1950, young singers and actors could receive training at the BC Institute of Music and Drama, another initiative of the Park Board. The University of British Columbia (UBC) established a Department of Music in 1946—Harry Adaskin was appointed chair and Edwina Heller joined the teaching staff. A few students were admitted to the small department, but for the most part, the training of singers and musicians was a private affair.

Opportunities for paid employment were meagre, but the musicians who continued to play and sing in amateur groups were to be an important factor in the BC music scene of the 1950s. When the time was ripe for establishing a resident professional opera company in the province, these local artists formed the foundation of its orchestra and chorus.

During the war, an important impetus to the arts took place: in 1943 a public-spirited Vancouver industrialist, W.J. Van Dusen, pledged $10,000 and encouraged nine other wealthy men and women to do the same, to establish the Vancouver Foundation, a community fund with one of its goals being to "support endeavours which improve life in the community." It took seven years for their objective to become a reality, but during those years, as members of the armed forces returned from abroad with an expanded view of the world, and post-war European immigrants introduced a new level of sophistication to the province, British Columbians began to emerge from their pioneer, colonial mentality to place value on the visual and performing arts as a means of nourishing the spirit of their towns and cities.

The next important development took place in 1945. The Junior League of Vancouver sponsored the publication of *The Arts and Our Town*, a report by Virginia Lee Comer, a consultant on community arts. A direct outcome of Comer's report was the creation of the Community Arts Council, whose objective was to increase and broaden the opportunities for Vancouver citizens to enjoy and participate in cultural activities. Arguably the most influential cultural organization ever formed in Vancouver, the early initiatives of the Community Arts Council supported events and organizations that were to be of lasting significance to the arts in this province: the establishment of the Department of Music at UBC (1946) and its expansion to the School of Music with degree-granting status (1959); the Vancouver International Festival (1958–68); the Vancouver Opera Association (1959); the opening of the Queen Elizabeth Theatre (1959); and the establishment of the Community Music School of Greater Vancouver (1969), now known as the Vancouver Academy of Music, to name a few.

The Massey Commission report (1951) and its recommendation for the formation of the Canada Council for the Arts, accomplished in 1957, together with the creation of several of the first private philanthropic foundations in the province, two of which were the Chris Spencer Foundation (1949) and the Leon and Thea Koerner Foundation (1955), proved a great boon for emerging arts organizations by providing them with a source of grant money, hitherto in very short supply. (A third, the Hamber Foundation, which also supported the arts, was not formed until 1964.)

Opera lovers in Vancouver were following these developments with keen interest, especially after learning that, because of escalating costs, the San Carlo Opera Company would no longer be visiting Vancouver after 1945. The vacuum was filled occasionally by Vancouver impresario Gordon Hilker, whose company, Hilker Attractions, brought singers from the Metropolitan Opera or from other notable houses to star in a week-long season, beginning in September 1945. Also filling the void was the Northwest Grand Opera Company of Seattle, begun in 1953 by the legendary Glynn Ross, founding director of Seattle Opera ten years later. The clipping files of the Vancouver Public Library Fine Arts Department trace the company's performances staged in Vancouver between 1953 and 1956: *La Bohème*, *La Traviata* and *Rigoletto* in 1953; *Madama Butterfly* and *Carmen* in 1954; *The Barber of Seville* and *Tosca* (Puccini) in 1955; *La Traviata* in 1956. Northwest Grand Opera was apparently a first-rate touring company. Singers from the Metropolitan Opera were cast in the principal roles—for example, the celebrated American mezzo-soprano Regina Resnik sang the title role in *Carmen*. The company drew on local talent for minor parts, the chorus, the orchestra and various technical personnel, which made it very popular in Vancouver. Unfortunately, the company folded in 1957, and the implication of this news was reported by Stanley Bligh (*Vancouver Sun*, March 30, 1957): "That [Vancouver] is opera-conscious has been proven by the San Carlo Opera Company, which for years came each season and played to capacity houses. Increased cost in transportation and general travelling expenses caused these visits to cease. The North West Group failed mainly for the same reason . . . Keen disappointment was expressed by hundreds of opera lovers at the cancellation of the North West Opera performances." The article's heading, "Time Opportune Now to Start Grand Opera Here," must have struck a strong chord of approval with similarly minded readers.

The Vancouver International Festival was next on the scene. Early in 1954 the Community Arts Council Board had been approached by one of its most enthusiastic members, Iby Koerner, about an idea for a festival of the arts that she and her friend, well-known Toronto musician and impresario Nicholas Goldschmidt, had dreamed up during Goldschmidt's visit to Vancouver to develop an experimental Summer School of the Arts at UBC during the early 1950s. Koerner had come to Vancouver from Europe in 1939 with her husband, Otto Koerner, and members of his family to escape persecution by the Nazis. She had been a patron of the arts in Vienna and shared Edwina Heller's view of the sad state of culture in her new home. Almost immediately she became involved in artistic circles in a volunteer capacity and became known as a person who not only got things done, but also inspired others to share her dreams of a vibrant cultural community. After consultation with local arts organizations and community-minded men and women, the Community Arts Council endorsed the concept of an annual festival of the arts and delegated Koerner to set up and head a festival committee. This led to the incorporation of a permanent organization, the Vancouver Festival Society. The first business of the board was to commission Tyrone Guthrie, the British theatrical director who had been instrumental in setting up the Stratford Festival of Canada in 1953, to come to Vancouver to conduct a feasibility study. His report to the Vancouver Festival Society in 1955 contained the following opinion: "[Vancouver] is still a frontier city where material needs have hitherto, and needfully taken priority of spiritual. As such it owes itself and to posterity the expression of something besides material prosperity . . . As I see it, this should be a Coming of Age Party of a phenomenally rich and potentially powerful heir."

Encouraged by Guthrie's report, the festival board began at once to make plans for the first Vancouver International Festival to take place in the summer of 1958, three years hence. Excitement reached a fever pitch among opera lovers when they learned that the inaugural program was to include Mozart's *Don Giovanni*, featuring the Metropolitan Opera star, Canadian bass-baritone George London, as Don Giovanni, and Canadian tenor, the late Léopold Simoneau in his signature role as Don Ottavio. Joan Sutherland, the Australian soprano who was getting attention in London in Covent Garden productions, was to make her North American debut in the production as Donna Anna. There were twenty-eight events in the ten days following the gala opening concert on July 19, 1958; the opera was performed on July 26 to a capacity audience and received rave reviews in the press.

The next year the festival opera was *Orpheus and Eurydice* (*Orfeo ed Euridice*, Christoph W. Gluck) starring American soprano Mary Costa, Canadian soprano Marguerite Gignac and Swedish mezzo-soprano Kerstin Meyer. These two performances were undoubtedly the most important operatic events to take place in the province to date. They demonstrated to the community the enormous opportunities for employment and career advancement for local musicians, singers, technicians, stagehands, costumers and so on, many of whom were hired for both operas, and they galvanized the opera-lovers' community into action to realize their long-simmering desire for a resident professional opera company. Some years after the Vancouver International Festival had fallen on

hard times and been abandoned after the eleventh, in 1968, arts critic Ray Chatelin wrote, "[the festival's] most visible outgrowth was the fledgling opera company."[2]

At the time of the festival performance of *Don Giovanni*, two separate amateur groups of Vancouver opera enthusiasts, the Grand Opera Society and the Opera Players of British Columbia, were among those who longed for a richer, more constant menu of opera. The Opera Players put on concert performances, but the Grand Opera Society was more ambitious, as the following archived report of the Vancouver Opera Association shows: "The Grand Opera Society . . . began operation in November 1955 with three performances of 'A Prologue to Grand Opera' at the Georgia Auditorium. Fully staged and costumed excerpts from 5 operas . . . were presented at each performance, in order to utilize as many talented artists as possible. In May 1958, the Society presented two performances of Puccini's 'La Bohème' to capacity audiences, again in the Georgia Auditorium . . . In both the 1955 and 1958 productions all the artists, with the exception of the symphony musicians, donated their time and talents."

In the fall of 1958, the Grand Opera Society, located at 508-1035 Comox Street, Vancouver, was registered formally as a non-profit organization, and an executive committee was formed: headed by Mrs. John T. McCay as honorary president;

Bravo!

Brian Hanson, acting president and first vice-president; Gail McCance, second vice-president; Mrs. Harriss Goad, secretary; Robert Harrison, treasurer; and the Honourable Ralph Campney, honorary legal counsel. These people, especially Mrs. McCay, were well known in the community for their devotion to and knowledge of opera. The first extant minutes of the executive committee are dated December 15, 1958, and the remarks of the chairman, Brian Hanson, set the agenda for the society's main objective: "The Chairman felt the time has come when Vancouver should have a 'resident' Opera Society and we should look ahead to the time—five to ten years hence—when this Opera Society would be professional."

▲ The late bass singer, Jan Rubes, in the buffo role of Sir John Falstaff in the Vancouver International Festival's 1963 production of *The Merry Wives of Windsor*.
BARRY GLASS PHOTOGRAPH

The meeting also discussed plans for membership and fundraising campaigns, and the opinion of Robert Philips, a director at large, was recorded, that in selecting a board of governors, people "whose names *mean* something in the city" should be approached.[3]

The next meeting took place on January 12, 1959, at which the following motion was approved: "Mr. Gideon Grau to be appointed musical director of 'La Traviata' for a fee of $600." Evidently, the plan to present *La Traviata* was in the works, though details were not finalized until a later meeting. However, the executive committee was forced to meet again on January 18, 1959, "to consider what steps should be taken to prevent Opera Players of BC, and the ticket sales personnel acting for them, from informing the public that they had produced 'La Boheme' [in May 1958] and that at the time of such production this Society was 'merged' with the Opera Players of BC and had since broken away." The secretary was instructed to place a notice in the two Vancouver papers and to advise the Opera Players of the notice and state the Grand Opera Society's complaint against them by registered letter.

According to the minutes of the meeting of March 8, 1959, there were to date seventeen paid-up members of the Grand Opera Society, and those present passed a motion to produce *La Traviata* on December 17, 18, and 19, 1959. At subsequent meetings, this small band of activists made momentous decisions that changed the course of operatic history in the province of British Columbia and put the city of Vancouver on the map as an emerging centre for professional productions of grand opera.

First, on April 13, 1959, the society met and unanimously passed the following resolution: "That we change the name Grand Opera Society of BC to Vancouver Opera Association." This change was meant to "eliminate confusion with other groups"—i.e., the Opera Players of BC—and "to broaden the scope of our activities." Next, at the meeting of May 11, 1959, Secretary Jo Goad was instructed to write and ask Irving Guttman, a young man residing in Montreal and making a name for himself in the East as a talented newcomer to the ranks of opera directors, if he would be available to direct the forthcoming production of *La Traviata* in Vancouver. Finally, Secretary Goad informed the meeting of June 8, 1959, that the name was now officially changed, and that Guttman had replied that he was free to direct *La Traviata*, for his fee of $500, plus transportation costs. Exit the Grand Opera Society; enter the Vancouver Opera Association.

An undated document under the heading "Vancouver Opera Association (Formerly the Grand Opera Society of British Columbia)" lists the directors for the 1959–60 season, and sets out the aims of the association, as follows:

Vancouver is fortunate in having many fine artists living in and around the city. Some are Canadian, and some come to us from other lands. All have a great deal to contribute to the musical life of our city.

In order to increase the opportunities available for these many talented people, The Vancouver Opera Association is working on two projects of major importance:

a. Establishment of a resident opera company to provide Vancouver with a regular season of opera, comparable to that provided in eastern Canada by the Toronto Opera Festival

b. Establishment of an opera workshop, which will provide instruction and experience for many of our young artists, and the opportunity to perform under actual stage conditions

As a start toward achieving the first of these, our 1959/60 season will open on December 18th and 19th, in the new Civic Auditorium [the Queen Elizabeth Theatre], with two presentations of Verdi's "La Traviata." This will be a memorable production because it brings together two of the city's active opera groups. Plans are being made to produce a second opera in March 1960, also in the new theatre.

These inspiring objectives ushered in a new era in the cultural life of the province, but, as might be expected, the going got tough along the way.

Act I

VANCOUVER

1960 to 1974

THIS ERA IN THE EVOLUTION OF WHAT WAS, AT THE TIME, THE ONLY professional opera company in the province should rightly be considered "the Guttman years." Irving Guttman's name is inextricably linked with the fledgling Vancouver Opera Association (VOA); indeed, he has been called "the father of opera in Western Canada," referring to his formative influence on Edmonton Opera, Manitoba Opera and Calgary Opera as well as his tenure with the VOA as its first artistic director.

Guttman described in an interview his situation when he received the letter from the VOA inviting him to direct its first opera:

> I was living in Montreal at the time [and had] just arrived home from New Orleans where I'd done Johann Strauss's *A Night in Venice* for the New Orleans Opera, and found this letter from Josephine Goad from Vancouver saying they were trying to start an opera company and wanted to do *La Traviata* with local singers, and I had been recommended to come out. Would I come? My friends in Montreal said, 'What do you want to go out there for? There's nothing out in Vancouver,' but I never refused anything in those days . . . I was just starting my career.

The VOA Board had intended to do *La Traviata* with an all-local cast but was having second thoughts about the quality of such a production. The directors had decided that *Carmen* with imported singers in the lead roles would be a better choice as the first offering of the new company, and wrote to Guttman advising him of this change. Guttman replied, releasing the board from its commitment to him for *La Traviata* and expressing interest in directing *Carmen*, which prompted the board to renew its invitation to him to stage the new choice. Guttman recalls the journey to Vancouver in October 1959 to talk to the directors:

◄   Russell Oberlin as Oberon and Mary Costa as Tytania in their stunning costumes for
A Midsummer Night's Dream, the 1961 Vancouver International Festival's opera offering.
BARRY GLASS PHOTOGRAPH

"I came here on a lark. I arrived in Vancouver after flying all night on a North Star, and they seemed so excited to see me. I was given the royal greeting and all that sort of thing . . . I met a lot of very interesting and nice people . . . and I said [to them], 'Well, let's try' . . . not that I knew anything about starting an opera company, but I was young . . . I loved the idea of pioneering."

Guttman spent the next four days auditioning "everyone in Vancouver who could sing, 180 in all," and was very impressed with the quality of the voices: "I was able to build a first-class chorus with no problem." He was also very upbeat about the fact that Vancouver had a well-established symphony orchestra and a new

theatre suitable for opera performances, and he went back to Montreal full of excitement and confidence for the forthcoming production scheduled for April 1960. He returned to Vancouver in early March 1960 to begin rehearsals with the chorus and the dancers, all locals; rehearsals with the principals— American mezzo-soprano Nan Merriman as Carmen, Canadian baritone Louis Quilico as Escamillo, American tenor Richard Cassilly as Don José and BC soprano Joyce Perry Crist as Micaëla— began two weeks before the opening date, April 2, 1960.

The energy and enthusiasm within the company was palpable. A small group of volunteers worked tirelessly running

▲ Director Irving Guttman at work during a rehearsal of *Carmen*, Vancouver Opera's inaugaural production, 1960. BARRY GLASS PHOTOGRAPH

errands, providing transportation for the visiting principals, making and serving sandwiches and coffee for the cast at rehearsals, persuading friends and neighbours to buy tickets and generally helping out wherever needed. Board members were equally busy. Since a deficit was budgeted for *Carmen*, guarantors were sought to offset the anticipated shortfall; seven people pledged a total of $16,000. Numerous unexpected glitches arose, requiring hasty consultations and decisions. Publicity and ticket sales continued to the last minute, by which time volunteers and board members alike were in a high state of nervous anticipation.

Their hard work paid off. For a debut production, *Carmen* was an unqualified

▲ In the death scene in act 4 of *Carmen*, Don José, played by Richard Cassilly, kneels over the dead body of Carmen, played by Nan Merriman, whom he has just killed in a jealous rage. BARRY GLASS PHOTOGRAPH

▲ Nan Merriman, a voluptuous, seductive Carmen, was one of the two imported "names" for Vancouver Opera's first production. The other was Richard Cassilly. BARRY GLASS PHOTOGRAPH

Bravo!

success in the opinion of the opera-going public, the company and the media critics. Audiences were on their feet, applauding the performances. Ticket sales resulted in over 93 percent capacity houses; the guarantors were required to meet only 51 percent of their undertakings, reducing the company's net loss on the four performances to a modest $8,663. To everyone's surprise the reviewers of the opening night were remarkably kind. Desmond Arthur (*Vancouver Sun*, April 4, 1960) wrote, "Vancouver Opera Association faced its moment of truth Saturday night with the opening performance of 'Carmen' and emerged victorious . . . Some of the cape-work and passes were inept and reckless, and there were brushes with near-disaster, but strength and youth and courage won the day." He went on at length to praise the performances and vocal talents of the principals and some of the supporting cast, the dancers and the sets, but also had this to say by way of gentle criticism: "Occasional disagreements on tempo between pit and stage, and some near-disintegration of chorus singing, are matters which can be solved in later performances by tightened command." There was great rejoicing at the opening night after-party at the home of Edwina and Paul Heller—Edwina being one of the first directors of the VOA and Paul a guarantor for *Carmen*. Everyone involved with the production was well satisfied that the Vancouver Opera Association had been launched with distinction.

However, hiring Guttman to do *Carmen* presented the VOA Board with its first minor crisis: Gideon Grau had been appointed musical director for *La Traviata* for a fee of $600 at a meeting of the Grand Opera Society on January 12, 1959, and he was upset by the decision to abandon *La Traviata* and do *Carmen*, using Guttman instead of offering it to him. Grau attended a meeting of the society on October 7, 1959, and his position was recorded: he had not been properly informed of the decision and believed there had been "no real attempt by the Board to finance 'Traviata,' and no Board leadership for the large numbers of people willing to help." He demanded full payment of $600 as though *La Traviata* had been performed, but, since the organization had virtually no financial resources at the time, the board offered him only $300. At a subsequent meeting on April 21, 1960, the impasse was turned over to the board's honorary solicitor and by November 17, 1960, the board was informed that the matter had been resolved, with no record of the

▲ Newly appointed Vancouver Opera artistic director Irving Guttman meets Beverly Bower, the star of Vancouver Opera's 1961 production of *La Traviata*, as she arrives at the Vancouver airport to begin rehearsals.
BARRY GLASS PHOTOGRAPH

settlement amount in the minutes.

As a result of the success of *Carmen*, Guttman was offered, and accepted, a contract as the company's first artistic director. With the valuable experience gained from that production, the VOA Board was proceeding with plans for two productions in the coming season: *La Bohème* in November and *La Traviata* in May 1961. In his report to the guarantors and contributors to *Carmen*, Robert Philips, who became president in July 1959 after Mrs. McCay's resignation due to illness, outlined the board's objectives:

> We must have $12,000 in hand to meet all contingencies for "La Boheme." The budget has been completed and deviations are unlikely now that we have the experience of "Carmen" to guide us . . . We will pursue the same course as before of seeking guarantees in excess of the maximum potential loss . . . We have already submitted a brief for Canada Council, asking assistance, and our chances are said to be good, but a prerequisite of a grant is local support, and if the Council's money is added to the $10,000 we are seeking for "La Boheme" we can carry through several further productions without being a burden of any consequence on our local patrons and philanthropists.

Indeed a Canada Council grant of $10,000 was obtained and matching funds were raised, but Philips's seemingly curious attitude above toward fundraising was one that persisted during his presidency and likely accounted for his stand during the next crisis at the board: Guttman's intention to cast the Ukrainian baritone Igor Gorin in the role of Germont in *La Traviata*. Gorin, an internationally known singer, charged $800 per performance, a shocking sum for the VOA to contemplate in its production budget. The issue "provoked violent controversy among Board members," with Philips leading the opposition.[1] Since five performances were scheduled, Gorin's fee would take up more than 25 percent of the total cast costs, which seemed outrageous to those who agreed with the president. Guttman, however, refused to back down and recalled how he managed to convince the board: "The main problem was not that they didn't trust my judgment. President Philips was a lovely man, but he had a huge ego. His big thing was being fiscally responsible. Igor Gorin's fee was considerably higher than the standard of the day . . . [but] there was nobody around who could do the role. I stuck by my guns. They respected that and they allowed it to happen. I think they realized by then that I had a big talent for [casting], but at the same time there was apprehension. It was strictly financial." The financial statements for the year indicate that Guttman's tenacity was justified. Even taking into account that there were four performances of *La Bohème* and five of *La Traviata*, and that ticket prices for *La Traviata* were

Bravo!

▲ In act 2 of Vancouver Opera's *La Traviata*, Igor Gorin as
Germont tells Violetta, played by Beverly Bower, that
she must give up her scandalous relationship with his
son, Alfredo, for the good of the family name.
BARRY GLASS PHOTOGRAPH

increased by fifty cents for all seats, the excess of expenditure over income for the former was $7,211 and the latter, only $1,049. Attendance for *La Bohème*, starring Canadian soprano Irene Salemka, was at 90 percent capacity and for *La Traviata* it was over 94 percent, suggesting that Gorin was a big drawing card. His performance earned him the following kudos from Stanley Bligh (*Vancouver Sun*, May 5, 1961): "Igor Gorin in the role of Germont was superb . . . with his singing of 'Di Provenza' he almost brought down the house."

However, Guttman demonstrated in both operas, as well as in *Carmen*, an admirable pattern he adhered to whenever possible during his tenure with the VOA: he gave promising local singers a chance to advance their careers by casting them in the supporting roles. In *Carmen*, for example, he cast Joyce Perry Crist as Micaëla and her performance received glowing reviews. The roles of Benoit and Alcindoro in *La Bohème* were given to Karl Norman, the new business manager of the VOA, and Milla Andrew sang the role of Musetta.[2] In *La Traviata* Betty Phillips was cast as Flora and Norman was given the role of Gaston. Andrew, Phillips and Norman had all starred in many TUTS productions and had fine voices, as did other Vancouver singers like Audrey Glass and Sophie Turko, who appeared in solo parts in future VOA productions. Guttman was not governed solely by the obvious cost benefit of using local talent, though his

board must have applauded the practice and it likely also had a degree of box-office appeal. He truly believed in and enjoyed encouraging young Canadian talent and had an uncanny ear for a singer's proper place in a production. Reminiscing about all the good local talent, Guttman said, "If I couldn't use them in Vancouver, I could use them in Edmonton or Winnipeg. I brought them along with small parts to larger parts."

Some of Guttman's proteges, most notably mezzo-soprano Judith Forst and tenor Richard Margison, went on to achieve international fame. Forst, a member of the VOA Chorus, entered the newly created VOA training program in 1966, the same year Guttman cast her as Lola in the VOA production of *Cavalleria Rusticana*. Two years later, after winning two prestigious competitions in the interval, she auditioned for the Metropolitan Opera, was given a contract and made her debut there. Although Forst sang in other VOA productions during Guttman's tenure, she did not sing again under his direction until his brief return as artistic director in the years 1982–84; in the 1982 production of *La Bohème* she sang the role of Musetta. Nevertheless, her brilliant career began with the VOA and some of the credit for early recognition of her great talent belongs to Guttman.

Similarly, Guttman mentored tenor Richard Margison, long before the opera world paid any attention to him, by giving him comprimario roles (supporting roles)

Bravo!

and eventually casting him as Lensky in *Eugene Onegin* (Pyotr Tchaikovsky) in 1985. His glorious career took off shortly after that when he debuted with English National Opera in 1989 as Riccardo in *Un Ballo in Maschera*. Since then he has appeared in leading roles on the stages of all the major opera companies in North America and Europe, including a number of times at the Metropolitan.

Guttman also recognized the talent of West Vancouver–born soprano Heather Thomson (now Heather Thomson-Price) when she was still in her teens and trying out for the Vancouver International Festival opera, *The Magic Flute* (*Die Zauberflöte*, Mozart), in 1962. In an interview she recollected, "I got an early start [in Vancouver] . . . When I was seventeen, I auditioned for both Nicholas Goldschmidt and Irving Guttman . . . they gave me the first lady, which was quite an honour." Thomson went to Toronto to join the Canadian Opera Company's touring ensemble and study with Herman Geiger-Torel. Her fine future career was predictable when, at the age of nineteen, she was a finalist in the Metropolitan Opera National Council Regional Auditions and then won the San Francisco Opera Auditions.

By the end of the 1960–61 season the VOA had made a considerable impact on the artistic community and had made equally impressive strides to ensure stability within the company. The Vancouver Opera Guild had been established under the energetic leadership of director Mrs. Cyrus H. McLean, and President Philips was able to report to the board that membership stood at over 600. On the same occasion he reported that, owing to the efforts of VOA director David Spencer, the Vancouver Opera Endowment Trust Fund had been established and totalled $20,500. Spencer had made the founding contribution of $4,500 earlier in the year and was responsible for seeing the trust deed finalized. Philips concluded his report with the following statement: "[It is] the policy of the VOA, as far as possible, to avoid nagging people for money when already they have made generous contributions to other cultural organizations in the city." Whether this truly reflected VOA policy or whether Philips allowed his own apparent reticence to intrude in this statement is not known, but it certainly did not reflect the view of at least one VOA Board of Governors member and prominent supporter of the arts, Mrs. B.T. Rogers. It is baffling to read in the minutes of the board of directors in 1961 that Philips asked Mrs. Rogers to reduce her generous grant to the VOA; no doubt perplexed, she refused to comply. Nicolette McIntosh was on the board at the time, and from an interview her recollections provide valuable insight into this peculiar aspect of VOA management under Philips's leadership: "Bob [Philips] was very idealistic, and it was his belief, and he had quite a theory about it, that

the opera should be self supporting . . .
He objected to the constant fundraising
that went on in Vancouver, and felt that if
it had to be done, the beneficiary couldn't
really be wanted, or needed. The guild
did all the fundraising, and Bob counted
a lot on grants." However, by 1964 Robert
Philips no longer headed the board and the
new president, Otto Andreasen, appointed
four directors to form the first fundraising
committee.

The 1961–62 season began with a paper
surplus of just over $4,000, owing to the
benefit of writing off the balance of the
cost of the sets for *Carmen*, an accounting
procedure begun the previous year. Five
scheduled performances in October
1961 of *The Tales of Hoffmann* (*Les Contes
d'Hoffmann*, Jacques Offenbach), sung in
English, did little to improve the finances
of the VOA, partly because the first
performance had to be cancelled at the last
minute. The two lead singers, American
tenor Louis Roney in the role of Hoffmann
and his fiancée, Irene Salemka, cast to sing
the four lead soprano parts, claimed to
be ill with the same throat ailment. Both
had a reputation for being temperamental
and there was some conjecture about the
legitimacy of their claim, especially as
they were onstage and in full voice two
nights later. However, they were seen by
a physician who prescribed antibiotics for
what he diagnosed as twenty-four-hour
flu, which put an end to the rumours.[3] The
company put on a makeup performance
at the end of the run, but 16 percent of the

ticket holders for the opening performance,
which was sold out, asked for a refund,
which resulted in a considerable loss. The
season concluded without further incident
with five well-attended performances of
Rigoletto in March 1962; the cast included
American tenor John Alexander as the
Duke, Canadian baritone Napoléon Bisson
as Rigoletto, American bass Richard Cross
as Sparafucile and American soprano Reri
Grist as Gilda.[4]

Three operas comprised the 1962–63
VOA season: *Tosca*, *Faust* and *Aïda*. Richard
Bonynge, who was to figure prominently
in VOA affairs in the 1970s, made his first
appearance in the city as the conductor
of *Faust* and Mario Bernardi, who was
to become one of Canada's best known

▲ Napoléon Bisson in the title role of *Rigoletto*, staged by
Vancouver Opera in 1962, has his worst fears confirmed
when his daughter, Gilda, tells him she has been
seduced by the Duke of Mantua.
BARRY GLASS PHOTOGRAPH

and revered conductors, led the orchestra for *Aïda*. If one critic is to be believed, *Aïda* fell far short of the VOA's standard for excellence, but his was an opinion not shared by others, nor did attendance records indicate poor audience reaction. When asked about adverse reviews in the media in general, Guttman replied, "They didn't affect the company or me. I didn't think [the critics] were qualified to make the comments they made."

Guttman's ambitious plans for the next season provoked more controversy at the board level. If the directors thought Igor Gorin's fee was high, they must have been apoplectic to learn that Guttman proposed to bring Joan Sutherland back to Vancouver in October 1963 to sing the lead

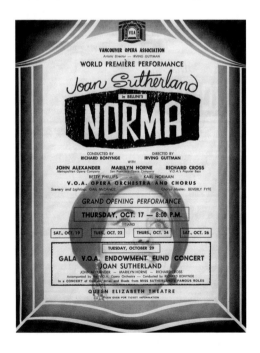

▲ An early piece of Vancouver Opera memorabilia advertising the 1963 production of *Norma*, starring Joan Sutherland, whose picture underlies the printing.
DONATED BY NICOLETTE MCINTOSH

in five performances of *Norma*, for a fee of $3,000 per performance. Readers will recall that Sutherland thrilled audiences in the Vancouver International Festival's production of *Don Giovanni* in 1958, and her international star status had been on the ascendancy ever since. Furthermore, her conductor husband, Richard Bonynge, had hitched his star to his wife's and was to lead the orchestra for the production; together their fees accounted for more than half of the total costs. Guttman proposed to cast American mezzo-soprano Marilyn Horne as Adalgisa and intended to use locals Betty Phillips and Karl Norman in the supporting roles of Clotilde and Flavio. Despite the projected production costs, which were the highest to date in the VOA's history, Guttman won over the board. President Philips hastened to assure the still-anxious directors that "the decision to present Joan Sutherland [is] not setting a new policy. The VOA would continue to engage young, relatively inexpensive artists for future productions." The production was a personal triumph for Guttman and a huge boost for the reputation of the association's ability to mount grand opera on a grand level. Casting Sutherland and Horne together was a stroke of genius; their voices blended magnificently, giving audiences one of the most memorable performances experienced in the Queen Elizabeth Theatre. All five performances of *Norma* were sold out and advance sales were the highest ever in the VOA's history, yet, when the final tally

was presented to the board, the profit from *Norma* was $14, hardly worth mentioning.

In fact, the rest of the 1963–64 season was not a financial success, as an August 29, 1964, article in the *Vancouver Province* confirms: "The VOA has gone into the red for the first time in its four-year history . . . The defeat is blamed on lack of a [Canada] Council and government grants this year and on the loss suffered by the Association's production of a modern opera *The Consul*." Prior to the ill-fated production of *The Consul* (Gian Carlo Menotti), the VOA had presented *The Barber of Seville* in February 1964, which had added $760 to its coffers, but a decision to follow that with *La Bohème* and *The Consul* running on alternate days during the same week in

May proved disastrous to the company; ticket buyers were given a choice and they chose the familiar over the unfamiliar. *La Bohème*, which had three exceptional young Canadian singers appearing in principal roles for the first time on the VOA stage—soprano Heather Thomson as Mimì, soprano Marguerite Gignac as Musetta and baritone Bernard Turgeon as Marcello—attracted a 94 percent capacity house as opposed to a 38 percent house for *The Consul*.[5] Both operas lost money: *La Bohème*, $5,911 and *The Consul*, $20,829. The VOA decision to present a modern opera so early in its development was a brave one, and the audience response might have been better had the opera not had to compete with *La Bohème*. Guttman considered,

▲ In act 2, scene 3 of *Norma*, Joan Sutherland in the title role beseeches her father, Oroveso (Richard Cross), the Head Priest of the Druids, to care for her children after her death. Members of the women's chorus as Druid priestesses form the background of this scene.
BARRY GLASS PHOTOGRAPH

Bravo!

and still considers, *The Consul* an artistic success. He recalls that there were standing ovations for the performances but acknowledges that Vancouver audiences were not ready to embrace the modern repertoire. As for the VOA, it reacted quickly and decisively to the message its patrons delivered and returned for the most part to the tried-and-true repertoire for the remainder of the decade.

It is not the writer's intention to list here every opera produced by the VOA between the years 1960–74. The reader who wishes to know these details is directed to Appendix A, which lists by season and title every opera put on since the company's beginning. In addition, the reader may wish to consult a useful early compilation covering the years 1960 to 1974, which may be found as Appendix I in David Watmough's book, *The Unlikely Pioneer*, already cited here.

However, there are several productions that warrant mention in some detail to chart the history of opera during the period covered by this chapter. The first of these is the presentation in early 1965 of *The Italian Girl in Algiers* (*L'Italiana in Algeri*, Rossini), starring Marilyn Horne as Isabella. Two errors in artistic judgment contributed to the failure of this production at the box office: first, overestimating the appeal of Horne as a star of adequate stature to fill the house for five performances; second, allowing Horne to sing in English because she had not had time to learn the Italian libretto.

Despite Horne's memorable singing in *Norma* the previous year, her reputation had not grown sufficiently to attract star-struck opera patrons in sufficient numbers, and Vancouver audiences had already indicated their preference to hear operas sung in the original language when *The Tales of Hoffmann* was performed in English in 1961.[6]

Two anecdotes about *The Italian Girl in Algiers* provide insight into artistic temperament and onstage, unscripted humour. Nicolette McIntosh recalled an incident that occurred during the piano rehearsal: "*The Italian Girl* was conducted by Henry Lewis, Marilyn Horne's husband. The tenor who sang Lindoro was being very difficult, complaining about being on his feet for so long. [Lewis] finally said, 'You're complaining, and this woman, (pointing to his pregnant wife), has been on her feet for just as long as you have,' and then he threw his baton at the tenor. It ricocheted off the piano over Harold Brown's head [the rehearsal pianist], and shot across the stage. It was very dramatic."

Those who were in the theatre for one unidentified performance of *The Italian Girl in Algiers* might not have been aware of an incident that occurred onstage and was recounted in Jack Wasserman's column in the *Vancouver Sun*, February 24, 1965: "During performances of the 'Italian Girl in Algiers' one of the bit players who spends virtually all his time on his knees, wraps his knees with rolls of toilet paper

for padding. So one end of the roll came loose and drifted down his pant leg. At this point, the unsuspecting player had to make one of his few moves across the stage. An equally unsuspecting singer was standing on the exposed end of the roll. The ensuing scene has seldom, if ever, been duplicated in the history of opera. Company manager Karl Norman claimed a first: 'In this opera we have included a role that wasn't written by Rossini.'"

The Italian Girl in Algiers was followed two months later by a repeat of the VOA's original presentation, *Carmen*, noteworthy because for the first time, closed-circuit TV cameras were used to enable the chorus to get its cues accurately from the conductor via small monitors in the wings.

The apparent blot on Guttman's copybook from *The Italian Girl in Algiers* was soon forgotten when it was revealed that Joan Sutherland would sing the role of Lucia for six performances of *Lucia di Lammermoor* in March 1967. Either willing to risk again the financial burden of Sutherland's fee or unwilling to forgo

the prestige of presenting the Australian diva on the VOA stage again, the board chose to ignore its previous policy decision regarding the casting of high-priced singers. Unfortunately, VOA president Bjorn Hareid was obliged to report that despite special scaling of ticket prices and sellout performances, ticket sales did not cover the costs, which was an important measure of fiscal responsibility in those days. Sutherland's fee was again responsible for the shortfall and she did not sing again for the VOA until 1972. However, owing to a special grant from the Federal Centennial Committee and other substantial grants totalling $104,000, Hareid was able to report some good news: an end-of-season surplus of $118,868.

But in spite of there being many more highs than lows in VOA productions, discontent with the artistic director and pressing administrative problems were apparent at the board between the years 1965–68: three managers came and went within three years; Gail McCance, the VOA's redoubtable set designer, announced

▲ Vancouver Opera staged *La Bohème* in 1964, and cast Heather Thomson as Mimi and Ralph Porretta as Rodolfo. In this act 1 scene, Mimi sings her lovely aria, "Mi chiamano Mimi," which touches Rodolfo and stirs his first feelings of love for her. BARRY GLASS PHOTOGRAPH

Bravo!

in mid-1966 that for medical reasons, he would not continue beyond the following season; negotiations with Actors' Equity over chorus remuneration were not going well; outgoing President Andreasen had been replaced by Jo Walton (formerly Jo Goad), who resigned in protest after less than a year in office because of an executive decision made in her absence. Bjorn Hareid succeeded Walton and much to his distaste, as a supporter of Guttman, the anti-Guttman faction of the executive committee administered a seeming rebuke to Guttman, upset as they were by his frequent absences from the city and his increasing involvement with other opera companies. They passed a motion in October 1967 "that Mr. Guttman be given a three-year contract as artistic director, subject to his being advised that he will not direct all the operas." When this became public knowledge, Guttman was interviewed by the press. He justified his absences, explaining that he needed to spend time in the East to keep abreast of what was going on in the rest of the opera world and maintain his network—but to no avail. The board hired seven guest stage directors during the remainder of Guttman's tenure.

Although these internecine issues made good copy for the media, the course of opera was not duly harmed. Guttman continued to schedule and cast fine productions. The 1967–68 season went well and was made particularly noteworthy by the appearance on the VOA stage of the now legendary Plácido Domingo, then a new and exciting young singer gaining considerable attention in operatic circles. Guttman, to his credit, obtained Domingo at an early stage in his meteoric career to sing the role of Cavaradossi in *Tosca* for five performances in May 1968. The tenor was only twenty-seven years old and already much in demand. The previous year Domingo had made his debut at the Hamburg State Opera in the same role, and in September 1968 he debuted at the Metropolitan.

Peggy Mathisen, head of the women's committee of the VOA at the time and one

▲ An ensemble scene for the 1965 Vancouver Opera production of *The Italian Girl in Algiers*, which starred Marilyn Horne as Isabella, seen front centre, and Herbert Beattie as Mustapha, seated on the left.
BARRY GLASS PHOTOGRAPH

of its most devoted volunteers in the early days, tells an amusing anecdote about Domingo. She and her husband, Dr. Arne Mathisen, also a great supporter of the VOA, were renowned for their hospitality, hosting parties after the opening performance of every opera for many years. They owned a farm in the country and often invited visiting singers to spend a Sunday with them there to relieve them of a lonely day in the city. On one such Sunday Domingo told them that he had wanted to be a bullfighter but his mother would not hear of it. Upon spying a young bull in a nearby field, he asked if Mathisen had anything red; she produced a red bedspread and much to his hosts' horror, Domingo, bedspread in hand, climbed

over the fence and attempted to antagonize the creature into an impromptu bullfight. Mathisen recalls her understandable anxiety: "I thought, 'Dear God, *please* don't let anything happen.'"

Fortunately nothing did happen, and Domingo so pleased audiences and critics that he was brought back the following season in the role of the Chevalier des Grieux for five performances of *Manon* (Jules Massenet). However, a disappointing 55 percent of available tickets were sold for *Manon*, reinforcing what audiences had already demonstrated: the lesser-known repertoire did not appeal to them. Fortunately the other two operas of the season were crowd-pleasers, especially *Faust*, in which Heather

▲   Joan Sutherland as Lucia, dressed for her arranged
marriage to Lord Arturo, act 2, scene 2 of *Lucia di
Lammermoor*, staged by Vancouver Opera in 1967.
BARRY GLASS PHOTOGRAPH

Bravo!

Thomson, on the verge of her international career, returned to the VOA stage to sing the role of Marguerite.[7] Her performance received excellent reviews, but the headline for James Barber's column (*Vancouver Province*, February 21, 1969) said it all: "Heather Thomson was unbelievably perfect in the role."

The VOA marked its tenth anniversary season, 1969–70 by presenting four productions instead of the usual three. Two of them, *Salome* (Richard Strauss) and *The Elixir of Love*, were unpopular at the box office, with the result that a deficit of $66, 263, including the previous year's deficit, was reported at the end of the fiscal year, causing pundits to forecast another year or two of well-loved standards in the future.

For the production of *Aïda* in October 1970, the sets were rented from Seattle Opera and, although they were not up to past set designer Gail McCance's standard, they saved the company a lot of money. Co-operation with other companies, especially for sets and costumes, was beginning to be recognized by most opera management as an economic necessity, something that Robert Philips first brought up during his presidency in the early years. VOA sets, built by Harold Laxton, were rented during the season to Edmonton, Seattle, Portland, San Diego and Houston.

The February show of the 1970–71 season was *Madama Butterfly* and offered for the first time a children's matinee performance. Two more similar events

took place in February of 1972 and 1975 but were discontinued thereafter, presumably because of the Opera in the Schools initiative, which began in 1973.[8]

On the VOA stage for the first time since 1966, Judith Forst sang the role of Nicklausse in *The Tales of Hoffmann*, directed by Bliss Hebert. It was the last production of the 1970–71 season, which ended on a more positive note than the previous one. The deficit had been reduced to $23,979 and first-time grants from the Municipality of Burnaby, the City of New Westminster and the District of New Westminster were a welcome indication that municipal governments were at last becoming aware that people in their communities comprised part of VOA's audience base.

The 1971–72 season presented the double bill of *Cavalleria Rusticana* and *Pagliacci* (commonly referred to as *Cav-Pag* in opera-speak). Heather Thomson returned to the VOA stage to sing the role of Nedda in *Pagliacci* to critical acclaim. Max Wyman (*Vancouver Sun*, February 18, 1972) wrote, "Miss Thomson combines both vocal and dramatic resource in extensive measure. She creates a seductive, wholly credible Nedda . . . There is a light silveriness to her tone, and a warmth and purity too, that both intrigues and satisfies—with a flowing line that binds all neatly together."

Wyman took the opportunity to vent his spleen on the opening night audience: "Thursday's crowd was the ultimate in

boorishness and provincialism—complete with numerous late-comers, persistent talkers and whisperers, and the usual array of compulsive clappers. If you are one of those who persists in treating opera as an accompaniment to dressing up and being seen, may I suggest that in future you stay home, put on a recording, and stand in your finery by your lighted front window." Fortunately patrons, including any leftover boors, filled over 90 percent of the house for subsequent performances.

Turandot (Puccini) followed *Cav-Pag* to close out the season. When it became apparent that Filipina soprano Evelyn Mandac, cast in the role of Liù, was unable to perform due to illness, Ruth

Huang, a member of the VOA Chorus, was called upon at the last minute to replace her. Huang made the most of her golden opportunity, singing and acting extremely well.

The next season was memorable because of its blockbuster opener, six performances of *Lucrezia Borgia* featuring the husband-and-wife combination of Richard Bonynge as conductor and Joan Sutherland in the title role, and directed by Guttman.[9] The opera was an unusual choice, since it had been performed only twice in North America in the twentieth century, in 1904 and 1967, but it likely had a lot to do with Bonynge's growing interest in promoting the revival of the

▲ Nancy Tatum as Tosca and Plácido Domingo as Cavaradossi, the ill-fated lovers in *Tosca*, staged by Vancouver Opera in 1968. BARRY GLASS PHOTOGRAPH

Bravo!

bel canto operas of Donizetti, Bellini and other eighteenth- and nineteenth-century composers. However, there was likely another, less obvious, reason: by Sutherland making her role debut on the VOA stage, she and Bonynge were able to get the bugs out of the performance, thus sparing themselves debuting it in a more prestigious house and exposing themselves to a more critical reception. Although Sutherland was the undisputed star, the rest of the cast—which included principals Louis Quilico as Alfonso, John Alexander as Gennaro and Canadian mezzo-soprano Huguette Tourangeau as Maffio Orsini—was up to the challenge. By all accounts it was a splendid show, attended by a capacity audience.

Irving Guttman's long and distinguished career with the VOA ironically ended with the opera originally intended to be the association's first under his direction: *La Traviata*. Doubly ironic is that all five of the productions under his direction in the last two seasons of his tenure were popular and successful

at the box office. Nevertheless, what had been set in motion by the board during the late sixties came to pass in June 1974 when Guttman, knowing within himself it was time to move on, did not renew his contract.[10] Max Wyman (*Vancouver Sun*, April 26, 1974) bid Guttman a critic's adieu with the following compliment: "Irving Guttman's swan-song with the Vancouver Opera Association could hardly have been more impressive if he had deliberately set out to leave behind him, after 14 years, one last enduring impression to be remembered by . . . [*La Traviata*] brings together what one remembers as the best elements of Guttman's work . . . and blends them into what is, by a good distance, the finest production of the current season." Evidently, opera patrons thought enough of the show and of the outgoing artistic director to attend in near-capacity numbers: almost 97 percent of the tickets were sold.

In addition to the productions of the VOA during the period covered by this chapter, the Vancouver International

▲ Marilyn Horne (Rosina) listens demurely to Napoléon Bisson (Dr. Bartolo), her guardian, who tells her in act 1, scene 2 that he is on to her wiles. Vancouver Opera staged this production of *The Barber of Seville* in 1968.
BARRY GLASS PHOTOGRAPH

Festival also included an opera in its annual program of arts events. The 1960 festival, which ran from July 22 to August 16, opened with a production of *Madama Butterfly*. Teresa Stratas, a young Canadian soprano making a name for herself at the Metropolitan, sang the role of Cio-Cio-San and Canadian tenor Richard Verreau was cast as Pinkerton. Stratas has been likened to Maria Callas for her fine voice and acting ability, and the production was a huge success, drawing a capacity audience. Also on the festival program that year was the children's opera, *Noye's Fludde* (*Noah's Flood*, Benjamin Britten). Christ Church Cathedral in downtown Vancouver was the venue for the performance, which was directed by Joy Coghill, a well-known Vancouver actress and director; conductor, pianist and CBC personality John Avison was the musical director. The cathedral was sold out for the performance on July 30 and people were lined up outside beforehand, hoping to get last-minute tickets. The ambitious agenda for this third festival also included the Peking Opera, received with great enthusiasm despite the Chinese cast being urged by locals to defect and the production being picketed and boycotted by various groups.

The festival committee obtained the rights to present the North American premiere of *A Midsummer Night's Dream* (Britten) as the opera for the fourth festival, July 14 to August 19, 1961. It was a tour de force: Metropolitan Opera star Mary Costa was cast as Tytania

and American counter-tenor Russell Oberlin reprised the role of Oberon that he had sung at Covent Garden in 1960; Joy Coghill earned much praise in the speaking role of Puck. Unfortunately, although recording the largest attendance of all previous festivals, the fourth year concluded with a deficit of $52,000.

For the 1962 festival, the board of directors attempted to stem the financial losses by programming *The Magic Flute* and two Gilbert and Sullivan operettas. Although the opera played to a capacity crowd, it alone could not pull the festival out of deficit. The following year, Vancouver audiences did not respond in large numbers to *Macbeth* (Verdi), the opera chosen to open a reduced sixth annual festival. Although the cast and the production were of a respectable standard, the opera had never before been performed in Vancouver and was unfamiliar to many. Also, it followed close on the heels of the VOA's production of five well-attended performances of *Aida* between April 27 and May 11, 1963.

Sadly, the festival society and its remaining five festivals entered a downhill spiral financially. The seventh, 1964, did not feature a full opera production, presenting instead the concert opera,

▲ Richard Bonynge and Joan Sutherland in Vancouver for her debut performance as Hannah Glawari in Lehár's *The Merry Widow*, April–May 1976. Bonynge conducted the production.
PHOTO COURTESY VANCOUVER OPERA

Bravo!

The Damnation of Faust (La Damnation de Faust, Hector Berlioz). No opera was on the program of the eighth festival, but the ninth featured *Hansel and Gretel,* an opera suitable for children, in keeping with the festival's informal theme of a salute to youth. It was the first of two operas produced for the festival society by the VOA and directed by Irving Guttman, the second being *The Girl of the Golden West (La Fanciulla del West,* Puccini), starring American soprano Dorothy Kirsten and presented during the eleventh and last Vancouver International Festival in 1968.

Before moving on to the next phase in the history of opera in the province, five important opera-related initiatives during the period 1966 to 1974 must be mentioned:

the Young Singer Training Program; BC Opera Ensemble tours to communities outside the Lower Mainland; the Resident Artist Program; the Opera in the Schools productions, begun as a project of the Vancouver Opera Guild; and the formation of the Vancouver New Music Society.

The Young Singer Training Program was initiated in 1966 by the VOA to provide promising local singers, most of them members of the VOA Chorus, with free voice and acting instruction to enhance their performances onstage. Students were auditioned and they became members of what was called the BC Opera Ensemble. Many went on to good careers in opera and a few graduates, including Judith Forst, Riki

▲ Artistic director Irving Guttman puts the finishing touches on the final scenes of *La Bohème* at the dress rehearsal of the opera, presented by Vancouver Opera in 1964. BARRY GLASS PHOTOGRAPH

Turofsky and Lyn Vernon, won national competitions and scholarships and left Vancouver for some time to further their careers in larger North American centres and abroad. However, while they were still in the program they were given the opportunity to take leading roles in the touring productions of the BC Opera Ensemble, for which the VOA obtained funding from the provincial government in return for 66 percent of the box-office receipts. The first of these was *Hansel and Gretel*, which toured a number of small towns in BC before it was presented as the Vancouver Festival opera in 1966. In the cast were Judith Forst as Hansel, Sophie Turko as the witch and Christine Anton as Gretel. The tour was considered a success despite uneven attendance at the thirty-two centres it visited. Next, the ensemble took Offenbach's *Orpheus in the Underworld* to a number of central and southern interior towns, beginning in the fall of 1967. However, because of late funding, the advance publicity suffered and consequently so did the tour. During this period the ensemble also presented several studio operas, but by the time the VOA president gave his annual report two and a half years later, the Young Singer Training Program and, with it, the BC Opera Ensemble had been dismantled; the reason given in the annual report was "a lack of talented singers to merit the teaching facilities required." The real reason was more likely the worrisome deficit.

Taking its place was a new VOA initiative: the Resident Artist Program. The intent was to create the nucleus of a permanent resident opera company in Vancouver, admitting singers by audition and providing instruction and a subsistence income. The "residents" were able to earn additional money by singing in supporting roles for the VOA. The program foundered when Irving Guttman left the VOA in 1974 but was revived shortly after when Richard Bonynge became artistic director. Bonynge

▲ Ensemble scene from *A Midsummer Night's Dream*, featuring Oberon, King of the Fairies, (Russell Oberlin) and Tytania, Queen of the Fairies, (Mary Costa), presented as part of the 1961 Vancouver International Festival. BARRY GLASS PHOTOGRAPH

▲ Well-known Vancouver theatrical personality Joy Coghill applied her acting talent to the speaking role of Puck in the Vancouver International Festival's production of *A Midsummer Night's Dream* in 1961. BARRY GLASS PHOTOGRAPH

Bravo!

conducted auditions in late 1974 and for a fee of $750, successful candidates were guaranteed a yearly income and roles in VOA, Edmonton Opera and Manitoba Opera productions. However, by 1976, despite support from the Vancouver Foundation, the program was losing too much money and the financially troubled VOA Board closed it down.

Opera in the Schools (OIS) was the brainchild of members of the Vancouver Opera Guild who saw it as a way to make opera appealing to young children and thus generate future audiences for VOA productions. The first opera chosen to begin the program in the 1972–73 school year was *The Marriage of Figaro*, presented in a forty-five minute version with a small ensemble of singers who were members of the chorus, an accompanist and volunteers to assist with costumes, makeup, portable

sets and so on. Since then the format has varied only slightly, but artistic and administrative responsibility for OIS passed from the guild to the VOA at the end of the 1980–81 school year. What began as a free educational venture for the first two years, apart from a modest performance fee of $50, now costs approximately $700. A union wage is paid to the singers and other professionals involved, who comprise what is now known as the Vancouver Opera Touring Ensemble. The guild continues to support OIS with volunteers and financial assistance and the program has grown to be one of the largest and most popular in Canada. While continuing the student productions and maintaining the same truncated format, it has expanded into local communities, attracting family audiences to performances in gymnasiums

▲ In act 1, scene 2 of the Vancouver International Festival's 1963 production of *Macbeth*, Lady Macbeth (Mary Curtis-Vernon) and Macbeth (Frank Guarrera) hatch their murderous plans for Duncan after hearing the witches' prophecy. BARRY GLASS PHOTOGRAPH

and community centres throughout the province. Still operating, it is the longest-standing outreach enterprise of the VOA and the Vancouver Opera Guild.

The Vancouver New Music Society (VNM) was formed in 1972 by a group of people prominent in the local music world, including Ian Hampton, at the time principal cellist of the Vancouver Symphony Orchestra and the CBC Vancouver Chamber Orchestra; George Laverock, CBC Radio producer; Phyllis Mailing, mezzo-soprano soloist and voice teacher; and Simon Streatfeild, conductor. As its name indicates, the society's aim was to promote and support the creation and performance of new music, including opera, primarily by Canadian musicians. Although during the early years the operatic works presented were not composed by Canadians, Vancouver musicians and singers were employed to stage VNM's first two offerings, *Down by the Greenwood Side* (Harrison Birtwistle) in 1973 and *Renard* (*The Fox*, Igor Stravinsky) in 1974. As we shall learn in later chapters, VNM turned increasingly to compositions by Canadians for its opera productions.

▲ *Hansel and Gretel* was produced by Vancouver Opera for the ninth Vancouver International Festival in 1966. Pictured are Christine Anton, Sophie Turko and Judith Forst, members of the BC Opera Ensemble that toured the production throughout the province prior to the Festival staging. BARRY GLASS PHOTOGRAPH

Interlude
VOA 1974 TO 1979

JUST AS THE PREVIOUS PERIOD IN THE HISTORY OF OPERA IN THE province might have been called "the Guttman years," the brief period covered by this chapter might well be termed "the Bonynge years." Richard Bonynge, the Australian conductor who first appeared with the VOA as the conductor of *Faust* in 1963, succeeded Irving Guttman as artistic director for the VOA in 1974. During his tenure, extreme and unfortunate circumstances brought the association to the brink of financial ruin. It would be simple, but incorrect, to lay the blame wholly on Bonynge's shoulders, as many did at the time. The board of the association was equally responsible for a rapidly deteriorating situation, as the following account will show.

Bonynge's contract, signed in June 1974, was for three years with a further two at the VOA's option. However, the company understood that Bonynge, who had many commitments elsewhere, would not be available full-time until the 1975–76 season, meaning the board would have to make other arrangements for 1974–75. Accordingly, Henry Butler was secured as stage director for the fall production of *Lucia di Lammermoor*; Norman Ayrton directed *Rigoletto* in January and February 1975; Herman Geiger-Torel, the renowned general director of the Canadian Opera Company, directed four performances of *Die Walküre* (*The Valkyrie*, Wagner) in March; and Bliss Hebert directed four performances of the operetta *The Gondoliers* (Gilbert and Sullivan) in April and May. Hebert was known to Vancouver audiences, having directed *The Elixir of Love* in 1969, *The Tales of Hoffmann* in 1971 and *Cav-Pag* in 1972. The only appearance of Bonynge during the season was in February to conduct the Resident Artist Program's presentation of *La Buona Figliuola* (*The Good-Natured Girl*, Niccolò Piccinni) in the Playhouse Theatre. The 1974–75 season comprised four productions instead of three for only the second

◄ Heather Thomson as Cio-Cio-San awaits the arrival of Lieutenant Pinkerton in act 1 of Puccini's *Madama Butterfly*, which opened Vancouver Opera's 1978 spring repertory season.
PHOTO COURTESY VANCOUVER OPERA

time, the first being in 1969–70. The explanation may be that the last event of the season, *The Gondoliers*, featured singers from the Resident Artist Program in the leading roles. As reported in the press the previous fall, the Canada Council had given the Resident Artist Program only $8,100, referring "slightingly to it as an 'apprenticeship' program."[1] Presenting the operetta in the Queen Elizabeth Theatre as a bona fide part of the season and charging full ticket prices was seen as an error in judgment by Bonynge and the VOA, and added insult to injury to many patrons who considered the production second-rate at best.

The ensuing brouhaha took the board aback and caused the directors to retreat to their usual defensive position when faced with controversy: stick to the tried-and-true. That type of programming, however, could not have been more at odds with the new artistic director's plans for the company. Bonynge had made it known that he intended to show Vancouver what good opera really was and, quoted by Max Wyman (*Vancouver Sun*, May 9, 1975), he made it clear that he would tolerate no interference from his board in artistic decisions: "I am entirely against the idea of sticking to safe operas. If that's what they want they don't need an artistic director, and I for one would have no intention of staying here." In his view the board's job was to raise money, and he had quite a bit to say in public about the shortage of that commodity: "It's a terrible state of affairs here. There is no money—and I come from a country where the government finances opera for the whole year." And in answer to the question of whether he was aware of this situation before he signed on: "Certainly not as aware of it as I am now." Bonynge went on to say that raising money was not his job: "That's not what I was hired for—if it was, it was surely a

▲ Richard Bonynge, Vancouver Opera's artistic director and conductor, on the set of Rossini's *Semiramide*, the opening production of the 1975–76 season.
PHOTO COURTESY VANCOUVER OPERA

mistaken idea—they can get somebody else."[2] What Bonynge said about a lack of funds was true. The VOA was finding it more and more difficult to get grants from the three levels of government in the province, as president W.R. Steen reported at the 1974 annual general meeting, and the board's fundraising program was not even close to being capable of financing Bonynge's plans for the company.

The board was rudely jolted from its naivety when Bonynge announced his plans for the 1975–76 season, which were obviously going to be costly. The opening fall production was to be the bel canto opera *Semiramide* (Rossini), starring American soprano Marvelee Cariaga in the title role, Canadian mezzo Huguette Tourangeau, who had made her Metropolitan Opera debut in 1973, as Arsace, and American James Morris, the leading bass-baritone at the Metropolitan since 1971, as Assur. The next production was to be *The Queen of Spades* (Tchaikovsky) with Regina Resnik, of Metropolitan and international fame, in a new career as stage director and also in the leading role of the Countess; followed by *Faust*, with Heather Thomson, by then much in demand in North America and abroad, reprising her 1969 VOA appearance as Marguerite; and Canadian bass, Don Garrard, as Méphistophélès. *The Merry Widow* would complete the season, with Joan Sutherland in her debut performance as the widow, Hanna Glawari, and bass Jan Rubes of the

Canadian Opera Company as Baron Zeta. *Faust* was the only one of these four operas to have previously been put on by the VOA and fell into the tried-and-true category; *The Merry Widow* was not an opera, but an operetta, which would not escape patrons already testy about *The Gondoliers*.

Bonynge and the VOA Board did not see eye to eye on other matters:

▲ Regina Resnik played the Countess in Tchaikovsky's *The Queen of Spades* in addition to her role as stage director for the 1976 Vancouver Opera production.
PHOTO COURTESY VANCOUVER OPERA

Bonynge insisted on a minimum of three weeks for rehearsals as opposed to the customary eight or ten days. When he learned that the company had rented what he considered "tatty" sets from the Canadian Opera Company for *The Merry Widow*, he was outraged: "I consider my wife's appearance here an important event that merits a new production. Certainly it deserves better treatment than that. It shows no style at all."[3] Despite considerable dissension, the board deferred to him in these matters and put on a brave face. VOA general manager Brian Hanson was the company's spokesman in the press (Ray Chatelin, *Vancouver Province*, December 13, 1974): "The Vancouver Opera Association

1975–76 season gives promise of being one of artistic and box-office success. It can be truly said that as the VOA goes into its 16th season it does so with the knowledge of having reached even greater professional achievement."

However, the forecast of a brilliant season turned out to be wishful thinking. Ticket sales accounted for only one-half of the costs of production and were lowest for *The Queen of Spades* and highest for *The Merry Widow*, not surprising considering Joan Sutherland's great drawing power. Even the usually popular *Faust* failed to ignite audience and critic enthusiasm, despite Heather Thomson's brilliant performance as Marguerite, which, according to one reviewer, was

▲ Joan Sutherland, wearing a beautiful blue dress and hat, and company in an ensemble scene from Lehár's *The Merry Widow*, Vancouver Opera 1976 production. Miss Sutherland's costumes were made by Barbara Matera Ltd., New York. PHOTO COURTESY VANCOUVER OPERA

the only redeeming feature of a ho-hum production. Thomson's superb singing was the paradoxical outcome of a backstage incident on opening night that left her badly shaken:

I came into my dressing room and there was an envelope lying on my dressing table. I thought nothing of it . . . because frequently people will write and say how much they are looking forward to a performance. As I was reading it . . . things started to blur . . . it was a horrible letter that some nutcase had written. He said that I looked like some hot bitch . . . and that he belonged to a motorcycle gang and that they were going to kidnap me and take me up to their clubhouse, and what they were going to do to me . . .was horrible . . . I was shaking, and I took it up to the stage manager . . . The police came, and they hung around while I was in the theatre . . . and I remember standing in the wings waiting for my first entrance in the dark there, and I thought, 'Who can this be? It could be some person who's already in the theatre, or maybe some person who, when I step out on the stage, is going to stand up in the audience and shoot me.' And something took over and I just decided, 'Well, they're either going to shoot me, or I'm singing the best damned performance in my life,' so I marched out onstage, and I hung on to that last note in the aria forever—here I am! [The police eventually caught the culprit.]

The season's deficit of $42,258, when added to the previous year's, brought the two-year total to $131,806; higher administration expenses and losses associated with the Resident Artist Program contributed to the red ink. When reporting this bad news to the membership in 1976, president W.R. Robson said, "I think it only fair to say that one area in which your board has been remiss in this past season is in the area of continuing open and frank communications with Mr. Bonynge." The casualties associated with this period were heavy and included the loss of a long-standing board member and past-president, Bjorn Hareid, a respected member of the Vancouver legal community and a knowledgeable opera devotee. After more than ten years' service, Hareid resigned from the board in 1976 when his attempts to curb Bonynge's costly productions and the board's enthusiasm for them failed. In an interview he recalled those days clearly: "I resigned because I didn't agree with the policies at the time. Bonynge came and said he was going to put on world-class opera and [the board] gave him a free hand. I was not going to be a part of that. We used to have budgets, and Irving Guttman had to stay within that budget, but not Mr. Bonynge. I had some talks with [Bonynge] . . . I wanted to tell him exactly . . . we couldn't afford [his productions]. He promised that he was going to do something about it, but he didn't, and when the board decided to keep him, I said, 'Well, I don't think I have a

general meeting that a formal meeting with Bonynge would take place on October 30. Whatever transpired at that meeting is not on public record but it obviously had no effect on the calamitous course of events.

During the fall of the 1976–77 season, an unpleasant surprise was in store for the Vancouver Symphony Orchestra (VSO), which had been the pit orchestra for the VOA from the start. The bombshell exploded one day when Michael Allerton, the manager of the VSO, learned from a newspaper that the VOA was performing on dates that coincided with VSO scheduled concerts:

> [Allerton] wanted to believe it was a printing error, but it wasn't. Without warning, Bonynge had thrown the VSO out of the opera pit, and was hiring freelance players and creating his own opera orchestra. Allerton suspected he was looking at a *fait accompli*, and that gave him plenty to worry about.
>
> The opera represented roughly seven weeks of work for the VSO, a very significant portion of the total number of weeks for which the musicians were contracted. The society had just signed a new master agreement that promised the orchestra an increase from thirty-six to forty-three weeks. Losing the opera services meant that the management now had fourteen weeks of new concerts to sell to the public, rather than the seven that they had originally planned on.[4]

place on this Board anymore.'"

Hareid's wife, Lori, herself an opera lover and one of the first volunteers with the women's committee of the VOA, had these remarks to add to Bjorn's: "We had wonderful opera before Bonynge came. There were people on the board . . . so awed with Bonynge they let him do anything he wanted."

Adding to the general uproar in the Vancouver opera community were the local critics' near-unanimous negative opinions of the artistic merits of the season. The ultimate sacrilege occurred when prima donna Joan Sutherland was criticized for her lack of acting skills. To deal with the internal situation, President Robson informed the assembled at the annual

▲ *Faust* was Vancouver Opera's third opera in its 1975–76 season of four offerings, and starring as Marguerite was local favourite Heather Thomson, shown here in act 4, scene 1, saddened by Faust's neglect and performing the spinning song, "Il ne revient pas."
PHOTO COURTESY VANCOUVER OPERA

When the news broke, the season was already underway with *La Bohème* as its first offering, and the musicians of the VSO were in the pit. Bonynge did not return to Vancouver until the next production, *Mignon*, was staged in early 1977, at which time he was not only on the podium but also in the hot seat. Despite the symphony society's strenuous protests that, in allowing Bonynge to act in so harmful a way to the VSO, the VOA Board was being reckless and gutless, the decision was a *fait accompli*. Bonynge's stated reasons for his seemingly arbitrary action was that he did not want to have to accommodate the VSO's schedule when planning the VOA's and wanted more rehearsal time with the musicians,

but apparently there was another factor in the dynamics, which he naturally did not acknowledge: "VSO players had very little respect for Bonynge and took every opportunity to show it . . . To them, playing for Joan Sutherland's husband in a cramped and uncomfortable bunker under the stage was demeaning."[5]

Evidently there were plenty of excellent freelance professional musicians willing to play for Bonynge, and when *Le Roi de Lahore* (*The King of Lahore*, Massenet) opened on September 23, 1977, the new Vancouver Opera Orchestra was in the pit. Sharman King, long-time bass trombonist in the VO Orchestra, was there and recounted in an interview how he came to be one of the charter members:

▲ Spiro Malas as Indra, Joan Sutherland as Sita, and Huguette Tourangeau as Kaled in the 1977 fall repertory season opening production of Massenet's *Le Roi de Lahore*. Richard Bonynge conducted the newly formed Vancouver Opera Orchestra, which was in the pit for the first time. PHOTO COURTESY VANCOUVER OPERA

Bravo!

▲ The lovers, Ron Stevens as Alim and Joan Sutherland as Sita, in a tender embrace in Massenet's *Le Roi de Lahore*, which opened the Vancouver Opera's fall repertory season in 1977. The Vancouver Opera Orchestra, conducted by Richard Bonynge, made its debut amid considerable controversy.
PHOTO COURTESY VANCOUVER OPERA

▲ Constanza Cuccaro as Marie in the title role leads members of the regiment in a lively march in Donizetti's *La Fille du Régiment*, the second production in the Vancouver Opera 1977 fall repertory season.
PHOTO COURTESY VANCOUVER OPERA

At the time in Vancouver the freelance non-symphony music business was very good for musicians . . . in fact, it was advantageous to a string player not to be in the symphony because there was so much other work, and in general it was better-paying work, so there was a large body of musicians outside of the symphony available. Zena Wagstaff, who was the first contractor for the opera orchestra, was a friend of the Bonynges—that's what she called them—and he had approached her about putting an orchestra together. We were playing a recording session at Little Mountain Sound . . . with a large orchestra . . . and during a break, Zena walked up to a bunch of us and said 'Would you be interested in playing in an orchestra to play for the operas?' We were all standing around—well, [the operas] are spread out over a lot of time . . . so it means you don't work that much, so you don't get paid that much . . . but it was Dave Robbins and, I believe, Donny Clark, a trumpet player, who said, 'You know, we're spending all our time playing all this different music. Why don't we do this, this should be fun.' So we all said, 'Okay, fine, we're in,' so Zena contracted the orchestra for the first performance, which was Massenet's *The King of Lahore*, with Joan Sutherland in the leading role . . . The orchestra never really had a learning curve. It started out . . . a fine orchestra from the beginning, and having Bonynge as a conductor

was good, because he was such a communicative musician. I don't believe anyone would accuse him of having the best technique as a conductor, but he didn't need it. Because he was such a good conductor, you just knew what to do, and I look back on those times with great fondness . . . Of the fifty-five people who played the first show, there are still thirteen of us in the orchestra this many years later.[6]

During this tumultuous period, the VOA was in the midst of implementing another major change: becoming a repertory company, beginning in the 1977–78 season. Rumoured to have been introduced for Bonynge's convenience to allow him to fulfill his international commitments, and perceived by the board as an innovative way to conserve resources and increase revenues, the plan was doomed from the beginning, in spite of the varied works planned: *Le Roi de Lahore*, *La Fille du Régiment* and *Don Giovanni* for the fall season and *Madama Butterfly*, *The Magic Flute* and *The Barber of Seville* for the spring. On the strength of the repertoire alone, the venture might have been a success but the board, its general manager, Barry Thompson, and Bonynge seriously misjudged the public's reaction to such a revolutionary change to their long-established opera-going pattern. Coupled with generally poor reviews of the artistic merits of the productions, attendance

Bravo!

was significantly lower, which in turn
translated into a crippling accumulated
deficit of over $400,000 for the company
and an abrupt end to Bonynge's position
as artistic director. Even before the end
of the disastrous repertory experiment,
the VOA issued a press release dated
March 31, 1978, to announce that Barry
Thompson's resignation had been accepted
and that, "After recent discussion with
Mr. Bonynge held in New York, the
board has agreed that he will remain
as consulting artistic director through
to June 1980 despite the fact that his
extensive commitments elsewhere prevent
his presence in this city." It was clear to
all that this new title was nothing more
than face-saving for Bonynge and an "out"

for the board. The remaining two years
of Bonynge's contract were to be paid out
over time and there is no evidence that his
services as a consultant were ever called
on. His parting advice to the board, which
it heeded, was that it should not revert to
using the VSO as the pit orchestra. The
VO Orchestra proved to be Bonynge's
most important legacy to the company, or,
as former artistic director Irving Guttman
put it, "Ricky [Bonynge] was right."

Down but not out, the VOA Board
took further decisive and drastic actions: it
closed down the Resident Artist Program;
it abandoned its repertory experiment; it
put on three operas guaranteed to please
Vancouver audiences the next season—*Aida*,
starring Polish soprano Teresa Kubiak as
Aida, *Carmen*, with Vancouver's own Judith
Forst singing the title role and *La Traviata*,
with popular Canadian baritone Bernard
Turgeon as Germont—all playing to sold-
out houses; and it undertook for the first
time an aggressive fundraising campaign.
By the end of June 1979 the deficit had
been reduced, not by enough to satisfy the
auditors, but enough to encourage the board
that the VOA could survive to carry on
with the next season after all.

It should have been clear from the
beginning that Bonynge and the VOA
were not a good match. If Bonynge
was looking to advance the restoration
of bel canto opera in Vancouver, as
many believed, he must have been very
disillusioned; and if the VOA was hoping
to see its stature raised to the level of

▲ The Don (James Morris), left, and Leporello (Spiro
Malas) are up to no good in act 2 as the Don plots to
seduce Donna Elvira's maid, Zerlina, who is betrothed
to Masetto. The production, Mozart's *Don Giovanni*,
closed the Vancouver Opera's fall repertory season in
October 1977. PHOTO COURTESY VANCOUVER OPERA

the great opera houses of the world, the Bonynge years were a sobering reality check. In an interview David Lemon, an opera enthusiast who became a member of the VOA Board in 1983, provided his view of how things went so wrong, and defended Bonynge:

> We had as good from him as he got from us. Getting Joan Sutherland and Huguette Tourangeau here was a real advance for Vancouver. The problem Vancouver Opera [Association] had is that it always tried to punch above its weight. New artistic directors came here and it all looked very expensive and shiny, and they got treated well by people who had beautiful homes . . . and they got the impression that there was tons of money here, and they were always disappointed. If you bring in someone of [Bonynge's] stature, you have to be ready to pay for what they want to do. Guus Mostart [artistic director 1989–92] had the same huge disappointment. Opera is not core to the culture of the place. The board thought you could work some kind of operatic magic with these tiny little budgets. The whole notion of aggressively pushing for sponsorships was absolutely unheard of. The company had plugged along on government money and patrons like Mrs. Rogers and lots of little private donations, which is why I say Irving [Guttman] did miracles with tiny amounts of money.

Richard Bonynge is scheduled to conduct *Norma* in November 2009, the first opera of the 2009–10 season. In an email sent to me on March 18, 2009, Bonynge recalled his time in Vancouver "with great affection." He is justly proud that he introduced to Vancouver a number of previously unheard operas and brought many famous singers to the city. He believes that his most lasting achievement was the formation of the VO Orchestra, and he gave much credit to Zena Wagstaff for her help. He concluded by saying, "Apart from the odd battle with the board (I never minded a good fight) I loved my time in Vancouver."

Fortunately for the history of opera in British Columbia, the VOA was not only rescued from the very real prospect of bankruptcy in 1979, but also went on to produce some fine opera in the following years, though not without a few more rides on the financial roller coaster, as we shall see in a later chapter.

Act II

VICTORIA

1979 to 1996

WHILE THE UNFORTUNATE EVENTS OF 1974 TO 1979 DESCRIBED IN THE
previous chapter were playing out in Vancouver, a more positive
development in the history of opera was unfolding across the Strait of
Georgia in the capital city of Victoria. As recounted in Overture, although
Victorians were devoted to opera, they had not seen many fully staged
professional performances since the turn of the century. Victoria had
many fine resident musicians and singers, so not surprisingly a number of
amateur companies formed to fill the void, and some of these staged very
good performances by all accounts. And although operetta and light opera
were the usual fare, some, such as the Victoria Grand Opera Association
and the Victoria Civic Opera had staged grand opera on several occasions
between 1935 and 1942 and were noteworthy for keeping the genre at the
forefront in Victoria during some lean years. The Canada Opera Touring
Production, the first touring branch of the Canadian Opera Company,
visited Victoria in 1976 and gave a matinee and an evening performance
of *La Traviata* on November 21. The company came again in 1978 to
present *The Marriage of Figaro* on November 22 and 23, and during the
1988–89 season to stage *The Tales of Hoffmann*. Amateur groups continued
to flourish in the city and one of them, the Vancouver Island Opera
Society, became the vibrant professional company known today as Pacific
Opera Victoria.

The Vancouver Island Opera Society (VIOS) was founded in 1975
by local singers, teachers and musicians, including Bruce More, the
founding president of the society; Catherine Young, the founding artistic
director; and Selena James, Erika Kurth and Karen Smith. The company
was quasi-professional, since many who took part in the productions had
professional experience, for example, conductors, members of the Victoria
Symphony Orchestra and several singers; those who did not were usually

◀ In act 5 of Pacific Opera Victoria's production of *Roméo et Juliette*, 1991, Roméo (Kevin
Anderson) stands over the seemingly lifeless body of Juliette (Kathleen Brett), not knowing of the
potion she has taken, and believing, mistakenly and with dire consequences, that she is dead.
DAVID COOPER PHOTOGRAPH

students of the Victoria Conservatory of Music or the University of Victoria School of Music. The VIOS staged several productions between 1976 and 1979; the first for which there is documentation in the form of a program was *The Marriage of Figaro*, presented in the McPherson Playhouse on November 3 and 4, 1976. Bruce More was the musical director, Dale Read of the Victoria Conservatory was the dramatic director and Stanley Chapple, from the University of Washington Faculty of Music, conducted the Victoria Symphony Orchestra in the pit. Bruce More was the production manager for the next offering, *Amahl and the Night Visitors* (Menotti), on December 21, 22, 23, 24 and 26, 1976. Two productions were mounted the following year: *The Beggar's Opera* (John Gay) in March and *The Magic Flute* in September. In the latter production, Selena James sang the role of the Queen of the Night and Erika Kurth was cast as the First Lady. Kurth also sang the role of Esmeralda in the society's 1978 production of *The Bartered Bride* (Bedřich Smetana), and native son, tenor Richard Margison, at the time a student of Selena James, made what was likely his first appearance on the stage of an opera company in the role of Jeník. *The Bartered Bride* was conducted by another native son of Victoria, Timothy Vernon.[1] Kurth, Margison and Vernon were to be important players in Pacific Opera Victoria. The last performance by

the VIOS before it became professional was *The Yeomen of the Guard* (Gilbert and Sullivan) in the spring of 1979.

Encouraged by the response of the community, the company decided that, despite lacking the large population base usually required to support a professional opera company, it would attempt to become a viable second source of opera in the province. And it succeeded, against all odds, because the founders proceeded according to a plan adopted during the formative years: the principal role of the board of directors was to raise the money needed to support the productions of the company; the artistic director would have complete authority to make all decisions regarding the repertoire; the company would feature established and emerging Canadian singers, conductors, stage directors and technical personnel in all its productions; the Victoria Symphony Orchestra (hereafter referred to as the VSS) would be the pit orchestra for all performances; the chorus would be made up of non-professional volunteers chosen by audition principally, but not exclusively, from students at the Victoria Conservatory of Music and the University of Victoria School of Music, and would receive an honorarium for their services; the company would construct its own sets because, owing to the small stage of the 814-seat McPherson Playhouse, the home theatre at the time, renting sets from other companies was not practicable. The company also adopted a new name, Pacific Opera

Association ("Association" was changed to "Victoria" in 1987, and hereafter, the company will be referred to as Pacific Opera Victoria, or POV).

POV was fortunate to be able to draw on several local sources of emerging vocal talent, in addition to those already mentioned above. A new talent incubator, Canada Opera Piccola, began in the summer of 1982: twelve auditioned young singers were paid a living stipend and received advanced vocal and performance training in opera for three months every summer. The program was started by Léopold Simoneau, a Canadian tenor of international repute, particularly in the Mozart repertoire, and his equally well-known Canadian wife, soprano Pierrette Alarie; during the height of their careers, they were known as Mr. and Mrs. Mozart. Simoneau had retired from the operatic stage in 1965 and he and his wife moved to Victoria in 1978, where they took up teaching responsibilities at the Shawnigan School of Arts. Their standards for Opera Piccola were very high and their training was thorough. Simoneau was the voice teacher and Alarie directed the productions, for which a professional orchestra was used, led by prominent guest conductors, including Timothy Vernon. The program was one of the most successful of its kind, and it became an operatic "farm club" for many professional companies, including POV. At least one of its participants, Richard Margison, who was coached by Simoneau, became even more famous than his illustrious mentor. Regrettably, Opera Piccola was forced to close in 1988 because of cutbacks in government funding. Its swan song was two performances of *Così Fan Tutte* sung in Italian with English surtitles, accompanied by the Victoria Festival Orchestra led by Maestro Vernon in the Royal Theatre on August 25 and 27, 1988, as part of the Victoria International Festival.

The first move toward establishing POV was to elect a board of directors and to plan and raise money for the first transitional season, 1979–80. The board comprised president George Heffelfinger, a Victoria businessman who was part-owner and general manager of *Monday Magazine*, an independent weekly with a strong arts component; Karen Smith, the past-president of VIOS; vice-presidents Erika Kurth and Mary Jane Scott; treasurer James Munro, and seven directors at large. Cathrine E. Lowther was hired as general manager, and fundraising for the season's planned productions began immediately. Although the goal of $9,000 was not reached, twelve corporate donors were obtained and total monies raised, including grants from eight foundations and other granting bodies, totalled $7,612, enough to encourage the board.

The first production, *The Merry Wives of Windsor* (Otto Nicolai), to be sung in English, was scheduled for September 13, 14, 15 and 16, 1979. All went well until ten days before the first performance, when the company found itself with neither a

Bravo!

conductor nor director. Fortunately, an exceptional stroke of good luck found conductor Timothy Vernon, who had recently returned to his hometown from the East, available to take over both roles in the nick of time. His ability to put the pieces back together earned him kudos from Richard Todd (*Monday Magazine*, September 21–27, 1979): "In a field of many heroes, the one who deserves the lion's share of the credit is surely Timothy Vernon who . . . made it possible for everyone else's hard work to bear such sweet fruit." Those involved in performing and staging the work were the usual mix of professional and non-professional talent: the VSS provided the music; Richard Margison made his professional debut as Fenton; Jane Heffelfinger, a former actress and married to the president of the board, acted as drama coach; the chorus master and accompanist were locals Rory Hammond and Robert Holliston, respectively; the dancers were students of the Wendy Marlow School of Dance; the Victoria Senior Secondary School Drama Department was responsible for the lighting; and the Spectrum Senior Secondary School Drama Department worked as the backstage crew.

La Bohème, also sung in English, was performed in the spring of 1980 as the company's second offering of its first season. Dr. Paul Freeman conducted the VSS, Peter Mannering directed the production assisted by Jane Heffelfinger, and general manager Cathrine E. Lowther

was the producer. Freeman encouraged the company to engage two professional artists for the first time and, as a result, soprano Margarita Noye, a member of the touring company of the Canadian Opera Company, was cast as Mimì and Aaron Bergell, an American tenor of considerable operatic experience, sang the role of Rodolfo. The performance received a fairly positive review from Richard Todd (*Monday Magazine*, February 29–March 6, 1980): "The company landed firmly on its feet, at least as far as artistic and popular success were concerned . . . The principals, three of them professional singers from out of town, all turned in pleasing performances, though several could have done better . . . Despite its shortcomings, this *Bohème* was a major achievement for Pacific Opera."

The transition to full professional status was completed in 1980 when the company was incorporated and Timothy Vernon accepted the post of artistic director. The previous board was re-elected and Vernon worked on finalizing the first fully professional season. He decided on *The Barber of Seville* as the September 1980 offering, to be followed by *Madama Butterfly* in February 1981.[2] Vernon was on hand to conduct the Victoria Symphony Orchestra for *The Barber of Seville* and Glynis Leyshon, who was then the assistant artistic director at the Belfry Theatre in Victoria, made her operatic debut as the stage director of the production. Richard Margison, by then a member of Actors' Equity, sang the

role of Count Almaviva. Other Actors' Equity singers in the cast included Donald Collins as Figaro, Derek Del Puppo as Doctor Bartolo and Joel Katz as Basilio. The local non-union members of the cast were Stephen Bouey as Fiorello, Elizabeth Taylor as Rosina and Erika Kurth as Berta.

A near-disaster involving Kurth occurred onstage during one of the *Barber* performances and has survived as one of the earliest anecdotes in the POV collection. In an interview, Kurth herself made little of it, recalling it as an amusing example of what can go wrong in areas other than those involving singing or acting: "I was onstage as Berta and was about to run up a flight of stairs, as I was supposed to, when one of the singers called out urgently from the wings, 'Look out, Berta!' I didn't know it, but some of the stairs had collapsed." Not only the stairs, but also the balcony above had collapsed. Kurth was seemingly unaware that another peril was imminent, recalled many years later by Maestro Vernon: "Indelibly

memorable was Erika Kurth's virtually definitive Berta, who endured what could have been the ultimate indignity—finding herself alone onstage beneath a collapsing set and a curtain which threatened to land on her head—with unforgettable panache."[3] When Kurth was reminded of Vernon's account of the incident, she said, "He always called it *Berta of Seville* after that."

Madama Butterfly was the company's first production to be sung in the original language. Jacklyn Moffat, a student in the voice program at the University of Victoria, debuted with POV as Kate Pinkerton, and cast in the principal roles of Cio-Cio-San and Pinkerton were two up-and-coming African-American singers, soprano Delcina Stevenson and tenor Vinson Cole making his debut in the role. Apparently, artistic director Vernon was counting heavily on the audience's willing suspension of disbelief in the second act: when Sorrow, Cio-Cio-San's child, appeared onstage, the audience could not fail to observe that he was unmistakably Caucasian. The incongruity returned to

▲ POV's first professional production, *The Barber of Seville*, was staged in 1980. From left to right the principals were Derek del Puppo, Joel Katz, Donald Collins, Richard Margison, Elizabeth Taylor and Erika Kurth. RICHARD TODD PHOTOGRAPH

BravO!

haunt the company when the following appeared in a review by Jerry Richards (*Times Colonist*, October 20, 1995) of a later production of the opera: "Do not think me unkind to Pacific Opera Victoria. It's an admirable organization even if it does sometimes test the forbearance of its audiences to the utmost. I'm thinking of their 'Madama Butterfly' some years ago when they arranged for a black officer in the US Navy (an impossibility for the time represented) to consort with an Asian [sic] Butterfly and produce between them a strikingly blond offspring."

Behind the scenes, in the sponsorship, fundraising and marketing department, a formidable head of steam was building under the leadership of Jane Heffelfinger, who, at the request of Timothy Vernon, had taken on the responsibility for this crucial element of the fledgling company's ability to thrive. She explained in an interview her willingness to do what surely was going to be a huge job: "Tim asked me because he knew I had been head of development at Simon Fraser [University]. I took that marketing and fundraising task on for him, and took it very seriously. It became almost an obsession with me. I believed in Timothy completely. He had a vision . . . I felt he was someone I wanted to work with."

And work she did. Awareness of the magnitude of the task before her came almost immediately during a large promotional breakfast reception organized for her by Mel Cooper, the owner of

CFAX radio station. Cooper had invited all the important people in Victoria, and he turned the floor over to her to tell them about the company she was hoping to interest them in. She described what happened: "I remember some man standing back in a corner who said, 'Well who in the hell ever heard of Pacific Opera Victoria?' And I knew then that we had this huge branding exercise to do . . . but I was really gung-ho and determined to get the word out. Remember, we were starting with a blank canvas in Victoria. Very little was happening in the arts, very little aggressive fundraising and marketing." Listening to Heffelfinger describe the various branding strategies she employed to make POV a household name in Victoria is akin to taking a crash course in fundraising and marketing: opening-night performance parties at the theatre, billed as "A Sense of Occasion," to get "fun party-people with deep pockets into the theatre, frequently to see their first opera," without pressuring them to donate, which had the desired result in the long run of increasing the donor pool considerably; gala fundraising concerts at the Royal Theatre featuring famous singers—for example, Canadian tenor Ben Heppner, Richard Margison, Canadian soprano Tracy Dahl, Vinson Cole and Judith Forst—who donated their talent "to help the kids," as Forst put it, and often stayed on to sing in a POV production; and luxury Mercedes-Benz car lotteries. Heffelfinger also arranged the more common marketing methods

such as personal contact with potential sponsors, selling POV merchandise in the lobby opera shop, putting up eye-catching advertising posters all over town, targeted fundraising letters and direct-mail marketing, one of which—a city-wide mail drop of a stunning brochure to over 100,000 homes—was very costly, risky and "scary" to Heffelfinger and her board at the time. They needn't have worried. The response was overwhelming, Heffelfinger recalled: "I couldn't believe that we doubled our subscriptions. Piles of letters and envelopes with cheques in them came in. Barbara [administrative assistant Barbara Newton] said 'How are we going to deal with all this?' There was no one in the office except Barbara and myself. No computers, no donor base—we kept our donor list in a shoe box under [her] desk." Although a newcomer to Victoria (the Heffelfingers arrived in 1977), Jane Heffelfinger's charm, energy, enthusiasm and knowledge of the theatre and how to go about raising money, identifying potential sponsors and donors, and then getting them to open their chequebooks proved invaluable to the organization. Indeed few would deny that without her volunteer contribution to the cause, POV would have been unable to survive financially. However, she gives a great deal of credit to the others who worked with her: "I can't tell you how fantastic the volunteers . . . were. They worked their hearts out." Heffelfinger was chair, POV Foundation Bravo Society, and she

joined the board of directors in 1983 and served as president from 1989 to 1995. In addition to her board duties, she acted in a volunteer capacity as POV's general manager for nine months in 1989–90. Heffelfinger continued her involvement in fundraising, but in her penultimate report as president of the board in 1994, she acknowledged her co-workers again: "Our volunteers power most of the fundraising."

The opening opera of the 1981–82 season was *The Abduction from the Seraglio* (Mozart), a brave choice because of the demands the difficult music places on the singers—not one of whom was up to it, according to the critics. The season took another beating in the press in February 1982 over *La Traviata*, this time because of the sets and the staging. However, the next season got off to an excellent start with *Die Fledermaus* (Johann Strauss II), starring Richard Margison as Alfred, Canadian soprano Susan Sereda as Adele and Margarita Noye as Rosalinde. The team of Maestro Vernon and director Glynis Leyshon applied their own comic touches to the production, and Margison was singled out for praise for both his acting and vocal ability. There were five performances of the opera, and the houses were near sellouts at 92 percent capacity.

▲ Richard Margison as Alfred, the singing teacher, and Glyn Evans in the tenor buffo role of von Eisenstein, ham it up in Pacific Opera Victoria's production of *Die Fledermaus*, 1982. JEFF BARBER PHOTOGRAPH FOR INFOCUS PHOTOGRAPHY

Bravo!

Victoria audiences loved it and showed their appreciation by attending the five performances of the final opera of the season, *Tosca*, in equally large numbers. The casting for *Tosca* was a mix of name singers, including professionals Delcina Stevenson as Tosca and Canadian tenor Paul Frey as Cavaradossi, the up-and-coming Canadian baritone Cornelis Opthof as Scarpia and local talents in the comprimario roles, including the fourteen-year-old head chorister at St. Mary's Church, Ian Bullen, as the shepherd boy.

Subscriptions for the next season increased from 580 to 700, and all seemed to be going well, despite a niggling deficit. The board was gratified to receive a Canada Council grant for the first time

(after an earlier attempt to get permanent grant status was denied), and felt confident enough to increase staff to three full-time people, as well as two part-time summer students at the end of the season.

By rights, the POV 1983–84 season should have built on the success of the previous one, but, for some reason, the repertoire did not appeal to Victorian audiences. The first production was *The Elixir of Love* and, as Jane Heffelfinger put it, "it was tough to get bums in the seats" despite a good cast and the added new attraction of a pre-show lecture in the lobby by a local opera expert, Dr. Anthony Jenkins. (Pre-show lobby lectures became a permanent promotional feature from then on.) Heffelfinger and her volunteers tried

▲ Delcina Stevenson in the title role of *Tosca* struggles against the villainous Scarpia, sung by Cornelis Opthof, in act 2 of the opera staged by Pacific Opera Victoria in 1983. LECH JANASZEK PHOTOGRAPH

to spark ticket sales by word of mouth for the remaining performances by passing out little potions of "elixir" to those waiting in the lobby before the show, but the hoped-for response was not forthcoming. The seats were filled eventually, but only by vigorous volunteer effort. However, Victorians responded with enthusiasm to the traditional Christmas production, *Amahl and the Night Visitors*, which took place in Christ Church Cathedral on December 19, 20, 21, 22 and 23, 1983. The Christmas productions were not regarded as part of the POV season, but were paid for out of the company's budget. Two musicians and an organist provided the musical accompaniment, and all performances were well attended.

In February 1984 Christopher Newton, artistic director of the Shaw Festival in Niagara-on-the-Lake, Ontario, came to Victoria to make his debut in the art form as the director of *Carmen*, the second opera of the season, and caused a sensation. Set in Nicaragua, the piece began when a teenager walked onto the stage carrying a ghetto blaster playing loud rock music. A performance of *Carmen* was then announced in Spanish, and the entire prelude followed, not from the pit, but from the ghetto blaster. Although that made headlines and was filmed and shown by the CBC on "The National," the audience did not like the production and the small houses played havoc with the company's finances. The deficit grew to over $100,000, almost one-half of the entire operating

budget for the year, causing great concern for the future of the organization. The board took immediate economy measures: full-time staff was reduced to two from five; there would be only four performances of the next season's productions instead of five, and the planned Christmas production was held in abeyance. Although these actions undoubtedly eased the pressure somewhat, one of Jane Heffelfinger's fundraising projects really saved the day: "I talked Frank Hertel [owner of the Mercedes-Benz dealership in Victoria] into donating an imported Mercedes-Benz, a dear little red vintage car for a lottery. It sounds common now, but it was very rare then, and it was a sensation. I called on the manager of the Empress and persuaded

▲ *The Elixir of Love*, was staged by Pacific Opera Victoria in 1983, and featured local Victoria tenor, Richard Margison, as Nemorino and Barbara Collier as Adina, the object of his unrequited love, shown here in act 1 outside Adina's farmhouse. LECH JANASZEK PHOTOGRAPH

him into letting us station ourselves in front of the hotel where we could catch all the visitors off the [cruise] ships." Heffelfinger and her army of volunteers went everywhere, including Granville Island in Vancouver, to sell lottery tickets, and as a result not only raised the profile of the company, but also a lot of money: $75,000.

The crisis was averted but the next season's budget was much reduced. Timothy Vernon got a call just as he was going into an early rehearsal for the fall production of *Rigoletto* telling him that there was just enough money to pay the singers who had been hired, but nothing but a few thousand dollars left for the rest of the show—sets, costumes and so on—and that he should consider cancelling

it. That didn't sit well with Vernon, who devised a plan with the co-operation of director Peter Wylde and others involved in staging, which not only allowed the production to go ahead, but also allowed audiences to exercise their imagination to the fullest. Vernon described the solution during an interview: "We decided to give [*Rigoletto*] a minimalist treatment and tell the story with as much force as we could. We had good lighting. We dressed the cast in black leotards and got sixty lightweight cane-back black chairs, which we put in a semicircle facing the audience—and that was the set. The chairs were moved about on the stage and became [whatever was required by the story]. The audience went nuts. They loved it. I loved it. It was very theatrical . . . and people got it. It was the art of the possible." One reviewer, James Kennedy (*Monday Magazine*, September 20–26, 1984), had this to say: "The intended sense of ritual in the staging was best conveyed by the company entrances: sixty dark bodies file on stage, take their places behind their chairs, and sit down simultaneously, but with no visible signal. They remained seated during the playing of the prelude. It is an eerie effect . . . There is onstage a silent female chorus ever present as witness to Gilda's, or all women's suffering." Bernard Turgeon as Rigoletto and American soprano Iris Fraser as Gilda headed up a fine cast that contributed mightily to the success of what has become a legendary performance in POV's history.

▲ Pacific Opera Victoria's 1984 *Carmen* departed from the traditional rendering as this shot of Janet Stubbs as Carmen sitting on a pinball machine in Lillas Pastia's tavern demonstrates. LECH JANASZEK PHOTOGRAPH

Like the previous season's production of *Carmen* by Christopher Newton, the February 1985 production of *Faust* was another example of the relatively recent twentieth-century trend in opera staging— opera as the director's art—wherein attention to the traditional interpretation, previously dominated by the composer, the conductor and the singers, gives way to the director's view of how the work should be presented. David Walsh directed this *Faust* and deviated from the traditional in a number of ways. First, the setting of the piece was nineteenth-century France instead of sixteenth-century Germany, which removed the story from the association with Goethe's play and placed it in the realm of allegorical fantasy. There was no costume distinction between Faust and Méphistophélès, implying that they were one and the same, representing two sides of human nature. The physical transformation of Faust into a young man never occurred onstage, and at the end of the opera, when he and Méphistophélès met their end together by disappearing down a trap door, Faust emerged in character as though it had all been an old man's dream in which he had relived the desires and pleasures of his youth. The performance was significant for another reason: it was sung in French, and English surtitles were used for the first time, making POV only the second opera company in the world to do so (the first being the Canadian Opera Company).

The choice of *Faust* was an unusual

instance of the board intruding onto the artistic director's turf with undesirable consequences. Vernon recalled that the production was not one of his most satisfying: "We did *Faust* because the board wanted *Faust*. They wanted *Faust* so badly they held my foot to the fire and said, 'Okay, you want to do Benjamin Britten, do *Faust*.' Well, I haven't got much regard for *Faust*. I like the score melodically, but I'm such a Goethe fanatic, and I think it's such a pale shadow of Goethe . . . We did it, and I know it wasn't as good as it should have been because my heart wasn't in it. I'm not going to blame our director or any particular thing—there was some fine singing. I just know . . . my own investment in it was not at the level I know now must be [present] every time." *Faust* has not appeared since in the POV repertoire.

As a result of the austerity measures and a successful season at the box office, a surplus was recorded at the end of the year, and the proceeds of the lottery reduced the accumulated deficit

▲ Iris Fraser as Gilda and Bernard Turgeon as Rigoletto perform in front of the black-clad women's chorus in this cash-strapped Pacific Opera Victoria production of *Rigoletto*, 1984. LECH JANASZEK PHOTOGRAPH

Bravo!

considerably. POV moved into the next season with confidence, buoyed by the restoration of some of the grants that had been withdrawn in previous years. It was during this period that Vernon had a seminal discussion with his board, which he recalled as follows:

Within five years it became clear that we could not just repeat the top ten [operas], so I went to the board. It was the most important discussion in the history of the company, I think, and was the one around, Do we just go back and repeat or do we start to step outside? Now, it took several years, but . . . once you open it up, . . . then the artistic director's sensibilities can really come into play and be useful

to the company's development . . . My own understanding, such as it was, I could put into the service of each project . . . and not just safeguard the company's better interests through a succession of seasons, but really think about shaping it, forming it, giving it a particular profile, offering a more sophisticated range of options for the audience. That's when it became personally engaging . . . It then became more about the works and less about individual accomplishments . . . Opera is mostly about ensembles . . . finding the dynamic and the energy of the group where they . . . respond to each other, and where something emerges that has a focus and a direction—that is thrilling.

▲ *Il Trovatore*, produced by Pacific Opera Victoria in 1986, starred Vancouver singer Audrey Glass in the role of the gypsy, Azucena, shown here after being captured by Count di Luna's men in act 3, scene i, singing her aria "Giorno poveri vivea." LECH JANASZEK PHOTOGRAPH

This discussion resulted in a decision to "step outside" by expanding the traditional repertoire every season from then on to include at least one work outside the top ten. As Vernon said, several years were to pass before it became really obvious to audiences that new theatrical experiences were being offered to them, but when the 1987–88 season was announced and people learned that they would see POV's debut productions of *Lucia di Lammermoor* and *Fidelio* (Beethoven), there was no doubt. The distinctive profile that identifies the company in the opera world today was launched that season, but not without some setbacks along the way, the *Lucia* production being the first one.

The previous season's production

of *Il Trovatore*, noteworthy as director Robert Carsen's Canadian full-production debut, was described by James Kennedy (*Monday Magazine*, October 2–8, 1986) as the finest ever done by POV, one that would be "outstanding in any house in Canada." Carsen, a Canadian, was at that time earning kudos for his work as a talented young stage director in England and on the continent. Now renowned, he is much in demand internationally. His *Il Trovatore* featured a striking set designed by Allan Fellows; a fine cast of Canadians Heather Thomson (Leonora), Cornelis Opthof (Count di Luna) and Audrey Glass (Azucena); American tenor Augusto Paglialunga (Manrico); and excellent singing by an augmented chorus led by

▲ The finale of *Fidelio* opens with the arrival of the state minister, Don Fernando, played by John Dodington, who, in the ensuing action, has Florestan released from his chains and restored to freedom. Pacific Opera Victoria heightened the drama of the scene by having Dodington enter on horseback in this 1988 production.
LECH JANASZEK PHOTOGRAPH

Bravo!

the new chorus master, Michael Gormley, formerly of the Vienna State Opera.

By contrast, if the same reviewer is to be believed (*Monday Magazine*, October 1–7, 1987), *Lucia* was one of the worst: a set so steeply raked it was perilous, a "stand still, walk on/off" chorus that bore no resemblance to the group that had added so much to *Il Trovatore*, and an orchestra that struggled along with almost half of its players new to its ranks. The one redeeming feature was the singing of the principals, headed by internationally known American coloratura Sally Wolf in the title role. Timothy Vernon's contribution to the account of the apparent disaster is an anecdote involving Richard Margison, who sang the role of Edgardo: "It came to the stabbing. Glynis [director Glynis Leyshon] had personally gone shopping for condoms at the drugstore to fill with the stage blood, so that when he stabbed himself, the blood would go on his shirt. Well, he stabbed himself and nothing happened. Finally, he goes on the deck and tries to break it—it's in his sleeve—he's banging his arm down there trying to get the damn thing to break. When he left the stage, he had not shed one drop of blood . . . I sat down and wrote a testimonial letter to the manufacturer of the condoms."

If *Lucia* was the setback we are led to believe, *Fidelio* was a great step forward in the 1987–88 season. With another year of experience and a growing reputation to his credit, Robert Carsen returned to Victoria from London, England, to direct

the production and repeat his *Il Trovatore* success. He also translated the libretto, since the work was to be sung in English. Paul Frey, the Canadian tenor whose international career was taking off, arrived from Europe to sing the part of Florestan, a role he had wanted to do for some time. Another Canadian tenor, Michael Schade, whose career has since reached meteoric heights, appeared as Jaquino, making his historic operatic debut on the POV stage. Others in the splendid cast included mezzo-soprano Gaynor Jones as Leonore, Don Garrard as Rocco, Susan Sereda as Marzelline, Bernard Turgeon as Don Pizarro, Canadian bass John Dodington as Don Fernando and Simon Norton and Philip Heal as the first and second prisoners. It was, by all accounts, an operatic tour de force; it played to packed houses and got rave reviews. Board member Jane Heffelfinger, who was also on the board of KCTS 9 at the time, alerted the Seattle public television station to the production. It sent a crew to Victoria to film two performances for later broadcast nationwide as part of a documentary on POV and Victoria. The production was also recorded by CBC Radio for later airing on "Saturday Afternoon at the Opera."

Over the next six seasons, POV's plan continued to unfold with gratifying success on the stage and at the box office. In late February 1989, *The Flying Dutchman*, POV's first Wagner offering and Victoria's first since the Victoria

Civic Opera performed *Lohengrin* in 1935, was presented on the small stage of the McPherson Playhouse to critical acclaim. Neither the stormy onstage drama that awaited the audience, nor the snowstorm on opening night discouraged them from filling the 814 seats in the house. Everyone marvelled at the verismo effects that director Peter Symcox obtained by projecting onto the set a video he had made of waves breaking on Vancouver Island's west coast. One interesting anecdote involving casting for *Dutchman* that does not come directly from Timothy Vernon's seemingly inexhaustible supply concerns Ben Heppner: "One of the few up-and-comers POV missed out on was tenor Ben Heppner . . . Heppner was booked to sing a minor role in *The Flying Dutchman* . . . 'Six months before the production, he calls and says he has to cancel,' says Vernon. 'And the reason he has to cancel is that he has to sing at La Scala [Milan]. Of course, I should have said, "That's fine, Ben, but in two years you're singing this role at this fee." But I didn't.'"[4]

Before single tickets went on sale for the next season, POV had recorded an increase in donations, a 90 percent renewal rate for existing subscribers, and 200 new ones; the concern was that there would be a shortage of single tickets. Tchaikovsky's *Eugene Onegin* was the work chosen as the second production of the season and, once again, Victorians had to brave a February snowstorm to get to the theatre. Every seat was sold and anticipation was high,

because famed Metropolitan Opera bass Jerome Hines was cast as Prince Gremin, Richard Margison was cast as Lensky and Canadian soprano Deborah Jeans was to sing Tatyana. The day before the opening performance, Jeans came down with a virus that seriously affected her voice, and a replacement for her had to be found in a hurry. Jane Heffelfinger was the company's volunteer general manager at the time, and it fell to her to get someone to fill in. Fortunately, an excellent substitute in the person of New York soprano Beverly Morgan was available, had done the same English version and agreed to leave for Victoria as soon as the travel arrangements were made.[5] Heffelfinger recalled the stress for both the singer and herself: "[Beverly] left New York on the day of the opening, landed in Toronto in a blizzard and landed in Vancouver in a fog. I managed to get her a stateroom on the ferry to enable her to warm [her voice] up. We delayed the curtain, and by 8:41 p.m. she was in the pit singing, while Deborah mimed the role onstage. The whole thing went off beautifully. At the intermission I was explaining to my guest, David Lam [lieutenant-governor of BC at the time], what had happened, and he said, 'That must have cost a fortune, Jane. Send me the bill.'" A young Victoria singer who was destined for a great career, tenor Benjamin Butterfield, distinguished himself in the comprimario role of Monsieur Triquet.

However, not everyone who attended a performance was hearing the same thing.

Timothy Vernon overheard a conversation that still amuses him: "We were singing *Onegin* with a lovely cast—after all, we had Jerome Hines—in English, but because English is hard to sing and understand at the best of times, we surtitled it in English. At one of the intervals I'm sitting at the bottom of the stairwell in the vomitorium [the corridor around the sides and back of the stage] where you can hear conversations up in the corridor by the washrooms. These two ladies, archetypical Victorian ladies, come out of the washroom together, and one said, 'You know, it's wonderful to have the text spelled out. You can actually follow every point of the plot without worrying about the language,' and the other said, 'Well, yes, my dear, but you know the diction of these singers is so remarkably clear that at times I fancy I can understand the Italian.'"

The next "step outside" was *Roméo et Juliette* (Gounod), the second opera of the 1990–91 season. Irving Guttman, familiar to BC audiences for his Vancouver Opera Association work, and at the time, the

artistic director of Edmonton Opera, was contracted to direct the production. He reduced it from five acts to three and gave audiences what was termed an elegant evening in the theatre. He recalled the exhilaration of directing the two leads, Canadian soprano Kathleen Brett as Juliette and American tenor Kevin Anderson as Roméo: "They were just beautiful together—totally believable as young lovers. Audiences went wild." He learned afterward that many older members of the audience were so moved by the performance that they were overcome with nostalgic memories of their own young loves.

The 1991–92 season put pressure on POV to consider a move to the 1,400-seat Royal Theatre to accommodate the increased demand for tickets—the productions at the smaller McPherson Playhouse regularly sold out. The company decided to stage the third production of the season, *Die Fledermaus*, in the Royal despite Timothy Vernon's reluctance. Although the Royal had been designed

▲ Ensemble scene from Pacific Opera Victoria's 1992 production, *The Abduction from the Seraglio.*
DAVID COOPER PHOTOGRAPH

for opera, its acoustics and pit were substandard: sound did not reach many of the seats under the balcony, and the pit, in Vernon's words, "is not even a pit, it's what I used to refer to for years as a 'depressed area.'" As an experiment, the new location certainly solved the ticket shortage but was apparently not successful enough to warrant a permanent move at that time. However, from 1992–98, the largest production of every season, usually the third, was staged in the Royal, and after 1998 the company returned to the McPherson on only two occasions.

Two productions were notable in the 1992–93 season. One was the first in the season's sequence: *The Abduction from the Seraglio*. Recorded on video by freelance filmmaker and producer Robert Chesterman, it was aired ten times between 1993 and 1997 by the Knowledge Network, BC's public educational television channel. The second, Timothy Vernon's choice of newer repertoire for the season, was Benjamin Britten's *A Midsummer Night's Dream*. Some years later, it was referred to as one of two milestones in the company's growth.[6] Timothy Vernon explained why:

> It is my contention that there is no greater setting of Shakespeare than *Midsummer Night's Dream*. First of all, it's in Shakespeare's own English, and the level of invention is spectacular. It's moving and funny and it's got everything that the play has . . . the romance, the mystery of the forest, the dark side of the fairies and the mad, comic basic humour of the mechanicals of the last act, and it's got them all nailed—nailed! I think it's a real masterpiece—the highest accomplishment in our art, among many great works he [Britten] created for opera . . . It was an important thing for the company, because we were able to bring a sense of that particular achievement. People came away with a real sense that here was a fellow genius with Shakespeare.

The production and its Canadian cast, which included tenor Benjamin Butterfield and baritone Russell Braun making his POV debut, earned the following high praise from Peter Symcox (*Monday Magazine*, May 18–24, 1993): "This was theatre co-operation at its finest and all concerned—conductor, director, singers and designers—share in the very great success of the evening."[7] The show was recorded by CBC Radio for later airing on "Saturday Afternoon at the Opera"; it was

▲ Kevin Anderson as Roméo and Kathleen Brett as Juliette weave their stage magic as the star-crossed lovers in Pacific Opera Victoria's *Roméo et Juliette*, staged in 1991. DAVID COOPER PHOTOGRAPH

the second POV production to be singled out for this national exposure.

Although the 96 percent capacity attendance exceeded the budget expectation, which was for 85 percent full houses, the artistic and box-office success of the show was not enough to resolve POV's mid-season financial position: a deficit of $75,000, caused by cost overruns and a 50 percent reduction in projected revenues from the company's major fundraiser, a raffle for a BMW automobile. The situation called for stringent economies and heroic fundraising. Circle of Stars II, a gala concert held in the Royal Theatre on March 26, 1993, with name singers Ben Heppner, Judith Forst, Heather Thomson, Canadian baritone Theodore Baerg, Vinson Cole and others generously contributing their time and talents, raised $50,000. Nevertheless, a tiny surplus of $28 for the June 30 year-end was all that the vice-president of finance could report to the annual general meeting of November 24, 1993. Also discouraging was the news that subscriptions had fallen by 200, only

marginally offset by a slight increase in single ticket sales, but there was good news too: by November the company had accumulated a surplus of $29,000, owing to the success of *Don Pasquale*, the 1993–94 season opener, in which the celebrated Canadian bass-baritone Claude Corbeil, in the title role, delighted audiences with his talent for comedy.

Up to this point, POV's steps outside the tried-and-true repertoire had been unerring in terms of choice, but that was about to change with the production of *Der Freischütz* in February 1994. Since its premiere in Berlin in 1821, the work has been included in the standard repertoire of every major house around the world, has stood the test of time and has brought its composer, Carl Maria von Weber, lasting fame. Small wonder then, that POV chose to be the first Canadian company to present a full staging. However, the plot requires considerable suspension of disbelief when one of the characters, Max, accepts the offer of a rival's gun, loaded with a magic bullet

▲ Colin Heath as Puck, a speaking role in *A Midsummer Night's Dream*, staged by Pacific Opera Victoria in 1993.
PHOTO COURTESY PACIFIC OPERA VICTORIA

that never misses its mark, to succeed in a shooting trial and thus win the hand of his beloved. In a Faustian twist, Max risks eternal damnation by accepting the gun, and receives salvation and wins his beloved only at the end of the opera. Unfortunately, the POV's presentation of *Der Freischütz* did not bring the company the accolades it had earned previously. Timothy Vernon explained why, despite his complete commitment to the enterprise and attendance records of 96 percent capacity, he considers it a disappointment:

> *Der Freischütz* is one of the great operas in history. It's the great pivotal opera between *The Magic Flute* and Wagner . . . the pillar of High Romanticism, and it's a visionary musical accomplishment by [Weber] . . . I didn't stop to think, Why has it never been staged in Canada? I just thought, Gosh, it's never been staged in Canada. Well, sometimes you only find out by doing it, and in this case, some of the real difficulties . . . [like] the suspension of disbelief . . . where you have this mythological stuff that looks so much like hocus-pocus on the outside [that] you need to explain too much, and when you do explain too much . . . the less mysterious it is, and so it loses its intrinsic interest. We didn't make it work. I think it was partly a failure of nerve on the part of our then director, who left town before we opened because he couldn't deal with it, so we were left

with a partial accomplishment which we then saw through to the stage. If I were to do it again, I would tackle it completely differently. I would make the presentation less explicit, more suggestive, more luminous.

Wisely, neither Vernon nor the board of directors let what they considered to be the artistic failure of *Der Freischütz* deter them from their chosen course, though they changed the repertoire for the coming season: *Ariadne auf Naxos* (R. Strauss) was postponed to a future season. *La Fille du Régiment* was substituted as the first production, followed by *Macbeth*, both taking place in the McPherson Playhouse, and then *La Bohème* in the Royal; *Macbeth* was the risky choice. It was a relatively lacklustre season, except for a beautiful *La Bohème*, which got rave reviews for the performance of guest conductor Leslie Uyeda making her debut on the POV podium, and lead singers Canadian soprano Christiane Riel as Mimì and Chinese tenor Ya Lin Zhang as Rodolfo.

The 1995–96 season, the last to be discussed in this chapter, was anything but lacklustre, mainly because it featured the Canadian premiere and a potential major revival of *The Love of Three Kings*

▲ In this ensemble scene from Pacific Opera Victoria's *A Midsummer Night's Dream*, 1993, Colin Heath as Puck demonstrates his acrobatic ability on the ball.
DAVID COOPER PHOTOGRAPH

Bravo!

(*L'Amore dei Tre Re*, Italo Montemezzi), a work so rarely performed in North America that the music had to be ordered from Milan. Apparently, when the season was announced, a number of devoted fans from all over the United States and Canada called POV for tickets. "We sold tickets to two people in Kansas . . . and Stuart Hamilton said he'd crawl over the Rocky Mountains on his hands and knees to see it—he came to four performances," said Timothy Vernon.[8] The press reported that a dozen opera companies were sending representatives, one of whom was expected to be the renowned director Lotfi Mansouri from San Francisco Opera. Local interest was stimulated by a symposium on the opera held at Victoria's Craigdarroch Castle on February 16, 1996, the day following the opening performance.

The reviews were unanimous in praise of Alison Green's set, the direction of Alison Greene (two different people) and the excellent choral work, but mixed for the performance of the principals.

However, one local reviewer, Adrian Chamberlain (*Times Colonist*, February 17, 1996), was unequivocal in his praise: "There are scenes of great beauty and passion, and some good singing—particularly from soprano Susan Porta and tenor Gary Rideout . . . One of the most memorable scenes is an extended exchange between Fiora and her lover Avito. On Thursday night, Porta (Fiora) and Rideout (Avito) sang with an unadorned emotional depth. Porta has a rich, luscious voice, while Rideout sings with compelling clarity and lyricism." Unfortunately, the production went into the red to the tune of $62,820.

The company also spent nearly $10,000 more than it took in to stage *Carmen*, the last production of the season, due in part to an unexpected glitch involving American tenor Clifton Forbis, who was cast in the role of Don José. Forbis developed an allergic reaction to something on or around the stage of the Royal Theatre and was unable to sing the last three of the five scheduled performances. He was replaced for one performance by American Fernando del Valle and for the remaining two by American Scott Flaherty. Both replacements sang from the pit while Forbis acted onstage. Criticism of the ability of mezzo Tania Parrish to carry off the role of Carmen vocally was offset by kudos to the POV Chorus for its fine contribution to this troubled production.

By this stage in POV's development, the chorus—under the new leadership of

▲ William Neill as Max eases the fears of his beloved, Agathe, played by Gaynor Jones, who worries about him going into the forest alone at night in Pacific Opera Victoria's Canadian premiere production of *Der Freischütz* in 1994. DAVID COOPER PHOTOGRAPH

chorus master Robert Holliston, a Victoria musician, teacher and POV's *répétiteur* who took over from Michael Gormley in the spring of 1995—was showing great improvement as an important element in POV ensemble work. Since the formation of POV, choristers have remained volunteers, but receive a stipend for each production—in 1996 it was $150 and by 2006 it had increased to $500.[9] The usual complement of twenty sopranos and mezzos and nineteen tenors and basses comprises singers who live in or near Victoria, many of them voice students at the Victoria Conservatory of Music or the University of Victoria School of Music. All are required to audition each year by preparing an aria, preferably in Italian, and must be able to sight-read. When a larger chorus is needed for a particular piece, candidates must also audition for a place. Beginning weeks before the production, music rehearsals with the chorus master take place twice weekly, increasing to five staging sessions a week with the stage director for two and a

half weeks before opening night. Clearly, being a member of the chorus involves a commitment not commensurate with the stipend, but POV's choristers are obviously rewarded by doing what they love and being an important part of the company. Many who intend to go on to a professional career value the stage experience gained from their chorus work.

▲ Peter Barcza (Manfredo) bids farewell to Susan Porta (his wife, Fiora) unaware that she loves another man. Act 2 of Pacific Opera Victoria's Canadian premiere of *The Love of Three Kings* in 1996. DAVID COOPER PHOTOGRAPH

BravO!

Act III

WITH A NEW GENERAL MANAGER, HAMILTON MCCLYMONT, IN CHARGE AND a selection of mainstream operas on the menu for the 1979–80 season, the VOA hoped for a smooth recovery from its 1974–79 troubles. *Cavalleria Rusticana* and *Pagliacci*, with Lyn Vernon, well-known local soprano in the role of Santuzza in *Cav* and Metropolitan Opera superstar American tenor James McCracken as Canio in *Pag*, opened the season as the fall production, followed by *The Bartered Bride*, and *Il Trovatore* in the spring of 1980. Both operas featured Canadian singers familiar to Vancouver audiences: Audrey Glass as Ludmila and Bernard Turgeon as Kru□na in the Smetana opera and in the Verdi, Cornelis Opthof as Count di Luna, Audrey Glass as Azucena and Canadian bass Pierre Charbonneau as Ferrando. Making his first appearance as guest conductor for the VOA was Timothy Vernon, who led the orchestra for *The Bartered Bride*. Vernon's career was just taking off and he would appear again on the VOA podium several times after taking on a very influential role in the history of opera in this province as founding artistic director of Pacific Opera Victoria. The season was a box-office success, enabling the company to reduce the deficit by $100,000 and gain a welcome boost to its morale.

After the close of the 1979–80 season, the VOA announced that Anton Guadagno had been secured as principal conductor with a two-year contract. Guadagno was well known to Vancouver musicians and audiences, having guest-conducted on five occasions between 1969 and 1975. He had conducted the new VO Orchestra in the last opera of the season, *Il Trovatore*, in March 1980. His first appearance under his contract was to be in March 1981 to conduct *Otello* (Verdi), an Edmonton Opera co-production with Irving Guttman, the VOA's former artistic director, as production director. However, owing to a municipal strike in Vancouver, the March dates were cancelled and the production could not

◀ The bedlam scene from Vancouver Opera's 1989 staging of *The Rake's Progress* with Wendy Hall as Anne Trulove and Benoît Boutet as Tom Rakewell in the foreground. Sets were by David Hockney. DAVID COOPER PHOTOGRAPH

go ahead until August; Guadagno shared the podium with Canadian conductor Pierre Hétu for the production, presumably because of his prior commitments. *Otello* is noteworthy because it marked the VOA debut in the role of Roderigo of one of the most famous tenors on the operatic stage today: Ben Heppner, a native of Dawson Creek, BC, a graduate of UBC's School of Music and, at that time, in the early stages of a great career.

Guttman and Guadagno teamed up again for *Turandot*, the first production of the 1981–82 season. However, the season did not do well at the box office, mainly because of the very unpopular and unsuitable choice of the Broadway musical *Man of La Mancha*, (Wasserman, Leigh and Darion) as the last of the season's five offerings. Hamilton McClymont, who was primarily responsible for the disaster, tendered his resignation and left the company at the end of the season. Although an able administrator, McClymont had no previous experience with an opera company and was not a good fit for that reason. Before leaving, he gave the same advice to the board as Bonynge had: "No matter what you do, keep the band."[1]

In damage-control mode again, the board asked Irving Guttman to return as artistic director, offering him a two-year contract, which he accepted. During this period, 1982 to 1984, the repertoire comprised operas and singers that had proven box-office appeal, to avoid any

repetition of the failure of the 1981–82 season. However, one departure from the tried-and-true was planned for the opening of the 1983–84 season: Verdi's *Nabucco* was performed for the first time on the VOA stage—and for the first time in the company's experience, audiences gave a standing ovation during the middle of the performances. Those in the audience who had never before heard the Hebrews' moving choral lament, "Va, pensiero," left the theatre with it forever imprinted in their memories.

Despite having personnel and money difficulties, the board's decision to bring Guttman back was a sound one. The second year of his tenure was particularly successful from an artistic and box-office standpoint; two productions, *Madama Butterfly* and *The Tales of Hoffmann*, the latter a co-production with Seattle Opera, were outstanding and demonstrated once again Guttman's ability to cast unerringly. Soprano Maria Pellegrini lived up to her growing reputation as one of the finest singing actresses on the operatic stage and was superb as Cio-Cio-San, and in *The Tales of Hoffmann*, local favourites Milla Andrew as Giulietta, Heather Thomson as Antonia and newcomer American soprano Cyndia Siedentop as Olympia earned high praise and standing ovations in a production that was hailed as the best in years.[2]

Maestro Guadagno's last appearance on the VOA podium was in January 1983. His career had reached new heights with his Metropolitan Opera conducting debut in November 1982, and he had accepted the position of music director with Florida's Palm Beach Opera, beginning the following year. During his VOA tenure he had endeared himself to the orchestra, not only for his conducting skills and sense of humour, but also for his down-to-earth involvement with practical matters that most conductors would have had no part of. One such occasion was recalled by musician Sharman King:

> I was on what we called "the chairs and stands committee," an orchestra committee just for the logistics of things . . . We were having this meeting, and one of the issues . . . was getting the prompter's box out of [the middle] of the pit . . . and people from the city were saying, "This is an engineering problem. We'll have to do some studies, and its probably going to cost a lot of money." And Guadagno, being Italian and understanding concrete said, basically, "Bullshit. I'll get a jackhammer and take it out." . . . A person who conducted an opera would not be at a meeting like that and be that passionate about getting rid of that dumb chunk of concrete. After Bonynge, he was the guy. He was quite connected to us.[3]

Guadagno's no-nonsense attitude was enough to get the job done without him having to man a jackhammer, but King has no doubt that he would have if necessary.

Brian McMaster was engaged as artistic director after Guttman's contract expired, and Beverly Trifonidis became the new general manager. McMaster was well known as the managing director of the Welsh National Opera, a position he would continue to hold; Trifonidis, a local resident, was a teacher of business administration at Simon Fraser University in Burnaby. McMaster and Trifonidis inherited a company that was still experiencing financial difficulties, despite a profitable 1983–84 season. A grant for coming seasons from the VOA's largest donor, the Canada Council, had strings attached, which required more money and a change from the company's reliance on mainstream programming. The Council grant for 1983–84 was $275,000, one-quarter of all revenues other than ticket sales; without it, the company could not survive. Mindful that the future of the VOA depended on getting continued and, in view of the next season's higher budget, hoped-for increased funding from the Canada Council, McMaster's first season, 1984–85, was designed to deliver both quality and change. Of the four operas, only the season opener, *Un Ballo in Maschera*, had been seen in Vancouver. The others, *I Puritani* (*The Puritans*, Bellini), *Eugene Onegin* and *Così Fan Tutte*, were new to the VOA stage. The first three productions were imported from the Welsh National Opera (WNO), and the last was a VOA-WNO co-production. WNO conductors were used for the first three,

and WNO singers Suzanne Murphy and Dennis O'Neill, both of whom went on to fine international careers, took the lead parts in *Un Ballo in Maschera* and *I Puritani*. McMaster committed to using more Canadians in his productions and delivered on his promise. Three-quarters of the major roles in the season were sung by well-known Canadians such as Audrey Glass, mezzo-soprano Delia Wallis, tenor Gerhard Zeller, Phyllis Mailing, Don Garrard, Richard Margison, Cornelis Opthof and a new discovery of McMaster's, soprano Kathleen Broderick, who was cast as Fiordiligi in *Così Fan Tutte*. That opera was directed by David Walsh, also a Canadian, but better known at the time for his work in the United States

and Europe than in Canada, though he had directed, and was highly praised for, Pacific Opera Victoria's production of *Tosca* in 1983.

But even before the season began, problems became evident at the box office. The Welsh National Opera sets were designed for a much smaller theatre than the Queen Elizabeth and occupied only a portion of the theatre's huge stage. Consequently many seats had restricted view, particularly those on the orchestra centre-sides and sides. To compensate, ticket prices for the affected seats were significantly reduced and potential buyers were alerted to the problem, with the unfortunate outcome of empty seats and diminished revenues. However, when

▲ The VOA-WNO production of *I Puritani* featured the lead soprano of the Welsh National Opera, Suzanne Murphy, as Elvira, shown here in a state of acute mental distress over the flight of her intended bridegroom, Arturo, in the 1985 staging. DAVID COOPER PHOTOGRAPH

David Lemon, a VOA Board executive at the time, was asked in an interview about the effect this had on attendance at VOA productions using the WNO sets, he pointed out that there were a number of people who did not like the entire McMaster regime and expressed their opinion by staying away. He also reminds us that the 1980s were a period of financial hardship for many and, as a board member of the Vancouver Symphony Society and the Vancouver Art Gallery as well, he said these groups were experiencing the same reduction in membership and attendance as the VOA during the period.

Although McMaster's first season should have been a success, it was not. His operas were well directed, well cast, well sung and acted and did not stray into the far-out realm, but his style, which was more theatrical, more minimalist and more intimate than Vancouver audiences were used to, did not catch the wave of popular support it was experiencing in England. One of his blind spots was his aversion to introducing surtitles, which he viewed as distracting. Instead he preferred presenting his productions in the audience's spoken language, giving them the advantage of immediacy in uniting text and music. Yet, despite an opportunity to see Tchaikovsky's great work *Eugene Onegin* for the first time on the VOA stage and hear it sung in English, and despite a rave review from Stephen Godfrey of the *Globe and Mail* on March 11, 1985, following the opening performance, people

were not inspired to attend subsequent performances. It recorded the lowest attendance of the season, the houses averaging a dispiriting 71 percent of capacity.

But whatever the opera-going public chose to convey to the company about its 1984–85 season did not affect the Canada Council grant. The Council did not, as feared, reduce or withdraw its support, leading Vancouver Opera (VO)—during this season the company dropped "Association" from its name—to assume it was doing something right. Its plans for the next season were along the same lines as the previous one, though not quite so adventurous—one piece new to the VO stage, *Fidelio*, to open the season, and three mainstream favourites, *The Barber of Seville*, *The Magic Flute* and *Carmen*, to follow. Sets for *Fidelio* and *The Magic Flute* came from the Welsh National Opera, and although their minimalism suited the bleakness of the prison setting of *Fidelio*, it did nothing to convey a sense of other-worldliness so essential to *The Magic Flute*. Stephen Godfrey (*Globe and Mail*, March 12, 1986) described the scene thus: "This once-magic land now looks like a lumberyard rotting under a sickly sun." For *Fidelio*, the smaller size of the WNO sets was augmented

▲ Mark Pedrotti (Onegin) rejects and humiliates Joan Rogers (Tatyana) in act 1, scene 3 of Vancouver Opera's *Eugene Onegin*, 1985. DAVID COOPER PHOTOGRAPH

to attempt to fill the Queen Elizabeth Theatre stage by the addition of four large columns on which were mounted spotlights, meant to symbolize oppression at the outset and becoming the symbolic light of freedom as the plot unfolded. The cast of *Fidelio* included four Canadians: Lyn Vernon in the soprano role of Leonore, tenor Frederick Donaldson as Florestan, baritone Victor Braun in the role of Don Pizarro and soprano Irena Welhasch as Marzelline, the jailer's daughter.[5]

The fourth VO production, *Carmen*, was designed and performed five times as part of Expo 86, the stunning festival that set the city of Vancouver on the way to becoming a world-class tourist destination. It is not an exaggeration to say that the production also set VO on a path to new heights of controversy and ultimately to a new level of artistic maturity. Instead of the traditional setting and treatment audiences were expecting, what they got was so unconventional that many were shocked and furious. Escamillo sported a pompadour and was dressed in a white, studded outfit with tight pants reminiscent of Elvis Presley's stage costumes; his body language was as lewd and suggestive as that of a rock star, provoking frenzied females onstage to rip the shirt off his

back. Carmen exhibited what was thought to be an excessive degree of whorishness. Micaëla was played as a blind, pregnant ballerina whose maudlin sentimentality was epitomized at one point by a model of a Basque village atop a rickety wagon dragged onstage and trailed by "grimy children with stick-on angel wings in mock reverence," according to Stephen Godfrey (*Globe and Mail*, May 6, 1986). Don José appeared in camouflage battledress, causing the audience to wonder which banana republic was the setting for this travesty. Lighting and sets further added to the bizarre theatrical effects. The audience reaction was a surprise: the traditionalists hated it—no surprise there—but it attracted a sizeable group of hitherto unidentified modernists who loved it, saying it was the most exciting thing ever to be done in Vancouver.

At least one member of the board at the time, David Lemon, who was firmly in the latter camp, still remembers the production enthusiastically: "I think they actually got to the end of it, and everyone was very polite [up to then], but [at the end] there were a huge number of catcalls and boos mixed in with the cheers. It was our own little European opera row. I remember Len Lauk [also on the board] saying that

▲ BC soprano Lyn Vernon as Fidelio (aka Leonore) enters a subterranean prison cell and discovers her husband, Florestan, played by Frederick Donaldson, in a pitiable condition. In this scene in act 2, scene 2 of Vancouver Opera's 1985 *Fidelio*, they sing a joyful duet, "O namelose Freude," celebrating their reunion. DAVID COOPER PHOTOGRAPH

▲ VO used the sets from the Welsh National Opera for its 1985 production of *Fidelio*. The pillars supporting the lights on each side of the set were added to extend it into the empty spaces on the large Queen Elizabeth Theatre stage. DAVID COOPER PHOTOGRAPH

in twenty years there will be 8,000 people who say they were there that night. It was a fascinating experience, very exciting—it was visceral to be there that evening. [Canadian mezzo-soprano] Jean Stilwell was a marvelous Carmen. This notion that Brian McMaster was interested only in . . . theatrical effects and not in singing qualities was just wrong." The furor resulted in sold-out houses for the whole run, confirming director Lucian Pintilie's opinion that *Carmen* was the only opera he considered capable of surviving radical modernization.[6]

As a consequence, the company had enough money to stage the North American premiere of Leoš Janáček's last opera, *From the House of the Dead*, as the opener for the following season to take place during the last month of Expo 86. The work was considered risky because of its unfamiliarity, disturbing subject matter—life inside a Siberian penal colony—and the expense of a large cast. When the opera was being considered by the board, David Lemon found himself at odds with several of his colleagues' comments, which he described as "tedious" and attributable to a general lack of homework on their part. His view was, and still is, that as well as financial commitment, "there has to be an intellectual buy-in" by the board, of the notion that "this is a very dynamic artistic idea, it's going to meet opposition, but we should pay for this because it's something that is about the form, the value of opera, that is extended beyond what we already

know, that we can get our intellectual teeth into."

As if the dissenters and the risk were not enough, the opening performance nearly had to be cancelled. The weather in Vancouver that night, October 4, was cold and, as the first ticket holders began entering the theatre, a power failure plunged the whole of the Expo site and the Queen Elizabeth Theatre into total darkness, leaving over 2,000 people shivering outside for more than two hours. The performance, scheduled to begin at 8 p.m., finally got underway at 10 p.m. and, surprisingly, most of the audience was still around to hear Brian McMaster thank them from the stage for their remarkable forbearance. Fortunately, the opera is a short one—90 minutes—which made it possible to complete it before midnight. Despite the production and the nearly all-male cast (Canadian mezzo-soprano Kimberly Barber took the trouser role of Aljeja) receiving excellent reviews in the media, with one critic calling it a "must-see," the rest of the run was not well attended, confirming yet again the conservative taste of Vancouver audiences. In Lemon's opinion, *From the House of the Dead* was one of the most impressive of the Welsh productions, and he was pleased to learn during the board post-mortem that those originally opposed to the choice had become enthusiastic converts after seeing the show.

Expo 86 was good for opera in the province. *Carmen* was considered an artistic and financial success, and another

Expo operatic event, the La Scala opera company's travelling production of *I Lombardi* (Verdi) attracted capacity audiences to the Pacific Coliseum for its six performances from August 24 to September 4, 1986. Although the Coliseum has 15,000 seats, only 6,500 were used for the productions; the rest were obscured by floor-to-ceiling curtains on either side of the stage. Large video screens allowed people in the less expensive seats to see the stage action more clearly and also projected English surtitles, a first for Vancouver audiences as well as for the La Scala company. Approximately 39,000 people, more than an entire year's attendance at all VO performances in a very good year, saw the opera. Although it likely adversely affected the attendance of the VO Janáček production held during the last days of Expo 86, many who attended *I Lombardi* had never before been to an opera and, obviously pleased with the experience, subsequently signed up for the VO's mini-series of three operas offered for the remainder of the 1986–87 season.

One of the three was *Madama Butterfly*, in which American tenor Jacque Trussel was cast as Pinkerton. All was going well until shortly before the final performance when the singer discovered he had lost his voice. Occurrences like this are not uncommon in the risky business of singing, but finding a replacement at short notice puts an incredible strain on everyone, particularly the conductor and the director. With only hours remaining before curtain

time, American tenor John Stewart was flown in to sing the role offstage while Trussel lip-synched and acted the part onstage. Impressively, although Stewart had sung the role many times in Italian, he had never before sung it in English. If ever there was a compelling case for surtitles, it was then.

The 1987–88 season was vintage McMaster. The opener was the mainstream *La Bohème*, a WNO production, followed by two works new to Vancouver audiences: another Janáček opera, *The Cunning Little Vixen*, and Benjamin Britten's *The Turn of the Screw*. To close out the season, McMaster chose *Die Fledermaus*, which had been done once before, in 1977. All but the Britten work were WNO productions and, in one case, a Welsh and Scottish National Opera co-production. The repertoire should have been appealing to operagoers, but wasn't. Perhaps they were not excited about seeing *La Bohème* for the sixth time; attendance was only 76 percent of capacity. *The Cunning Little Vixen* got rave reviews, but that show did not sell well either. David Walsh returned to direct *The Turn of the Screw*, having done the last season's *The Marriage of Figaro*, but could not overcome the inappropriate venue and set. The Vancouver Playhouse Theatre would have been more suitable than the Queen Elizabeth for the scale of the chamber opera, and the sets, which, according to critic John Becker (*Georgia Straight*, March 18–25, 1988), "look like they've

been borrowed from an IKEA production of *Anne of Green Gables*," detracted from the brooding psychological tensions the music and text are meant to convey. The orchestra and the fine cast, which included Richard Margison as Quint, did their best, but the whole effect was not successful either artistically or at the box office.

Just before the curtain went up on the next season's opening performance of *Don Giovanni*, VO held a press conference to announce that it would be Brian McMaster's last, and that Guus Mostart was coming to Vancouver from the Netherlands Opera as VO's new artistic director. McMaster had given notice, stating that the hardship of travel between VO and WNO was taking too

great a toll. The real reason was a repeat of the Bonynge era problems: too large a difference between production costs and monies being raised. Although Mostart shared McMaster's opinion on the importance of the theatrical component of opera, he differed in his opinion of surtitles. Because they were becoming popular in North America as a way of building audiences, this suited those members of the VO Board who thought it was high time to introduce them, which Mostart said he intended to do. Mostart also made it known that he disapproved of stage directors "who highjack a score to do their own thing . . . I've seen this many times—especially in Germany. Directors are so full of their wonderful ideas that

▲ Two prisoners in chains in a Soviet gulag find a way to lighten their suffering by an intellectual division. Peter Barcza as Goryanchikov teaches Kimberly (Aljeja) to read in this poignant scene from VO's 1986 production of *From the House of the Dead*. IAN LINDSAY PHOTOGRAPH FOR THE *VANCOUVER SUN*

Bravo!

they try them out on any piece that takes their fancy."[7] VO audiences were unlikely to see a repeat of the Expo 86 production of *Carmen* or anything similar during his tenure.

Clearly, McMaster did not have the same aversion. On the face of it, the 1988–89 lineup was a decidedly atypical McMaster season, but three of the productions displayed their directors' departure from the usual, in either their setting or interpretation. Only David Walsh restrained himself and put on a traditional *Don Giovanni* sung in Italian by an excellent almost all-Canadian cast. Scottish director Giles Havergal transported *Ariadne auf Naxos* from eighteenth-century Vienna and ancient

Greece to Vienna during the First World War, and changed Ariadne from an inconsolable Greek woman living in a cave on the island of Naxos into an upper-class Viennese war widow mourning her dead husband during the last years of the doomed Hapsburg Empire. The other characters were updated and transformed to reflect the political realities of the era. Vancouver's popular Judith Forst sang the trouser role of the Composer as she had done in the Canadian Opera Company's production the previous year, and the rest of the cast delivered fine performances that found favour with audiences and critics. For *Rigoletto*, Keith Turnbull of the Stratford Festival and the National Arts Centre, Ottawa, used the two-level

▲ Richard "Doug" Devillier, a soloist and long-time member of the Vancouver Opera Chorus is transformed by Vancouver Opera's clever makeup artists for his role as the Badger in the company's 1988 production of *The Cunning Little Vixen*.
DAVID COOPER PHOTOGRAPH

set designed by Rick Roberts to the best advantage. His interpretation of the opera was a tragedy of fate in which the humiliations suffered by Rigoletto at the ducal court, instead of his own immorality, arrogance and hubris, led to his daughter Gilda's death and his own psychological disintegration. The closing offering, *La Traviata*, was the sixth repeat of the work by the company. Douglas Welch's exceptional lighting effects, the use of colour as a metaphor and a stunning set designed by renowned set and costume designer Carl Friedrich Oberle, featuring full-stage-height doors, all of which opened, were used to great effect by the equally renowned Swedish director Göran Järvefelt to indicate the scene shifts and moods of the Parisian demimonde and the bucolic French countryside.[8]

The program for *La Traviata* included "Notes from the Conductor," which gave readers insight into the decisions made by a conductor that only those with detailed knowledge of the score would notice. In discussing the nineteenth-century move from classic bel canto to romantic verismo, conductor Martin André wrote, "Singers began to insert and hold onto top notes that were not originally written or, indeed, ever intended by the composer. Consequently, we have cut out all unwarranted top notes, though our cast is perfectly capable of providing them. Violetta's 'Sempre libera' in act 1, for example, ends as Verdi intended it should, without a top E flat. The singers therefore

will not be obliged, as many still are nowadays, to omit several bars that Verdi *did* write to allow them to prepare for notes he never wanted."

La Traviata played on April 22, 25, 27 and 29, 1989, and the last two performances had to compete with the monumental International Opera Festival's production of *Aida* in BC Place Stadium, scheduled on the same nights. Readers are reminded of the Expo 86 La Scala production of *I Lombardi*, but the scale of *Aida* was much larger. Of the stadium's 60,000 seats, 37,000 were used, and local resources, including the Vancouver Symphony Orchestra, the Vancouver Bach Choir, Ballet British Columbia and 700 extras, were included in the big show. The beautiful African-American diva Grace Bumbry as Aida and conductor Giuseppe Raffa were huge drawing cards. As well, the company provided a spectacular set and an equally spectacular display of staging for the famous victory march in act 2—a parade of exotic animals, including camels and an elephant. People attended the production in unprecedented numbers, but VO did not appear to suffer from the competition. Indeed, co-operation was the order of the day, as reported by Ray Chatelin (*Vancouver Province*, April

▲ Judith Forst was cast in the trouser role of the Composer, and Gary Relyea was the Music Master in this scene from Vancouver Opera's *Ariadne auf Naxos*, 1989. DAVID COOPER PHOTOGRAPH

Bravo!

28, 1989): "Vancouver Opera provided the *Aïda* people with the 10,000-member mailing list. In exchange, it got 25 percent discounts on a block of *Aïda* tickets." International Opera Festival was the last blockbuster opera company to play Vancouver, leaving the field exclusively to VO and the new artistic director about to come on the scene.

Although many were sorry to see McMaster go, and nobody could dispute that he raised the opera bar to new levels, the prevailing mood at VO was optimistic, as was common at the onset of a new regime. Overall attendance for the 1988–89 season was 87 percent capacity, with seven of the sixteen performances sold out, resulting in a small surplus. There was more encouraging news: by early September 1989, approximately 70 percent of season subscribers had renewed; the accumulated debt of the company had been reduced by $90,510; Canada Council announced a grant of $100,000 for restoration of the Resident Artist Program; and VO president W.J. Wright announced the establishment of the Vancouver Opera Foundation.

These developments augured well for Guus Mostart's debut, as did the news that renowned British director John Cox would be on hand to direct the season's opening opera, *The Rake's Progress*, using the sets designed by the famous contemporary British artist David Hockney and employing surtitles.[9] The opera lived up to its hype. Critics, dazzled

by the Hockney sets and the performances of Canadian singers mezzo-soprano Sandra Graham as Baba the Turk, tenor Benoît Boutet as Tom Rakewell and baritone Allan Monk as Nick Shadow, waxed lyrical about the production, and people responded by attending in sellout numbers. The Stravinsky opera had never before been presented on the VO stage. Another "first" was the introduction of pre-opera talks in the theatre lobby given by knowledgeable people; designed for audience-building, the talks proved very popular and have remained so to the present.

Mostart's Canadian premiere production of the Baroque opera, *Alcina* (G.F. Handel), was chosen to open his second season, which was successful by all accounts. Reviewer Michael Scott made a prophetic comment at the end of his column in the *Vancouver Sun* on October 29, 1990: "Now that Vancouver Opera can claim Guus Mostart as its own, it must be careful to hang on to him." Nevertheless, in July 1991 the board took action that changed the course of VO significantly from then on and contributed to the departure of Mostart. VO announced that it had created a new position, general director, to be filled in September 1991 by Robert Hallam, who came from Edmonton Opera where he had been administrative manager during Irving Guttman's tenure. Next, David Agler, an American conductor with extensive international experience, was appointed music director starting in

▲ A domestic ensemble scene opens act 3 of Vancouver
Opera's 1990 production of *Werther*. Standing is Sunny
Joy Langton as Sophie. DAVID COOPER PHOTOGRAPH

▲ Judith Forst as Charlotte in *Werther*, staged by
Vancouver Opera in 1990. DAVID COOPER PHOTOGRAPH

Bravo!

September 1992, thus putting in place a team that was meant to give VO a new approach to artistic management.

Consequently, Hallam and Mostart were forced to work together with Hallam essentially in charge, a situation that provided considerable opportunity for professional differences. People in the know were not surprised to learn that Mostart told VO that he would be leaving at the end of his contract term in 1992 after only three seasons. However, it must be noted that Mostart's last season was one of VO's best: despite its largest budget to date, $3.5 million, the overall deficit was reduced to $75,410 and a $139,195 surplus was recorded for the 1991–92 season. A gratifying audience participation rate of 97 percent capacity houses was chalked up for the four productions. Thus, Hallam came on the scene when VO was on its uppers, thanks to his two immediate predecessors.

Two months into his job, Hallam served notice that new leadership was in charge by announcing the first-ever VO commission of a contemporary opera. Composer David MacIntyre and playwright Tom Cone, both Vancouverites with considerable creative experience, were contracted to create the new work, *The Architect*, scheduled for staging in the 1992–93 season after going through the workshop process. Funds for the venture came out of the operating budget, and members of the Resident Artist Program comprised the cast. However, the scheduled date for full production turned out to be optimistic. The first workshop

for act 1 took place at the Vancouver East Cultural Centre in June 1992, but there was a hiatus of two years before the premiere of the completed work was staged in the Vancouver Playhouse Theatre on June 11, 1994. Although the creative process took a severe toll on the friendship of MacIntyre and Cone, the wise counsel of conductor Leslie Uyeda usually resolved their numerous disputes over whose authority, the composer's or the librettist's, was paramount.

Hallam's criteria for the work were few: he wanted a lyrical piece; it was to be sung in English; the story was to be about a contemporary issue. MacIntyre and Cone also had their own ideas: they wanted to do an original, psychological piece that had nothing to do with the usual things, such as romance, that traditional libretti dealt with. The subject that best fit their goal was apathy, a contemporary malaise, and architecture was chosen as the medium to explore it. MacIntyre, having been a singer himself, set out to write a singer's opera and chose the harmonies of the blues as a sort of Wagnerian leitmotif to signal the appearance of malaise in the text. The drama concerns a successful architect, Sandra, played by American mezzo-soprano Gloria Parker, who befriends a beach bum, Even, sung by Canadian tenor André Clouthier. Sandra's relationship with Even leads her to question everything she has achieved and consider chucking it all over for a simple life. A dramatic intervention by Sandra's

friends and associates, during which
Even is murdered in order to remove his
"harmful" influence—harmful because,
with Sandra gone from the firm, their
futures are threatened—takes the piece to
a conclusion that leaves no doubt about the
complex emotions at work in the modern
world. Not surprisingly, critics found fault
as well as good things to say about *The
Architect*, but comments from a prominent
classical music reviewer, Lloyd Dykk,
(*Vancouver Sun*, June 25, 1994) struck the
best balance: "Yes, there are many clangers
in *The Architect* including the operating
room scene . . . Whatever you made of it,
I think it was a good experience since our
definition of opera has become old guard
. . . It continued a very old tradition in a

new way and at least tried to keep us in
time with the times. By commissioning a
new work and attempting to ensure that we
don't bury our own past, the architects of
Vancouver Opera were bravely responsible
in their duties." Kenneth Mahon, honorary
director of VO, was outgoing president of
the VO Board when he and his wife were
in the audience on opening night of *The
Architect*, and in an interview recalled an
experience concerning the local scene that
still amuses him:

> The grand opening production of *The
> Architect* was on a Saturday night,
> planned long before anybody knew that
> the Vancouver Canucks would make it
> to the Stanley Cup finals. That Saturday

▲ Baba the Turk in *The Rake's Progress* is a role well
suited to Sandra Graham's acting talents. She is shown
here in an ensemble scene from the Vancouver Opera
production in 1989. DAVID COOPER PHOTOGRAPH

BravO!

night, the Canucks played the New York Rangers in the sixth game of the finals in Vancouver . . . so downtown was completely packed with people, most of the 18,000-odd going to the hockey game and 600 going to our little opening of *The Architect* . . . When we came out of the Playhouse, the Canucks game was over and [they] had won. All the hockey fans were out in full force, driving up and down the streets, waving their Canuck flags, honking their horns, just making all sorts of noise, which is completely foreign to the atmosphere that . . . surrounded an opera . . . I'm a hockey fan, [and] I got a real kick out of this, because it was a completely different celebration and a different set of entertainment values . . . a real coincidence that the two events were happening on the same night.

The eight performances of *The Architect* averaged 85 percent full houses, not bad for a new work, and the production came in on budget. However, despite the generally favourable reaction of VO audiences to the

piece, and MacIntyre's hope that his work would become an enduring part of the contemporary repertoire, it has never again been produced.

The two seasons preceding the premiere of *The Architect* were very good ones for VO. David Agler and Robert Hallam formed a team whose productions were first-rate, resulting in gratifying box-office results and an enhanced North American profile for the company. Another change in the VO lineup in 1992 occurred when long-time chorus director Beverly Fyfe retired.[10] Fyfe had served in that capacity since 1961, and under his leadership the VO Chorus had matured into an ensemble on the threshold of first-class status in North America. Leslie Uyeda, the well-known Canadian conductor, composer and pianist, was Fyfe's replacement, and during her tenure, 1992–2004, the chorus earned that reputation.

During their first two years, the Agler-Hallam team introduced two works that had never before been staged by VO. One of them, *Dialogues of the Carmelites* (*Les Dialogues des Carmélites*, Francis Poulenc), remains in the memory of Bette Cosar, a long-time member of the VO Chorus, as being one of the most moving experiences she has ever had on the VO stage. The opera plot is based on factual events and deals with the testing of the faith of Carmelite nuns living in their convent at Compiègne during the Reign of Terror of the French Revolution. When their

▲ Vancouver Opera presented the Canadian premiere of
    Alcina in 1990, featuring Benita Valente in the title role,
    shown here in her stunning period gown.
    DAVID COOPER PHOTOGRAPH

order was declared illegal in any form, the sisters took a vow of martyrdom and were guillotined. It is a powerful work, one that makes great demands on the women's chorus, and in preparation for it, arrangements were made for the chorus and the principals to visit the monastery of the Sisters of St. Clare in Mission, BC. Cosar described the experience during an interview:

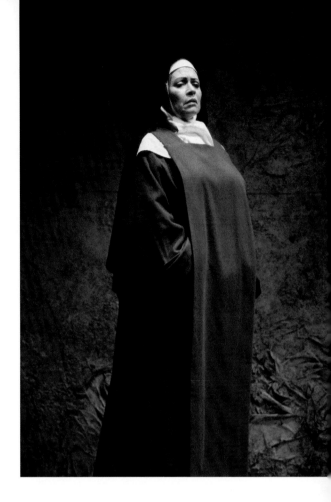

> This visit is so stamped in my memory. We were to go up there to exchange ideas and have tea with these cloistered nuns, and then take part in their five o'clock matins where we would sing . . . the Hail Mary. Most of us went; some were not free to go . . . I'm cynical, and I thought, "If we're going to get this holier-than-thou attitude from these women, I'm not going to be very pleased." But they were the most beautiful women. The Mother Superior—I have never seen [such] light in a face—and these women were so lovely . . . It was so interesting to get this feedback about what it was like to be a nun, and this was our prep for our role . . . When we sang the Hail Mary from the *Dialogues* . . . tears were running down everyone's faces. One of the nuns was young enough to have remembered the name "Judy Forst" [from] when Judy had won the Met Auditions, and at one point we said, "Well, you know, Judy's here with us," and in that matins in the church, I could see that young nun looking for Judy. After that we started rehearsing. We got the historical background, and we knew exactly who we were in these roles. It was just an incredible experience. We were totally lost in these roles. It was the finest thing I think they've ever done.[11]

Judith Forst was cast in the role of Mother Marie. Other Canadian principals were Kathleen Brett as Sister Constance, soprano Joanne Kolomyjec as Madame Lidoine and mezzo-soprano Lori Klassen, a member of the Resident Artist Program, as Mother Jeanne. The American soprano Patricia Racette sang the role of Blanche, and her fellow countrywoman, mezzo-soprano Karen Nickell, made her VO

▲ Judith Forst as Mother Marie in *Dialogues of the Carmelites*, staged by Vancouver Opera in 1993.
DAVID COOPER PHOTOGRAPH

debut in the role of Madame de Croissy. The performance was recorded for a future "Saturday Afternoon at the Opera" CBC Radio broadcast.

The other newcomer to the repertoire the following year was *Jenůfa* (Janáček), which had the added challenge for the performers of learning the opera in Czech. The opera was another highlight in Cosar's experience. Cosar stressed that performing new works are an essential part of maintaining an ensemble's vitality: "The unusual [operas] are the ones that feed us artistically. The first *Dialogues*, the first *Jenůfa* were real adventures—and *Peter Grimes* [Britten]—[they] are the real standouts in my memory as being the most challenging and involving." Judith Forst returned to the VO stage to sing the role of Kostelnička with Michaela Gurevich as Jenůfa; they and the performance earned high praise from the reviewers, one of whom, Michael Scott (*Vancouver Sun*, December 29, 1994), wrote, "If I were to pick a desert island performance from 1994, it would have to be Vancouver Opera's run at Leos Janáček's *Jenůfa* in January. Musically, dramatically, visually, emotionally, this production . . . soared past every expectation of what potent opera should be . . . 'Diva, diva,' people in the audience cried out at Judith Forst's curtain call opening night—the supreme Italian accolade. And with good reason. Forst reached deep into the character of the foster mother to produce a flesh-and-blood woman, horrible and comprehensible

in the same chilling moment." Like *Dialogues*, *Jenůfa* was recorded for "Saturday Afternoon at the Opera" and aired on October 24, 1994.

On the recommendation of Robert Hallam and the approval of the board of directors, VO moved to five productions per season, beginning in 1993–94. During the next two seasons, Agler-Hallam productions that were worthy of superlatives included *Peter Grimes* in January and February 1995, *Faust* in October 1995, *The Makropulos Case* (Janáček) in March 1996 and *Candide* (Leonard Bernstein) in June 1996.

Singing his first operatic role for VO since he appeared as a rising star in *Otello* in 1981, Ben Heppner, who by this time had achieved international fame, electrified Vancouver audiences with his powerful portrayal of the outcast, misanthropic fisherman, Peter Grimes. The intensity of the work proved to be too much for some, who left the theatre before the opera was over. Small wonder: described by Michael Scott (*Vancouver Sun*, January 26, 1995), "[Grimes] is probably the least likeable hero in all opera: an outcast fisher so violent and delusional that his death in the third act comes as a kind of relief. Along the way he reveals himself as an abuser of women and children, a brutal lunatic who contributes to the death of two young apprentices." Heppner talked to Scott before the opening and said, "It would be easy to dwell on the brutish side of the man. You can read some of his

abusiveness in the darkest way. But we are staying away from that . . . interpretation. We see the story as a more universal situation. One that teaches us about intolerance: here is a man who doesn't think the same as the people around him. He is as intolerant of them as they are of him." There is often a sexual innuendo associated with Grimes's abusiveness, which is what Heppner likely implied with the word "darkest." *Peter Grimes* was important for another reason: it was one of the few times when VO designed and contracted a company to build the sets and major props, instead of renting them. In an illuminating article in the opera's program about the set design for the opera, director Leon Major and set designer William Schmuck pointed out that illustrating the concept of intolerance with sets and costumes for *Peter Grimes* was a challenge.

Schmuck explained his starting point: "'I took the idea of the fishing net, which is so much a part of the action in the piece, as a wonderful metaphor for what was happening in the lives of the characters . . . They are all caught in their vices like fish caught in a net. Peter is trapped in the net of the town . . . This town thrives on gossip and accusation; cold, dry colours show the deadness of that kind of life. The simple costumes . . . are dark and roughly textured . . . the main character's wool sweater . . . comes from Mr. Big & Tall."[12] Although *Peter Grimes* may not have been everyone's cup of tea—it attracted the smallest houses of the season at 87 percent of seats sold—it was regarded as a milestone in the growth of the company, both artistically and administratively. Billed as the most ambitious production ever undertaken by VO, it cost nearly

▲ Judith Forst as Kostelnička (standing) lies to Michaela Gurevich, who plays Jenůfa, her stepdaughter, telling her that her baby has died when, in fact, Kostelnička has drowned it. The powerful scene takes place in act 2 of *Jenůfa*, staged by Vancouver Opera in 1994.
DAVID COOPER PHOTOGRAPH

$1 million to produce, required thirty rehearsal hours and extra singers for the chorus and fifteen hours of rehearsal for the orchestra, nearly twice the normal allotted. Besides Heppner singing the title role for the first time in North America, two singers from the United States were brought in to make up a powerful cast: soprano Patricia Racette as Ellen Orford and bass-baritone Alan Held as Balstrode. Canadian bass-baritone Robert Milne was cast as Swallow. For those in the audience who toughed it out, it was a riveting experience. Robert Jordan (*Georgia Straight*, January 27, 1995) said of the work: "As a trip into the dark night of the soul, magnificently expressed in Britten's music and Slater's [librettist Montagu Slater's] words, *Peter Grimes* is stage drama at its most powerful—all the more so in that it remains intensely personal throughout."

The poor public response to *Peter Grimes* was offset by some good news: the company recorded a modest surplus and an average attendance level of over 94 percent capacity at the end of the season. By October 1995 subscriptions for 1995–96 had increased by 11 percent to the highest level in the company's history.[13]

The 1995–96 season got off to a fine start with *Faust*, an old favourite in a new guise. Director Tito Capobianco, general director of the Pittsburgh Opera, made a number of changes that moved the pace of the piece along significantly. By cutting Marguerite's spinning song

(act 4, scene 1), the Walpurgis Night scene (act 5, scene 1) and the long ballet (act 5, scene 2), and making other modifications, he condensed five acts into three. Instead of adhering to the place in the middle of the Kermesse (an outdoor fair) in act 2 where Valentin usually sings his aria exhorting his friends to look after his sister, Marguerite, Capobianco moved it to the scene where Valentin is about to go into battle, which everyone agrees is where it belongs. Some of Capobianco's touches came close to high camp, for example, Méphistophélès onstage at the end of act 1 wearing nothing but a jockstrap sparkling with sequins. And, as if to show how far singers had progressed from the "stand and deliver" method, at the end of the show, Capobianco had Méphistophélès, in full voice, somersault into clouds of red vapour without missing a note. It brought the house down. Reviewing the piece for the *Georgia Straight*, October 26, 1995, James Barber said he couldn't recall ever having a better time at the opera.

Apparently no one could say the same for the production of *Carmen* in February 1996. Hallam was responsible for casting the show in Agler's absence and made the mistake of giving the lead to the French mezzo-soprano Magali Damonte. Given the lead time involved in opera casting, Damonte was likely not pregnant when she was first contracted, but there was no mistaking her condition when she arrived in town for rehearsals. Hallam apparently made no attempt to find a substitute, but he probably wished he had when the audience and reviewers expressed their opinions. Lloyd Dykk (*Vancouver Sun*, February 5, 1996) had this to say about Damonte's performance: "[it] had all the spit-fire passion of a Brownie on a cookie drive."

The season ended with two twentieth-century pieces never before staged in Vancouver: Janáček's *The Makropulos Case* and Bernstein's *Candide*. Purists regard *Candide* as a musical, but that hasn't stopped a number of opera houses from including it in their repertoire from time to time. VO chose to present the Chelsea version, so-called because it was first staged in 1973 by the Chelsea Theatre Center of Brooklyn with a new libretto by Hugh Wheeler, which transformed the original 1956 piece from an unsuccessful, heavy-going black comedy into a ribald farce that became a smash hit. Tyrone Paterson, the artistic director and principal conductor of Opera Lyra Ottawa, was the VO guest conductor, and David Gately returned after his 1994 appearance as director of *Die Fledermaus* to direct the production; together with an enthusiastic young cast, they put on a show that was a near sellout. The reviews were, for the most part, extremely favourable. The venue for the eighteen performances was not the cavernous Queen Elizabeth Theatre but the much more intimate Playhouse Theatre, which suited the scale of the show. As it had for *Peter Grimes*, the company contracted with Singular Productions of Toronto to build the sets.

Two weeks after the show closed, a VO news release reported a season attendance record of over 90 percent capacity and a subscriber base of 8,042 for the coming year. However, when the financial picture became evident, it was very bad indeed: a deficit of nearly $1 million had materialized seemingly overnight. Not only that, but all was not well within VO's administration, and the next few years proved to be stormy ones. What caused these problems and how VO resolved them will be revealed in the next chapter.

Before moving on, however, the contribution of Vancouver New Music to opera during this period is noteworthy. Four productions were staged: on September 30, 1988, the company

▲ Renowned BC tenor Ben Heppner appeared on the Vancouver Opera stage in 1995 as Peter Grimes in the opera of the same name. DAVID COOPER PHOTOGRAPH

Bravo!

performed the premiere of *No No Miya*, which it had commissioned Rudolf Komorous to write; the following year Michael Nyman's *The Man Who Mistook His Wife for a Hat* was presented; in 1990 *Kopernikus*, score and libretto by Claude Vivier, was the selection; and in 1994 *The Star Catalogues*, music by Owen Underhill, libretto by Marc Diamond, was staged.

Komorous was born in Prague but became a naturalized Canadian in 1974. He wrote his opera in Victoria, where he was director of the University of Victoria School of Music. *No No Miya* was a sellout, no doubt helped by the presence of Judith Forst and Canadian baritone Gary Dahl singing the leading roles, and glowing reviews in the media. Forst was cast as Lady Rokujo, a medieval Japanese noblewoman condemned to an afterlife as a spectre as punishment for her crime of passion. Dahl sang the role of the monk who helps her escape her sentence and return to the past, where she is able to find peace. Both earned these remarks in Ray Chatelin's review of the production

(*Vancouver Province*, October 2, 1988): "Forst and Dahl produce drama and music in a push/pull relationship that is perfectly proportioned to the task it undertakes."

Michael Nyman is a British composer, pianist, musicologist and librettist (he wrote the libretto for VNM's 1973 production of Birtwistle's *Down by the Greenwood Side*). His chamber opera is based on an essay by the neurologist Oliver Sacks about a man who suffered from visual agnosia, a neurological condition that makes one unable to recognize objects, places and people, hence the evocative title, *The Man Who Mistook His Wife for a Hat*. Taking such a complex case history and turning it into an opera was a brilliant paradox, because, in reality, the patient was eventually able to deal with his affliction by using his exceptional musical talents. Michael Scott, writing in the *Vancouver Province*, October 7, 1989, called it " a gem of inventiveness—a tiny perfect epic, movingly told."

Kopernikus, written in 1979, is the only opera in the musical works of Claude

▲ An ensemble scene from the 1994 Vancouver Opera presentation of *Nabucco*.
PHOTO COURTESY VANCOUVER OPERA

Vivier of Quebec, who, before he was murdered in 1983, was widely regarded as Canada's most original and controversial composer. Arguably, *Kopernikus* is less an opera and more a series of seven loosely connected scenes in which unrelated people from dreams appear to the central character, Agni, as symbols in a spiritual journey. It has been described as a strange piece, doubtless partly owing to the libretto being written in several languages, one of which Vivier invented. According to the artistic director, Owen Underhill, VNM's production depended on the clarity of Vivier's music to lead the viewer through any obscurities that the staging might not have addressed. One reviewer, Ray Chatelin (*Vancouver Province*, September 30, 1990), disagreed: "The stage values were exceptional. But— and it's a big BUT—by the time you've left this staging, all that you've heard musically will be forgotten. What will be left will be a boiling spring of unresolved mystical symbols . . . As theatre *Kopernikus* is a visual delight with imaginative sets

and costumes. As music, it's limited but pleasant enough."

About *The Star Catalogues*, Michael Scott (*Vancouver Sun*, October 24, 1994) wrote the following: "Vancouver New Music and composer-librettist team Owen Underhill and Marc Diamond deserve a sustained round of applause for their daring and finely wrought new opera, *The Star Catalogues*. This astonishing work of music theatre, which received its world premiere in October in a commandeered community hall, was so compelling, so masterfully allusive, so full of both poetic and musical passion, that if the world of contemporary opera were ranked along a Great Chain of Being, *The Star Catalogues* would find itself somewhere near the top, in the company of works by Poulenc, Britten and Janáček."[14] Clearly, VNM's productions were important and stimulating additions to the more traditional repertoire of the mainstream companies in Vancouver and Victoria.

▲ In act 1 of Vancouver Opera's 1996 presentation of *The Makropulos Case*, Mary Jane Johnson as Emilia Marty has entered the chambers of Dr. Kolenatý, played by John Fanning, to impart startling information about a case the lawyer is involved in.
DAVID COOPER PHOTOGRAPH

Act IV

VANCOUVER AND VICTORIA
1996–97 to 2008–09

THE DECADE FROM THE 1996–97 SEASON TO THE 2008–09 SEASON OF opera in the province was rich in drama, both onstage and behind the scenes. Before turning to the two major companies in the province, several other initiatives launched early in the decade deserve mention.

MODERN BAROQUE OPERA AND VANCOUVER NEW MUSIC
In the early 1990s, three young Canadians working as ushers at an opera house in London, England, discovered that they shared a passion for Baroque opera. Simon Capet, a conductor, Thomas Hassmann, a designer and Kate Hutchinson, a theatre director, lacked opera production experience, but, not letting that discourage them, they discussed the possibility of staging a Baroque opera.[1] Hassmann suggested a relatively obscure Austrian Baroque opera of which he was especially fond, *Le Cinesi (The Chinese)* by Gluck, and a bold plan took shape, explained by Hutchinson in an interview: "We just got it into our heads that we would stage an opera that summer, and that was back in 1995, so we staged *Le Cinesi* at the Battersea Arts Centre . . . and ended up extending the run, because we were completely sold out after the second week for three weeks." Despite the success of the venture, the trio realized that their professional futures in culturally rich London would be precarious at best, and so they all left: Hassmann to Mexico City, and Capet and Hutchinson to Vancouver, where Hutchinson grew up. She described what happened next:

> Within six months we were both getting kind of itchy to do something else, and so we decided to restage *Le Cinesi* here using Vancouver singers and the designer [Hassmann] who had worked with us in London . . . We had him fly up here from Mexico . . . We auditioned singers in the Vancouver

◄ Tarquinius, played by Phillip Addis, seeks a bed for the night at the home of Lucretia, played by Louise Guyot, with an ulterior motive: to test Lucretia's faithfulness to her absent husband in act 1 of Pacific Opera Victoria's *The Rape of Lucretia*, 2006. DAVID COOPER PHOTOGRAPH

laugh at and it was very approachable
. . . It was late May or early June [1996].
There wasn't a lot else happening, which
worked to our advantage.

The staging of *Le Cinesi* led to an
unexpected development when Duncan
Low, the new executive director of the
Vancouver East Cultural Centre (VECC),
who had seen the production, invited
Capet and Hutchinson to a meeting and,
much to their surprise, offered them
resident status at "The Cultch" effective
September 1996. Hutchinson recalled
her reaction as, "Okay, I guess we're
starting something here." She, Capet
and Hassmann, with considerable initial
support and guidance from Low and
VECC's business manager, got on with the
work of forming a company, which they
called Modern Baroque Opera (MBO).
The name seems at face value to be an
oxymoron, but the company's mission was
to present the eighteenth-century Baroque
repertoire in such a way as to make it
appeal to modern audiences by introducing
contemporary theatrical and orchestral
elements that the founders, especially
Hutchinson, had learned from English
National Opera productions.

MBO produced its first opera in the
300-seat VECC theatre in February 1997.
They chose *Orpheus and Eurydice*, another
Gluck composition, and a wise choice it
was, because it requires only three principal
singers and can be effectively staged with
a small chorus and orchestra. Although

community and came up with a new
Vancouver cast . . . Everything had to
be rebuilt because we had not brought
anything from England. We staged it
at what was then called the Gastown
Theatre . . . I think it sat sixty-eight
people . . . The orchestra was three
people—harpsichord, violin and cello.
Again we ended up extending the run,
because the same thing happened here
that happened in London . . . That
particular piece and the way I directed
it lent itself to people who had never
approached opera before . . . It's a sort
of reflection on different operatic styles
and different modes of performance that
existed in Baroque times and still exist
in opera today, and so there was a lot to

▲　The Modern Baroque Opera production of *Arcifanfano*
in 1999 featured Gregory Dahl in the title role and
Vancouver singer Phoebe MacRae as Semplicina, shown
here in this exuberant scene from the piece.
PHOTO COURTESY MODERN BAROQUE OPERA

the opera was well known to Vancouver audiences, and most performances were sold out, ticket sales and grants were not enough to offset a $10,000 loss on the production.

After *Orpheus and Eurydice* and *The Music Master* (Paisiello), MBO restaged *Le Cinesi* in the fall of 1997 and then staged ten more productions (see Appendix C), the majority of which were little-known pieces, such as the more obscure works of Handel, selected for reasons of economy. These resulted in uneven success at the box office—anywhere from 40 percent to full houses, according to Hutchinson—but, for the most part, received encouraging reviews in the media.

More than encouraging was the review for the comic opera, *Arcifanfano, King of Fools* by Karl Ditters von Dittersdorf, which played in May 1999, when the 29th Opera America Conference brought hundreds of opera people to Vancouver, the host city. MBO did itself proud alongside similarly scheduled performances by Vancouver Opera and Vancouver New Music, as the following comments of Christopher Dafoe (*Vancouver Sun*, May 7, 1999) demonstrate: "The cast of this musical dream or nightmare strikes just the right note, singing beautifully from time to time and knowing when a croak or a bray is needed . . . The production gives pleasure in so many unexpected ways." Singers in the principal roles, all Canadians who frequently appeared in MBO productions, included baritone Gregory Dahl as Arcifanfano, David Garfinkle in the mimed role of Divertimento, counter-

tenor Carl Strygg as Garbata and local soprano Phoebe MacRae as Semplicina. The performance was sung in English, using W.H. Auden's translation. The Pacific Baroque Orchestra, under the leadership of Marc Destrubé, provided the music and became the pit orchestra for all subsequent MBO productions.

The company expanded on its mission in 2001 when it became the recipient of an Alcan Performing Arts Award and the accompanying grant of $50,000, which was received the following year, to commission and stage a piece that was truly modern Baroque: *120 Songs for the Marquis de Sade*. Hutchinson recalled the effect this had on the company:

> Winning the Alcan Award in 2002 was a really major thing . . . We had applied with the idea of commissioning Peter Hannan to write *120 Songs for the Marquis de Sade*, and apparently the jury, hands down . . . decided this was a project they wanted to give this award to. That for me was a big moment of recognition . . . As soon as we got that money, a lot of organizations wanted to get involved, and we had Vancouver New Music come on board and give us an equal amount. It was the first time we were able to think a little bit larger . . . [such as] create more than one costume for a character . . . I would say that [*120 Songs*] was the company's most notable achievement, and for me it was probably the most challenging thing I'll ever do artistically.[2]

From the start to the premiere in March 2002, the production was a year in development. During that time, the CBC did a documentary on the process, and after viewing it, it's clear that Hutchinson was not overstating the challenge. Both the composer, Vancouver-based Hannan, and the librettist, Peter Hinton, were accomplished professionals with a good deal of solid work behind them, but creating and staging a piece based on the life and writings of the most notorious deviant in eighteenth-century France led them, and everyone else associated with it, into uncharted waters with the depiction of nudity and violence. Of the audience reaction, Hutchinson said, "The audience became really split. There were people who had loved our [traditional] Baroque stuff who also thought *120 Songs for the Marquis de Sade* was fantastic. They'd never seen anything like it. We also had some people who liked our Baroque stuff but were offended or shocked or thought it wasn't in keeping . . . The piece looked very period; . . . it was tricky trying to bridge the contemporary repertoire and the Baroque as far as the audience was concerned. That's when people became a little confused about what we were doing." Lloyd Dykk agreed (*Vancouver Sun*, March 5, 2002): "It is deadly, and I say this in sorrow, mixed with anger and confusion. Where the confusion comes in is how Sade, who apparently led quite an interesting life, could be turned into such a bore. Perhaps we should be content with

only reading the writings of Sade instead of seeing them turned into an opera—at least . . . an opera like this one, whose literal-mindedness verges on the amateur." Up to this point, Dykk had usually found positive things to say about MBO's productions.

The following year, MBO commissioned Peter Hannan to write *The Diana Cantata*, whose subject was the near-mythical Diana, Princess of Wales, and produced it with another short piece based on Georg Philipp Telemann's *Ino*. The company also commissioned composer Jeff Corness and librettist Michael Turner, both local artists, to create another piece, *Max & Moritz*, based on the German children's story of the same title, for presentation at the Vancouver International Children's Festival during May 2003. Five performances of *The Garden (Il Filosofo di Campagna*, Baldassare Galuppi) in the fall of 2003 turned out to be the last initiative of MBO, and Hutchinson explained why: "I was feeling a little bit burned out from fundraising all the time, but never being able to get to the point where I had enough operational funding to pay anyone other than an accountant . . . It was tiring in the long haul, and I was also at a place artistically where I had exhausted the possibilities of my imagination, and [my son] was just over a year old . . . so it was time to take a break." Hutchinson spoke to her board about the possibility of hiring someone to replace her, but its opinion was that the company and Hutchinson were too closely identified with each other to guarantee MBO's viability under a new artistic director. The board decided to allow the company to become inactive but still maintain its non-profit status by filing the required documents, which Hutchinson does every year. When asked about the possibility of MBO returning to the opera scene in the future, Hutchinson replied, "If someone came to me with an interesting idea and wanted to do the bulk of the running-around work, we might be able to do it . . . The way I'm feeling right now, I would not want to go back and run the company the way I did. It was a recipe for burnout all around." Since no one has come forward yet, the niche that MBO created in the provincial opera scene remains vacant.

Vancouver New Music (VNM), already introduced in Acts I and III, presented several new operatic works in the post-1996 period: Peter Hannan and Tom Cone's *The Gang* in 1997 and Rodney Sharman and Atom Egoyan's *elsewhereless* in 1999, as well as the co-production with MBO in 2002 described above. The venue for these productions was the Vancouver East Cultural Centre.

The Gang is set in 1947, and opens with a group of seemingly compatible people working together toward a common goal—construction of a beautiful glass house for them to live in—but the project ends in death, loss of sanity, and the triumph of tribal mentality. Reviewer Alexander Varty (*Georgia Straight*, June 12–19, 1997) offered the following insight into the composition of contemporary opera: "Both Hannan and Cone assert that if opera is to be more than a glittering relic it must shed some of its conventions, and in *The Gang* the most notable thing that is discarded is . . . the operatic voice. The eight singers Hannan has convened . . . sing with the dramatic skills of Broadway, the emotional authenticity of rock, and the lyrical suppleness of jazz." One would have to have been present to appreciate how this variety of style contributed to the whole piece along with the musical accompaniment of an amplified band, which included an electric guitar, two synthesizers and two percussionists playing vibraphone, marimbas, drum kits, tom-toms and tin cans. As is common with media coverage, some reviewers dismissed *The Gang*, whereas others found it exhilarating.

The chamber opera *elsewhereless*, Canadian composer Rodney Sharman's collaboration with filmmaker Atom Egoyan as librettist, was VNM's contribution to the 29th Opera America Conference in Vancouver. Its genesis was a commission from VNM in 1991, and work was begun in Victoria, where both Sharman and Egoyan were living at the time. The drama, set in an unidentified part of Africa, revolves around three male characters involved in a homosexual love triangle that ends in death and madness. Projected images, of Africans in varying poses suggesting brutality

BravO!

and genocide, introduced Egoyanesque elements of film into the work and helped to flesh out the drama without adding to its length. It received its premiere in Toronto by Tapestry Music Theatre in 1998, and was staged by VNM the following year in Vancouver in the Playhouse Theatre. Although panned by media critics, several of whom thought it should not be considered an opera at all, it has stood the test of time, having the unique distinction among contemporary Canadian operas of having been performed thirty-five times since.

VNM has been a regular presenter of numerous new music events in Vancouver since 1999, but opera had not been offered since *elsewhereless*. That was remedied in December 2007, when the company presented *Fig Trees*, a contemporary video-opera installation, details about which will appear in the next chapter.

PACIFIC OPERA VICTORIA

Before the doors to the McPherson Playhouse in Victoria opened in September 1996 for the first performance of *The Pearl Fishers* (*Les Pêcheurs de Perles*, Bizet), POV had sold every seat in the house for all five nights of the run. Doubtless, audiences were looking forward to hearing Canadian baritone John Fanning and tenor Ya Lin Zhang sing one of the most beautiful duets in all opera—"Au fond du temple saint"—and the singers did not disappoint. Fanning and Zhang were joined onstage by Canadian soprano Nathalie Morais as Leïla and Canadian bass Randall Jakobsh

as Nourabad. Morais's aria, "Comme autrefois dans la nuit sombre" in act 2 was, by all accounts, equally thrilling. (The four had also worked well together in POV's 1995 production of *La Bohème*, which received rave reviews.)

However, the mid-1990s were worrisome financially for POV. The accumulated deficit as of June 30, 1996 was $15,159, a result of excess expenditures over revenues from *The Love of Three Kings* and *Carmen* during the 1995–96 season. At the POV Board meeting of August 15, 1996, president Kathryn Stolle delivered a stern reminder to her colleagues in her president's report: "A POV Board member must possess the demonstrated ability to give money, get money, or contribute a significant amount of time and talent toward the bottom line of the company. It is the clear responsibility of each and every board member to be active and participatory." And at the annual general meeting of November 28, 1996, she reiterated her position, saying, "Our main objective over the next three years must be revenue generation." As an immediate response, a fundraiser called The Event was held on April 11, 1997, and raised $207,184, to be shared between the Victoria Symphony Orchestra and POV. POV's portion of the take not only retired the debt, but also contributed $35,000 to the POV Foundation and gave the company a working surplus of $60,000 for the coming seasons.

The next few years for POV were good ones in terms of repertoire variety and production quality, but were close to the margin financially. The company's twentieth anniversary season, 1998–99, got off to a brilliant start with *Un Ballo in Maschera*, which brought native son Richard Margison back to his roots to sing the role of Riccardo. Margison waived his fee—reported in the press as US$25,000 for a single performance—to assist the fortunes of the company that launched his fabulous career.[3] On the day single tickets for the opera went on sale, the number sold was seven times the previous record in POV's history. In addition to the excitement of hearing Margison in his prime, audiences were introduced to two newcomers making their debut: Margison's wife, Canadian Valerie Kuinka, directing a full production for the first time, and Barbara Livingston, a virtually unknown soprano except for occasional gigs in her hometown of Campbell River, BC, in the lead role of Amelia. Kuinka and Margison's daughter, Lauren, also made her stage debut in a non-singing role as Amelia's daughter.

Livingston had been persuaded by a friend in Campbell River to go to Victoria to take part in an audition not connected with the opera. Timothy Vernon was not present, but POV general manager David Devan was, and when he heard her sing, he called Vernon to get to the Royal Theatre at once. Vernon was overwhelmed at what he heard, and next

thing Livingston knew, she had agreed to be in the opera with Margison. She is what is known in the trade as a lirico-spinto soprano; her voice developed late, which is not unusual for its type, and had the added advantage of underuse, making it sound very fresh and youthful, though she was nearly forty years old.[4] Apparently she had something else going for her: a refreshing, down-home, no-nonsense attitude toward the task ahead of her. She contacted Selena James, her former voice teacher at the Victoria Conservatory of Music, to help her prepare for the role, and by the time she went onstage, was well able to hold her own with the star of the show, even after learning of the death of her mother in the middle of the run.[5]

One might wonder about Margison's reaction on learning that his leading lady was an operatic neophyte. Vernon dealt with that in an interview with Christopher Dafoe (*Globe and Mail*, August 7, 1998), during which he paid the following compliment to the tenor: "[Richard] is . . . very generous. A lot of guys of his stature

▲ Tenor Ya Lin Zhang and baritone John Fanning as Nadir and Zurga, the fishermen who love the same woman in Pacific Opera Victoria's 1996 presentation of *The Pearl Fishers*. DAVID COOPER PHOTOGRAPH

would be disconcerted to have someone like Barbara coming out of nowhere and looking them in the eye and singing at their level. But he's been nothing but supportive. He's been right there for her all the way."

Offstage, discussions were going on surrounding the production of a new opera, *Erewhon*, by a pair of Canadian cultural icons: composer Louis Applebaum and librettist Mavor Moore. Incorrectly reported as being commissioned by POV, production of the work was taken over by the company—against Tim Vernon's better judgment—when the National Arts Centre plans to stage it foundered. Some strong arguments by POV's general manager, who saw great potential in the project for the company, had the following effect on Vernon: "[*Erewhon*] was a millennium project that was born at the National Arts Centre, and when the regime [there] came a cropper, this fledgling piece that had had a workshop or two was left adrift, and we were approached by a well-standing person of some renown who told us that

if we took it on . . . he would guarantee us about a half a million dollars extra funding. If you want to know the truth, I looked at it, and said, 'no.' But the then general manager shut his office door and said, 'Don't say that. Look what happens if we do this—we get this [and] we get this,' and I allowed myself to be persuaded."

Inspired by two satirical novels by the Victorian author Samuel Butler, *Erewhon*'s libretto is quirky, to say the least, dealing as it does with the trials and tribulations of the central character, a Canadian named John Higgs, in a land where everything is contrary to mores and common practices in the rest of the world. Vernon described it to Tina Sudlow (*Vancouver Sun*, February 19, 2000) as "a sort of *Alice in Wonderland* meets *The Magic Flute*." It had its world premiere in the Royal Theatre in February 2000 and attracted more notoriety than any POV production before or since. The media had a field day with it. There were titillating advance reports of the bitter acrimony between the composer, the librettist and the director, nearly causing the latter

▲ Pacific Opera Victoria cast Joanne Hounsell as the Governess, shown here in a scene from *The Turn of the Screw*, 1997. DAVID COOPER PHOTOGRAPH

to withdraw from the project, and the runaway costs of production. Reviews of the artistic merits of the show brought forth extremes of opinion: it was described as magnificent, amazing, a peculiar piece, a farce and a production that sent people out the door at the first opportunity. Loyal fans, furious at the criticism, vented their spleens in support of the show via letters to the editor, adding to the already prodigious expenditure of ink.

All this publicity paled in comparison with *Erewhon*'s cost overruns, which put POV deeply in debt. Vernon described how it happened: "It was nightmarish . . . and it got worse as it went along. Every decision costs more the closer you get to curtain time . . . [and] that curtain's going up at eight o'clock on that day, and that's it, so there's an absolute that you can't fool around with, so you wind up spending for the additions, and that's what we did. We threw a bunch of money at it, we overspent, and it looked like ruination because we had a deficit of a quarter of a million dollars, roughly." Others say the deficit was $350,000—either figure represented an ominous threat to POV's continuing existence.

When asked his opinion of the show and its effect on the company, Vernon said, "It was an entertaining evening in the theatre—more than that I won't say. What was interesting, though, was the effect on the philanthropic situation, because the board was faced with this . . . whopping sum sitting there in red . . . Within a

couple of hours there was something in excess of $80,000 of board money on that table. Then the two Janes went out and raised just short of $400,000 in larger chunks than we'd ever received." The two Janes were Jane Danzo, president of the POV Board, and Jane Heffelfinger, whose importance to POV has already been described in Act II.

Vernon went on to describe the heartwarming outcome of his encounter with one particular operagoer, a third- or fourth-generation Victorian entrepreneur: "He saw the opera—didn't particularly like it—didn't hate it, but we talked about our situation and what had happened, and he said, 'Ah, I get it. That's venture capital. You're trying something different, something new. However, a Canadian work, who the hell wants to go to that? I'm not saying it's my favourite thing [but] you guys have done a great job. Here's what I'm going to do,' pulls out his chequebook, wrote out a cheque for $25,000 and handed it to me across the table."

What that response, and others like it, proved to Vernon and the others involved in the rescue operation, called Campaign 2000, was that there existed in the city and surrounding communities a solid and sizeable core of people who valued

▲ Barbara Livingston as Leonora and Sue Kelly as Ines, her confidante, in the 2000 presentaion of *Il Trovatore* by Pacific Opera Victoria. DAVID COOPER PHOTOGRAPH

Bravo!

▲ Jennifer Maines-Chamandy as Katarina, shown here
as a bride whose foul temper has been tamed by love
in the Canadian premiere of *The Taming of the Shrew*
presented by Pacific Opera Victoria in 2001.
DAVID COOPER PHOTOGRAPH

their evenings at the opera so much that the possibility of losing the company was unthinkable. They not only reached deep into their pockets to make sure that did not happen, but also subscribed in record numbers for the coming season. The company's year-end financial statements dated June 30, 2001, recorded an excess of revenue over expenditures of $407,181, mainly from a spike in donations to $509,152, most of which was raised during Campaign 2000.

Following *Erewhon*, Barbara Livingston returned to the POV stage to sing the part of Leonora in *Il Trovatore*, which finished off the 1999–2000 season. She shared the limelight with Canadian mezzo-soprano Marcia Swanston as Azucena, American tenor Philip Webb singing the role of Manrico and Canadian baritone John Avey as Count di Luna. Although Swanston received the greatest applause for her portrayal of the old gypsy, Livingston proved that her debut performance in *Un Ballo in Maschera* was no flash in the pan, confirmed by reviewer Robert Jordan in the *Globe and Mail*, May 1, 2000: "*Trovatore*'s Leonora is completely different from Amelia, of course, and Livingston relied almost entirely on her voice for characterization. Wisely so: Her thespian skills may need development but her vocal prowess is undeniable. She could cut loose with the decibels when required, but Livingston demonstrated admirable versatility by toning down her lusty lirico-spinto to a lighter and more delicate lyric

soprano than when she was Amelia." Indeed, Leonora became known as Livingston's signature role in subsequent performances with a variety of companies. Jordan wrote that the staging and the sets lacked "visual interest," but also had good things to say about the orchestra under Maestro Vernon and the "lusty" singing of the "well-trained" POV Chorus.

The next season was memorable on several fronts. First, there were three fine productions: to open the season, the company presented a rollicking *Barber of Seville*. The mood in the theatre on opening night matched the ebullience onstage after Jane Heffelfinger's announcement before the curtain went up of the success of Campaign 2000. The February 2001 offering, *The Taming of the Shrew* by a little-known American composer, Vittorio Giannini, had never before been staged in Canada. Regarded as the gamble of the season, it was completely sold out weeks in advance, much to POV's surprise and delight. *Nabucco*, the final production of the season, put the spotlight on the POV Chorus as never before. Not only does the work require the chorus to be onstage for two-thirds of the production, but also, singers had the greatest quantity to date of difficult music to master and, consequently, the most rehearsal time in the chorus's experience was required to ensure that the regulars and the extras, fifty-six in all, were up to the challenge. They were. Second, the company's morale was given a huge boost in May 2001 by the notification

Bravo!

with Susan Down (*Times Colonist*, October 11, 2001) before the opening, Vernon expressed his confidence in Dibblee's ability to portray the complexities of the role: "There are certain roles where as long as you sing pretty, that's all that's required. This is a far more profound examination of human nature. I'm absolutely convinced of her abilities to convey all the facets of the character. She has great depth of feeling."

Familiar to POV audiences from previous productions was Winnipeg tenor Kurt Lehmann, who sang the role of Alfredo. New Zealand-born baritone Mark Pedrotti, long a resident of Canada, was cast as Germont. Director Diana Leblanc, who brought with her a fine reputation from the Stratford Festival and the Soulpepper Theatre Company of Toronto and is equally well known as a fine actress, was also making her POV debut. The production featured traditional sets from the Virginia Opera Company and period costumes from Malabar Limited, the Toronto company that has supplied theatrical costumes to opera companies for many years. The orchestra was led by Giuseppe Pietraroia, who had occupied the podium for POV on several previous occasions, including the twentieth-anniversary presentation of *Un Ballo in Maschera*; he is presently conductor-in-residence for POV and the Victoria Symphony Orchestra.

Near-capacity audiences attended *Lucia di Lammermoor*, the opening production of the company's twenty-fifth anniversary

from Canada Council that POV's grant for the next three years would be increased by 19 percent to $146,000 per year. In its granting letter, the Council cited the company as an example to others of what can be achieved when everyone is working together toward the same goals.

One of Canada's finest sopranos, Sally Dibblee, made a double debut in POV's opening production of the 2001–02 season, *La Traviata*: it was not only her role debut as Violetta but her first Verdi opera. Dibblee (rhymes with "nibble"), who at that time was receiving a lot of attention as a young singer exceeding the promise shown in her early performances, is almost as fine an actress as she is a singer, and in addition, is lovely to look at, all of which made her ideal for the part. She was well known to Vernon, who had cast her in the role of Yram in *Erewhon*. In an interview

▲ *Nabucco*, produced by Pacific Opera Victoria in 2001, featured Kevin Maynor as Zaccaria, the High Priest of the Hebrews, shown here in part 1 with Allyson McHardy as Fenena, Nabucco's daughter, whom he threatens to kill if Nabucco destroys the temple.
DAVID COOPER PHOTOGRAPH

season, and the mood in the house was one of celebration. By enduring for twenty-five years in a community still far from the population commonly believed necessary to support a professional opera company (1 million), POV had beaten the odds, and all indications were that it would continue to do so. As well received by both audience and critics as *Lucia* was, however, the second offering of the season, usually the riskiest, was the most memorable anniversary production. POV staged the Canadian premiere of Lee Hoiby's *The Tempest*, regarded as a contemporary work, though written in 1986. Making his POV debut was French-born director Renaud Doucet, who moved to Canada in 1993 and quickly made a name for himself as a talented choreographer as well as a director. He received this glowing account from Ivan Munro (*Monday Magazine*,

February 19–25, 2004) for *The Tempest:* "[Doucet] brought out the inner actor in most of his singers, [making for] one of the most theatrically satisfying nights . . . POV has ever mounted." Lambroula Maria Pappas, raised in North Burnaby and a graduate of UBC's School of Music opera program, was cast in the lead female role, Miranda, and Vancouver singer Phoebe MacRae, who had distinguished herself previously in several Modern Baroque Opera productions, was singled out for her performance as Iris. The CBC taped the last two performances for later radio broadcast on "Saturday Afternoon at the Opera," and on those evenings, both Hoiby, the composer, and Mark Shulgasser, the librettist, were POV's honoured guests.

Regrettably, the season ended with the company in the red to the tune of

▲ Barbara Livingston, the virtually unknown soprano from Campbell River who was cast by Pacific Opera Victoria opposite "name" tenor Richard Margison in 1998, returned to the POV stage for the third time in a starring role to sing Norma in the opera of the same name in 2004. She is shown here in a scene with Anita Krause as Adalgisa. DAVID COOPER PHOTOGRAPH

Bravo!

$78,977. Increased revenues were offset by sizeable increases in production costs, salaries and benefits, and marketing costs, but by holding the line on expenses and raising more money, the company was able to achieve a surplus position, albeit very small, the following year. Despite budget increases, modest operating surpluses have been reported up to, and including, the 2007–08 season.

In addition to the company's financial and artistic well-being, there were several important developments arising out of the opera community that were of considerable importance to POV. First, Dr. Erika Kurth, a prominent singer and teacher and founding supporter of POV, and her husband, Dr. Burton Kurth, a noted scholar and writer, pledged $100,000 over three years to establish the Burton Lowell and Olive Kurth Young Artist Program, named in memory of Burton Kurth's parents, both well known in Canadian music circles.[6] The significance for POV was noted in the company's press release, dated February 24, 2004: "[It]

is established to provide development opportunities and vigorous professional training for young emerging Canadian artists. The program will provide employment and performance experience training to four . . . singers each year, and will increase the scope of POV's work nationally, as young artists from across the country advance from the program to major roles on Canadian stages." Alison Nystrom, Eric Olsen (the only candidate from Victoria), Colleen Renihan and Justin Welsh were the first entry singers chosen by cross-country auditions. They began thirteen weeks of intensive training in January 2005, and all were onstage in comprimario roles in POV's production of *The Cunning Little Vixen* in mid-February of that year. And before graduating, they gained additional performance experience during a three-week tour of *The Barber of Seville* to elementary schools in the Victoria area and on the concert stage. Each year since the program began, auditions have been held and four new singers given this great opportunity.

▲ A colourful ensemble scene from *The Cunning Little Vixen*, staged by Pacific Opera Vancouver in 2005. The action shows the Vixen attacking the Cock while the Hens watch in terror. TIM MATHESON PHOTOGRAPH

Next, a prominent Victoria philanthropist and devoted lover of opera, Alexander (Sandy) Shand, announced in September 2004 that he had made provisions in his will for a bequest of $1 million to the POV Foundation, to be held in the JONSAN Fund, named for Shand and his life partner, John Phillips, who had recently died. Shand died in May 2006, bequeathing the largest donation POV had ever received, one that ensured the continuing financial stability of the company.

Finally, in October 2005, RBC Financial Group announced a corporate pledge of $100,000, the largest ever made to a Victoria arts organization, to assist POV with its operating costs over the next three years, which enabled the company to stage some very fine productions, and doubtless helped achieve the above mentioned surpluses.

It is difficult to choose which productions from the last few POV seasons are especially noteworthy, because all were splendid, but a few had something special to make them stand out. The company had not done *Eugene Onegin* since February 1990 in the McPherson Playhouse, so when it was presented in October 2005 in the Royal, there was much more room onstage to create a set on a grand scale that better conveyed the vastness of Russia. To this end, a verismo Russian forest was built by bringing into the theatre twenty-eight recently cut trees from Port Renfrew, each 26 feet (8 m) tall,

and securing them by cable to an overhead grid capable of holding many tons. Head carpenter Don Buskirk discussed this feature and other unusual requirements of the set in the *Times Colonist*, October 2, 2005: "I'm quite an environmentalist and don't like cutting down trees, but these were leaning toward power lines and had to come down anyway . . . We have two palace scenes, a summer house, a Russian villa, bedrooms, an outdoor party scene, autumn leaves and almost a blizzard at one point." Two Canadian singers, both graduates of young artists programs, had the thrill of being onstage with superstar Welsh baritone Jason Howard: Frédérique Vézina, a graduate of the Canadian Opera Company's young artist program, sang Tatyana to Howard's Onegin, and Eric Olsen, the recent graduate from the Burton Lowell and Olive Kurth Young Artist Program, sang the act 2 comprimario role of Monsieur Triquet.

In February 2006, POV presented Benjamin Britten's mid-twentieth-century chamber opera, *The Rape of Lucretia*. The

▲ Lambroula Maria Pappas, the talented soprano from Burnaby, BC, was cast as the Vixen in Pacific Opera Victoria's 2005 production of *The Cunning Little Vixen*. Leslie Frankish designed the delightful costumes as well as the sets for the production.
TIM MATHESON PHOTOGRAPH

two-act work, not frequently produced, was performed without intermission by eight solo singers, two of whom act as the chorus, and an orchestra of thirteen players, as Britten scored it. Four young Canadian singers made their POV debuts in the all-Canadian cast: baritone Phillip Addis as Tarquinius, mezzo-soprano Louise Guyot as Lucretia, mezzo-soprano Mia Lennox-Williams as Bianca and soprano Sookhyung Park as Lucia. Diana Leblanc returned to direct the production. All worked together to produce a stellar result, as confirmed by J.H. Stape in *reviewVancouver*, February 2006: "The cast . . . gives a no-holds-barred performance of rare intensity: they are committed, have carefully thought out their roles, and are brilliantly directed by Diana LeBlanc . . . This performance has the usual panache one associates with Pacific Opera Victoria: so-called risky repertoire that wholly succeeds . . . The sets, in their austerity, and the clear, no-nonsense staging put maximum emphasis . . . on the interaction of the singers and on the sound Timothy

Vernon caressed out of the pit where the twelve [thirteen] players Britten scored this work for played their hearts out."

The brilliance of that production was repeated in February 2007, when POV staged the Canadian premiere of Richard Strauss's *Daphne*. The production is of special interest for several reasons, one of which is personal: it was the first time that this writer attended a POV production and experienced the difference between hearing opera in a small theatre as opposed to a large venue like the Queen Elizabeth. Readers are reminded that POV made a permanent move to the Royal in 2001–02, a decision that was not wholeheartedly endorsed at the time by Timothy Vernon. However, in the years that followed, he came to appreciate his new artistic home, as he explained:

> Our audience grew so well that . . . we had to move to a bigger house to accommodate them, . . . from my point of view with some reluctance, because it made that very, very intimate experience

▲ The Pacific Opera Victoria Chorus performs the Dance of the Peasants in this act 1 scene from *Eugene Onegin*, staged by POV in 2005. TIM MATHESON PHOTOGRAPH

[in the McPherson] a little bit bigger. [The Royal] is very like a European house; . . . the scale of the house relative to the stage and the proscenium is much more European . . . That conditions the kind of production we do . . . and we have to make sure that [everything] looks good . . . In a smaller house . . . we are able to offer younger singers more mature roles than they might feel ready for in a great big house where they really have to project their voices . . . A recent example would be Sookhyung Park singing Daphne. In my view she is almost perfect for the role. She looks beautiful, she has a wonderful, natural acting instinct and this beautiful, pure creamy lyric soprano . . . I don't know whether she would succeed in a big house with a big orchestra to the same degree.

The final comment about *Daphne* in the Royal concerns the score, which Vernon himself had to reduce for his orchestra of fewer than half of the ninety players that Strauss calls for, there being no commercial reduction available. Maestro Vernon explained: "We are . . . limited by virtue of the pit. Normally in opera you want flexibility. You want to be able to produce opera that requires anywhere from thirty, thirty-five, forty players up to one hundred players. Our absolute limit is forty . . . so there's a big chunk of the repertoire—I mentioned *Aïda*—that is really hard for us to do with any authority . . . When we get into the nineteenth

century, we find ourselves reducing the . . . string section, which is what a middle European house would do, so from that point on, most of what we produce is reduced." However, the reduction for *Daphne* was a lot more difficult than just reducing the strings; the wind section had to be substantially cut, and at least three uncommon instruments that Strauss's score called for eliminated entirely. Vernon took it on because he loves the piece and wanted very much to put it on the POV stage, and the result was brilliant. On the evening this writer was in the audience, the playing was so beautiful, and the listeners were so embraced by the music in the intimacy of the Royal, the size of the orchestra was irrelevant.

The closing opera of the 2006–07 season was *Don Giovanni*, which had the unique distinction of selling 103 percent of the seats in the Royal for every performance—a high in any opera company's experience. The 2007–08 and 2008–09 seasons included two works, *Regina* (Blitzstein) and *Thaïs* (Massenet) respectively, that are not often performed, and both proved to be thrilling choices. Sally Dibblee made an exciting debut as Cio-Cio-San in the familiar *Madama Butterfly* in February 2008.

▲ The rape scene from Pacific Opera Victoria's presentation of the *Rape of Lucretia* in 2006. Lucretia is sung by Louise Guyot, and the villainous Tarquinius is Phillip Addis. DAVID COOPER PHOTOGRAPH

In summing up, it is tempting to say that the remarkable success of POV is mainly owing to the stable artistic leadership, musical talents, vision and personality of Timothy Vernon. However, he is quick to point out that he does not operate in artistic isolation:

> We're so lucky here in Victoria. We have a group of artists that are second to none. Directors come as guests, and they're coming to a place they barely know, and they meet the people that handle us in the theatre, the people that build the props and the sets and design the work, and they're just knocked out, because [these people] are real artists and they take their work very seriously. They're very devoted to the company and its productions, and you can feel that when you're in the house. There is nothing here that has not been done [without] great thought and care towards getting the most out of every element. I have huge regard for those people.

When added to the equation are a well-focussed board and staff, a dedicated group of volunteers and the Victoria Symphony Orchestra musicians, all of whom are working toward the same goal, POV must be regarded as the sum of its interdependent parts.

VANCOUVER OPERA

Although there were many splendid productions mounted on the VO stage and covered in the media between 1996–97 and the two subsequent seasons, the attention-grabbing headlines had more to do with what was happening offstage. It all started during the early days of 1997, and three issues were at the forefront of the media frenzy.

First, representatives of the Vancouver Symphony and Vancouver Opera Boards announced in January 1997 that a merger of the two organizations was planned, confirming what had been in the works on an informal basis for some time. Cost-sharing one of the biggest expenses—the orchestras—was clearly the main impetus

▲ The celebration of Dionysian fertility rites is taking place in this scene from Pacific Opera Victoria's staging of *Daphne* in 2007. The god Apollo, disguised as a herdsman, offers Daphne a love elixir that she refuses.
TIM MATHESON PHOTOGRAPH

of the proposal for both the VSO and VO. Kenneth Mahon, a member of the VO Board of Directors from 1991–94 and president for his last year on the board, recalled this about the genesis of the proposal: "Those merger discussions began at least back in '93–'94, and I was involved initially . . . Generally, it was Rob Hallam, myself, [Nezhat Khosrowshahi, vice-chairman of the Vancouver Symphony Board] . . . I'm pretty sure that Yulanda [Yulanda Faris, VO Board member and president, 1996–97] was involved to a degree, but any of the meetings I went to, David Agler did not attend . . . I think it appeared to most people that were involved in those discussions that it was a great idea, but it wasn't likely to happen for a whole lot of reasons."[7] Nevertheless, both organizations took the "nothing ventured, nothing gained" approach and made the announcement, which distressed members of the VO Orchestra, who had the most to lose—one-third of their yearly playing income—and resulted in a groundswell of public support for the orchestra's position.

VSO players were unionized, but VO musicians had played for the company for nearly twenty years without a union contract. Sharman King provided the view from the VO Orchestra pit: "It was divisive in the short term, because first of all we had to fight for our jobs, and that was distasteful because we were fighting against another group of musicians. I'd say that we took as a position then that we would do nothing to harm either organization. Contentious situations, especially for people who are not used to dealing with them, as musicians aren't, especially of that importance to their future livelihood, are difficult. There were a lot of emotions, but the end result was wholly positive." VO Orchestra players organized a mail campaign asking for the public's support, and before the opening night performance of *Susannah* (Carlisle Floyd), which was the first production after the announcement, they took to the street in their white ties and tails to hand out leaflets and chocolates to people as they streamed into the theatre. When

▲ Kurt Lehmann as Pinkerton, Sally Dibblee as Cio-Cio-San (Butterfly) and Bruce Kelly as Sharpless meet in the house Pinkerton has leased for him and Butterfly after their "marriage" in act 1 of the production of *Madama Butterfly* staged by Pacific Opera Victoria in 2008.
EMILY COOPER PHOTOGRAPH

BravO!

David Agler took his place on the podium, the audience supported the orchestra with a standing ovation, while the string section waved their bows in thanks. Overwhelming public opposition to the proposed merger put an end to it: one month after the original announcement, the VSO and VO abandoned the plan. King explained why the end result was positive for the orchestra: "One of the benefits of the conflict between the symphony and the opera orchestra was that we got a collective agreement. David [Agler] and Rob [Hallam] negotiated the first agreement with Local 145 of the American Federation of Musicians. The AFM is a very large entertainment union. It defines our working situations and our fees. Our rate for playing a show is extremely good now. We have an incredible pension . . . and the payout of the pension is fabulous. Also, as a result of the collective agreement, the orchestra was involved in the selection process for a music director."

Although there were other factors at play, a casualty of the merger proposal was the working relationship of Agler and Hallam, and both departed from VO when their contracts expired in mid-1999. More about that to follow.

The next shocker to make headlines was the million-dollar deficit racked up during the 1996–97 season. On the face of it, it seemed to come out of nowhere, and although the press implied that Hallam was to blame, he would have had to be clairvoyant to foresee the outcome three years before, when the board of directors approved the budget. Kenneth Mahon described the process:

The budgeting for 1996–97 started as early as '92, and the budget numbers that were put together by staff showed an increase in expenses of almost a million dollars, from about $6.4 million to $7.4 million, and an equivalent increase in revenue . . . So, based on that budgeting . . . the board at that time approved going to five full productions in '95–'96, and we spent the money, because all those costs are virtually fixed costs for . . . the production . . . It doesn't matter whether two people show up or 22,000 people show up, it still costs the same to put the opera on, and what happened was that the gate receipts were not there—the estimate of what a fifth opera would bring in . . . additional ticket revenue. At the same time, if you recall, our economy in '96–'97 was not great . . . and so, as a result, the projections for sponsorship revenues, revenues from social events, the whole revenue side came up short by about a million dollars . . . The treasurer, in September or October 1996, reported that we were $200,000 off the budget. By December he was reporting that we were $500,000 or $600,000 off the budget. By March or April [1997] he was reporting that we were $700,000 or $800,000 short, and for the board at the time, and even for the staff, there wasn't a whole lot they could do about it . . . It

was just a bad combination of events, so the opera learned a tough lesson . . . Had we not had the VO Foundation, the opera company would have been in serious trouble.[8]

Mahon, who was by then past-president of the board and chairman of the VO Foundation, praised the board that had to deal with the deficit: "To their credit, the board at the time rolled their sleeves up and went back to work on the '97–'98 season and were able to produce a surplus. Now that's a pretty amazing turnaround from a very, very significant loss." There was still, however, the deficit to be addressed, and with assistance from two separate sources, a grant of $482,648 from the Vancouver Arts Stabilization Team (VAST), and a matching amount from the Vancouver Opera Foundation, to be spread out over three years, elimination of the deficit was virtually guaranteed by the end of 1998.[9]

That left only one issue to receive a disproportionate amount of ink: the

increasing internal dissatisfaction with Rob Hallam, evidenced by resignations from both board and staff, the acrimonious relationship between Hallam and David Agler, an increasing public awareness of the sagging morale within the company and the loss of support of several of VO's most loyal and generous benefactors. Understandably, nobody wants to revisit this discordant period by revealing what inside information he or she may have been privy to. It is best left in the past, and the wise words of Kenneth Mahon and Sharman King put the decision of the board to search for a new general director to replace Hallam in proper perspective. Mahon said, "The change that was made at the end of the '98–'99 season, not renewing the Hallam contract and doing the search for a new general director, is the kind of thing that happens in a lot of organizations. There's a feeling that there's a slightly different direction that the organization should be taking, not for one specific reason, but probably for a whole number of reasons . . . But those things

▲ David Pittsinger as the evangelical Rev. Olin Blitch leads his congregation at a service attended by Susannah Polk, played by Sally Dibblee, who is expected by Blitch and the members of his flock to seek absolution from them for her so-called sins. The Vancouver Opera 1997 production of *Susannah* was the Canadian premiere of the work. DAVID COOPER PHOTOGRAPH

happen in both artistic organizations and in business organizations, and so as long as the organization is progressing, and as long as the individual who was replaced ends up landing on his or her feet with a rewarding job or position to go to, then the way I look at it is, everybody's a winner."[10] King said, "It was a really tough time for the organization. They used it, as anyone should use a crisis, as a stepping stone to get up higher. As a result of that, they got this unparalleled general director [James Wright, who succeeded Hallam] and administration that we have right now." Important to note is that during this difficult, but relatively short, period, the quality of VO productions did not suffer from what was essentially an administrative problem. Hallam and Agler did their jobs as the professionals they were, and the shows went on as scheduled with the exception of the contemporary opera, *Savage Land*, by the Chinese composer Jin Xiang, which was cancelled as an economy measure during the 1997–98 season, as were any future plans for a fifth production. A concert of selections from opera, billed as X-treme Opera, was presented in place of *Savage Land*. The last opera to be staged before both Hallam and Agler left was the double bill, *Bluebeard's Castle* (Béla Bartók) and *Erwartung* (*Expectation*, Arnold Schoenberg), and a superb parting gift it proved to be. The transition in 1999 was smooth and without sensational publicity, and very quickly the offstage situation improved markedly.

James Wright came to VO from Charlotte, North Carolina, where he had been general director of the opera company for ten years. Before that he had been with Anchorage Opera in Alaska, and he had the same rebuilding job to do when he started with both those companies as he was facing with VO. He described in an interview how well briefed he was:

> Before I moved, I was very aware of the job in front of me—the rebuilding of the board *with* the board, regaining donor trust and business community trust and founders' trust to repair things and get the company back on the right track, and I felt that it was a really good fit for me . . . I knew what needed to be done and felt that I could bring a fresh perspective, and part of that perspective was having a clean slate at the top of the company, regardless of other people and who had been here before and whether they should stay or not . . . I felt, and still feel that the best thing to do was what I did— [be a] strong general director, [do a] music director search, and go from there.

Wright began work in August 1999, and one of the first things he had to do was fill in the gaps for the fortieth anniversary concert planned to occur early in 2000. The season was planned, but the concert needed immediate attention, as Wright described: "There were singers on hold, but there was no conductor, no programming . . . [and] no tenor for that concert. First thing I had to do was get a conductor and get a tenor." American tenor John Fowler was available, and so was Pacific Opera Victoria's Tim Vernon, and programming was arranged once those people were secured. Wright added his own twist to the event, which took place on April 4, 2000: "In my first two months here I felt that the company needed to pay a bit more attention publicly to Irving [Guttman], and so I decided to honour him at the fortieth anniversary, which had not been in the plans to my knowledge, and to also announce at the concert that we were naming him artistic director emeritus . . . So we announced that from the stage, and the singers all gathered around him and serenaded him . . . and I was pleased that I could bring a little extra something to it."

Wright also put his stamp on the organization at early staff meetings. Doug Tuck, who joined VO in November 1997 as communications manager, was present, and in an interview described how Wright did that:

> At the first staff meeting he produced a large cardboard box full of correspondence and files, . . . all the juicy correspondence between Rob Hallam and David Agler and letters to the editor, and whatever else there was [from] donors and board members—I don't even know what was in there—and he invited staff to look at it if they wished, but that in one week it would be destroyed, and it was. And no one looked at it. No one

wanted to look at it . . . and I thought that was a very good way to deal with it . . . The third thing he did, which I think was very wise, was that he did not countenance any continuation of the culture of self-pity. People tend to get stuck in ways of thinking and interacting when times are tough. There are perceived camps, and he didn't want that, and he wouldn't put up with it, so he just shut people down a couple of times when they started to go into that territory—he was focussed entirely on the future, and that's what he was here to do, and that's what he's done.[11]

With administrative issues firmly in control, and a staff that knew what was expected of it, Wright was able to turn his attention to the real business of the company: putting on good opera. He had a season to organize in short order, and recounted how he chose the first production:

> I talked to a lot of people, [used] my own good judgment and experience— expediency, for one thing . . . I had to get staff scheduled and I had to program something that I could get good singers for on short notice. I thought I needed to turn away a bit from the top ten repertoire . . . yet sell enough tickets to make sense. I think I wanted to say something about my tenure, say something about the kind of repertoire and singers that we'd be seeing, which

Brav O!

led me to think about . . . *Lucia* [*di Lammermoor*], and when I found out I could get [American soprano] Elizabeth Futral, who was just going to the top . . . that became a real easy starter . . . She'd never been here, I knew the audience would go crazy . . . That paid off.

His next choice, Stravinsky's 1951 work, *The Rake's Progress*, brought the board down on his head for committing what amounted to half the production costs of what was to be a co-production with Edmonton Opera—$50,000 or $75,000—without the board's permission. "That surprised me," said Wright. "I'd never had that kind of restraint put on me before as long as things worked within

the budget. We had a bit of a discussion about that . . . and we sorted it out, but . . . it was an opportunity to say, 'Okay, what kind of authority does this person have, financially?'" Wright knew the opera was not going to fill the house, but he was disappointed that it did not attract more single ticket buyers: "It's not our subscribers who don't like this unusual stuff. They want [it]. They've seen six *Butterflys*, six *Traviatas*, and often, when they travel, they see a lot of operas, and often the same thing . . . That 6,000-plus core is solid with us. It's the fickleness of the single ticket buyers . . . that go for what [they] know . . . It's the single ticket buyers that are hard to grab." Those who did not go to the production missed a grand show. Reviewer J.H. Stape (*reviewVancouver*, November 2000) did his best to improve box-office sales: "Ken MacDonald's stylish sets are dizzyingly lush . . . Michael Cavanagh's deft, even flawless, direction gives the evening a nervous energy that relentlessly teases out complex musical and dramatic values. No less imaginative are the costumes, all in primary colours and mingling eighteenth-, nineteenth-, and twentieth-century dress modes . . . The strong cast assembled for this visually stunning production provides first-rate ensemble work . . . Vancouver Opera's second production of the season shows the company on top form. This winner deserves to rake in the crowds." Both the Edmonton Opera and VO productions featured the same Canadian singers in

▲ Csaba Airizer is Bluebeard and Kristine Jepson is his fourth wife, Judith, the Bride of the Night, in Vancouver Opera's presentation of *Bluebeard's Castle*, 1999.
TIM MATHESON PHOTOGRAPH

the lead roles: tenor Benjamin Butterfield as Tom Rakewell and lyric-coloratura soprano Jackalyn Short as Anne Trulove. Andreas Mitisek, a native of Austria, now the artistic director of Long Beach Opera, was the distinguished guest conductor.

Wright's choice for the third production of the season was Wagner's *The Flying Dutchman*, staged once before in 1968. He was fortunate to find two internationally prominent American singers available to sing the leads, baritone Tom Fox and soprano Mary Jane Johnson, as well as a supporting cast of considerable eminence — Canadian tenor John MacMaster as Erik, Canadian mezzo-soprano Lucie Mayer as Mary, American bass Stefan Szkafarowsky as Daland and Philip Webb as the Steersman. Twenty voices from Chor Leoni, the nationally renowned all-male choir based in Vancouver, augmented the VO Chorus in that very important element of the work. Added to the Canada-US mix were American Maestro John Keenan, who distinguished himself in 1990 as the youngest conductor ever to debut at the Metropolitan, and was being considered for the position of VO music director; and Canadian director Roman Hurko, who had directed VO's production of *Don Giovanni* the previous season. Hurko gave audiences a traditional rendition of *Dutchman*, and the set, borrowed from New Orleans Opera, well suited his approach. The production received rave reviews and did well at the box office, which must have given Wright a good deal of satisfaction,

but he gave credit to one of the senior VO staff, Randy Smith, who provided valuable continuity during the transition from Hallam to Wright: "Randy was very helpful, because he'd been involved with some of the cast before — I hadn't — and at the same time we were undertaking a search for the music director — trying to put conductor candidates into the appropriate pieces."

Wright's first season closed with Mozart's *The Magic Flute*, for which Wright once again chose a cast comprising a mix of well-known Canadian and American singers. In addition, the much-respected and loved Canadian conductor Mario Bernardi was available to lead the VO Orchestra. All performances of *The Magic*

▲ Mary Jane Johnson as The Woman in *Erwartung*, staged with *Bluebeard's Castle* by Vancouver Opera in 1999, makes the horrifying discovery of her lover's dead body on a forest path. TIM MATHESON PHOTOGRAPH

BravO!

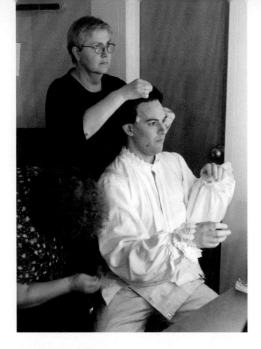

Flute were sold out, the season attendance average was 90 percent capacity, and when the financial reckoning was done, the season produced a surplus of $180,000, qualifying the company for the first of the grants from the VO Foundation and VAST over the next three years, provided the bottom line stayed black. The board of directors, the staff and Wright himself were committed to seeing that it did so.

Reassured also were those who feared the Americanization of VO under Wright's management. Wright was aware that there was initial uneasiness about his casting intentions, as he acknowledged:

> When I first came I know that there was concern that I'd be hiring all my American buddies . . . but I never had any intention of that . . . because I knew I didn't need to [and] I felt that an opera company . . . needed to be as much as it could be about where it is . . . And I know I had to overcome that initial skepticism from Canada Council, from local people, from singers, of course . . .

Early on I didn't know the Canadian singers as well, and when I did, I didn't know they were Canadian necessarily, and it's a very important part of our mandate, and our funders' mandate, especially Canada Council, that we hire a lot [of Canadians]. Early on Doug [Tuck] and others in the organization were very helpful. Everybody knows Richard Margison, but there's a thick layer of people underneath that I needed to get acquainted with."

Wright came up to speed very quickly, and came to appreciate the talent pool he has to choose from: "There's something in the water. It's amazing, the number of incredible Canadian singers . . . There have been great teachers for a generation or two . . . It must go back to training and opportunity . . . Canada Council has always been sure that [Canadian] companies supported the training and hired young singers."

The 2001–02 season opened with Jonathan Darlington on the podium as

▲ Benjamin Butterfield is fitted for his wig backstage in preparation for his role as Tom Rakewell in *The Rake's Progress*, Vancouver Opera, 2000. PAUL FREMES PHOTO COURTESY VANCOUVER OPERA

▲ Victoria Livengood is in makeup having a beard applied for her role as Baba the Turk in *The Rake's Progress*, Vancouver Opera, 2000. PAUL FREMES PHOTO COURTESY VANCOUVER OPERA

guest conductor for *The Marriage of Figaro*. Darlington, who is British, made his debut as a conductor in Paris in 1984, and was another of the candidates being considered by VO's search committee to fill the position of music director, vacant since the 1999 departure of David Agler. Wright described the process:

> I heard loudly and clearly from the orchestra that they felt underutilized in the selection of David Agler . . . We presented the search committee with a small group of finalists, . . . four or five to bring in and conduct. We also developed an evaluation tool for the chorus and orchestra to use—fifteen or twenty questions—technical things, leadership qualities, the final question: "Would you support this person as the music director? Yes or no." So we tabulated those . . . When we got to Jonathan it was absolutely unanimous—this is the guy we want . . . The whole process took a year before we announced it . . . I can't emphasize enough what a hands-down choice he was for everyone.

Darlington's appointment was announced backstage following the opening performance of *Of Mice and Men* (Floyd) on March 23, 2002. Trombonist Sharman King described the orchestra's part in the process and its reaction to the announcement: "As a result of the collective agreement, the orchestra was involved in the selection process . . .

Darlington came—it was a Mozart opera [with no trombones called for], so I wasn't there, but people said, 'This is the guy,' and they were right . . . I'm at the end of my career, and what a splendid note to go out on. [Darlington] is a superlative musician. He's the best orchestral trainer I've ever seen. All orchestras need training . . . He'll make us aware of that inner pulse in music . . . When we did the first thing [the orchestra's twenty-fifth anniversary concert on February 27, 2003], I thought, 'Wow, this is too good to last,' and he's still here." The orchestra broke into cheers when the announcement was made, and since then Wright has been hearing from all levels of musical expertise that the orchestra's improvement under Darlington is very noticeable. Darlington began his career as a vocal coach at Radio France, which explains why he is so attuned to the needs of singers. Bette Cosar had this to say about conductors and Darlington's rapport with the VO Chorus:

> If the chorus at times sounds ragged, it's because the conductor is too busy doing something else and doesn't give us our cut-offs . . . If something goes wrong, it's his job to rescue the production—it's a big, big responsibility. If something goes wrong, the eyes go "Phweet!" straight to the conductor in the pit . . . Before Jonathan Darlington came, we needed a musical director. We were putting our feelers out. A lot of guest conductors were interested in the job, so we got

BravO!

rehearsal time, and obtained Darlington to conduct two of the four performed since he began: *Pelléas et Mélisande* (Claude Debussy) on August 15, 2003, and *The Abduction from the Seraglio* on March 5, 2004.[12] In Darlington as music director, Wright has another colleague with whom he can confer about repertoire and cast, in addition to the in-house people he confers with. "Confer" is the important word, because the final responsibility in those matters is Wright's, as he explained:

> Those decisions, for good or ill, rest with me . . . Many opera companies, and probably the majority in North America, have a single head who is responsible for both administrative and artistic decisions. I think it's a system that works really well . . . because those decisions are made up through one person and presented to the board as a budget package, and it's "yes" or "no" . . . When I say it's my decision, I certainly don't want to leave the impression that it's not done without a lot of advice and help and consultation and negotiation. What it really means is that ultimately there's only one place to fix blame, and that's the way it should be.

evaluation sheets. Some we didn't like, but we just loved Jonathan. He is a singers' conductor. He gives cues, cut-offs . . . and [has] the power over the orchestra to keep them down so as not to drown out the singers. That's another mark of how we judge the conductors: by what they give us.

Darlington's contract specified that he would conduct only two of the four productions staged each year because most of his work is in Europe and Australia, he lives in Paris and he has a young family. To secure more time for him with the VO Orchestra, the company began to stage concert operas, which require less

Wright has likely not been called to account by his board since that very early incident, which was probably more attributable to residual fiscal anxiety on the board's part than to Wright's actions. The standard of VO productions has

▲ Marie Anne Kowan sings the trouser role of Cherubino, and Taras Kulish is cast as Figaro in the 2001 staging of *The Marriage of Figaro* by Vancouver Opera.
TIM MATHESON PHOTOGRAPH

been steadily rising to the point where it compares favourably with, and often exceeds, that of any company of the same size in North America, even that of larger, longer-established companies—even at times the Metropolitan. Doug Tuck, well aware, by virtue of his position in the company, that season ticket holders comprise a relatively static core and single ticket buyers fluctuate depending on the work being presented, put it this way: "Maybe we haven't done such a great job in bringing [other] people to the belief that they have an amazing cultural asset here in Vancouver Opera—that the quality of the productions are equal to or better than almost any regional opera company in North America, and even sometimes at the Met . . . Normally, people who travel and see other opera tell us repeatedly . . . that what they saw was no better than what we do here."

A glance at VO's productions listed in Appendix A between the 2002–03 and 2008–09 seasons will reveal what a rich cultural menu opera lovers have been offered. All were of the very best quality, musically and theatrically, that the company was capable of. Some were not as popular as others, but, as Jim Wright pointed out, "'failed' [at the box office] has very little to do with the quality of the work." Wright talked about the "failures":

> *Girl of the Golden West* [2003] [did] not [do] well, which is personally very disturbing to me, because I love the work

. . . It's a flawed work if you listen to all the critics and the musicologists . . . To me the melodies are haunting, the story is fascinating . . . but it's not a big seller anywhere. *Ariadne auf Naxos* last spring [2007] was very disappointing. We missed our goal by tens of thousands of dollars . . . I thought [it] was a beautiful production . . . It's a bit tough musically for some people, but I thought . . . the orchestra played so beautifully, Tracy Dahl, John MacMaster . . . sang so wonderfully. Another example: *Dialogues of the Carmelites* [2005] did not sell very well, but there are people—we know because they tell us—who increase their gifts because of works like that, and

▲ Jackalyn Short as Curly's wife encourages Ross Neil, who plays the simple-minded Lennie, to stroke her hair, which leads to tragedy in the barn in act 3, scene 1 from *Of Mice and Men*, a 2002 Vancouver Opera presentation. TIM MATHESON PHOTOGRAPH

they appreciate that they can see [them] in Vancouver instead of having to go to New York.

If the reader will tolerate a personal comment on each of the three "failures" discussed above, this writer was particularly looking forward to all of them for these reasons: *The Girl of the Golden West* had never before been staged by VO, and had the additional appeal of Mary Jane Johnson, as fine an actress as she is a singer, in the lead role of Minnie; Richard Strauss is a favourite composer, and *Ariadne auf Naxos* had been staged only once before, in 1989; *Dialogues of the Carmelites* was an opportunity to hear Judith Forst in the role of Madame de Croissy, the Prioress, and to be present when Measha Brueggergosman, the superb young Canadian soprano, made her VO debut as Madame Lidoine, with Jonathan Darlington on the podium. All were productions worthy of being termed successes, not failures.

Being forced to single out productions during this especially outstanding period is akin to taking a child to FAO Schwartz, the fabulous toy emporium in New York City, and allowing him to choose only one toy from the embarrassment of riches before his eyes; he wants them all. Nevertheless, the following shows stand out in personal memory: *Elektra* (2002–03); *The Threepenny Opera* (2003–04); *Der Rosenkavalier* (2004–05); and *Macbeth*, *The Magic Flute* and *Tosca* (2006–07). Although

they were not always huge successes at the box office, each had something special to make it stand out, and each usually received favourable reviews in the media.

Elektra was the first of the Richard Strauss operas to be featured in VO's Strauss cycle, planned to present one of the composer's major operas every two years over a ten-year period. Lotfi Mansouri, formerly general director of San Francisco Opera, and formerly the long-time general director of the Canadian Opera Company, accepted James Wright's invitation to direct the show, as he had accepted others since he left San Francisco: "I'm going to retire when I'm dead," said the much-respected director in an article about *Elektra* (Dan Rowe, *Vancouver Sun*, March 20, 2003). "I think retirement is for people who work in banks or insurance, stuff like that. In the arts, when it's in your blood, once in a while you need that infusion, you feel rejuvenated." Mansouri was well pleased with the lead singers, both beloved by VO audiences, Mary Jane Johnson in the title role and Judith Forst as Klytemnestra, and the rest of the cast, all of whom earned kudos for Mansouri and themselves. Mario Bernardi led the orchestra, augmented by more than half its usual complement to eighty-seven players who dealt expertly with the difficult score. To have Mansouri and Bernardi together applying their formidable talents to a Strauss opera was a guarantee of excellence not to be missed. Apparently others thought so too; the production was recorded by

▲ Susan Neves is Aida, shown here with Mark Rucker
as Amonasro, her royal father, and members of the
ensemble in a 2002 Vancouver Opera production.
TIM MATHESON PHOTOGRAPH

BravO!

CBC Radio for airing on "Saturday Afternoon at the Opera" at a later date.

The Threepenny Opera (Kurt Weill and Bertolt Brecht) is noteworthy because it was a distinct departure into the realm of music theatre, more suited to a cabaret venue than a cavernous opera house like the Queen Elizabeth Theatre. The first ten rows of seats were removed to extend the stage into the audience and to accommodate the fourteen-piece band, on the stage throughout. Morris Panych, well-known theatrical director, actor and playwright, was an appropriate choice to direct the piece. Although it is a risky, raunchy, edgy work for an opera company to take on, few can resist the tremendous appeal of Weill and Brecht's collaboration, which is undoubtedly what VO was banking on. The company knew that many in the audience had enjoyed singing along to the jazz-pop rendition of "Mack the Knife" made famous by singer Bobby Darin, or the version by the great American jazz musician, Louis Armstrong, and when the number came up in the show, there were more than a few who had to restrain themselves from joining in.[13] The show did very well at the box office: many theatregoers who were familiar with

Morris Panych's work bought tickets, as did those who were curious to see how VO would stage the piece. A few were indignant about the choice, but most sat back, relaxed and enjoyed a very unusual, well-done, quasi-opera night in the theatre.

The second selection for the Strauss cycle was *Der Rosenkavalier*, arguably the most stunning visual production mounted by VO in the 2002–03 to 2008–09 period. The curtain rose on act 1, a scene in the Marschallin's bedroom, where the Marschallin and her teenaged lover, Octavian (Quinquin), highlighted by clever lighting, were lying on her bed amid the tangled sheets in a position that left no doubt that passionate lovemaking had just taken place. It was obvious from the Canadian Opera Company's gorgeous set that this was going to be a traditional rendition of the piece, which was what gave the opening scene such startling verismo; few productions go as far as director David Gately and the principals did to engage the audience immediately. And engaged they were, from start to finish, enchanted by the music, the singing, the acting, the sets and costumes and the ensemble work. It was a deeply satisfying production, but one that nearly went off the rails before it opened. One of the opera world's foremost Strauss sopranos, American Deborah Voigt, was engaged for her debut role as the Marschallin, but during rehearsals it was obvious, particularly to Voigt herself, that she had not adequately prepared the role beforehand. Ten days before opening night, Voigt's agent informed VO in a prepared statement that she was withdrawing from the production. It was repeated in a VO press release, October 7, 2004: "Ms. Voigt was stretched too thin and exhausted. Like many people in Florida, her personal life was unsettled by the recent hurricanes and the subsequent interruption to her schedule left her unable to complete her personal preparations [for the role]." VO does not have understudies available, and Wright and Darlington, who was to conduct the show, went into high gear to find a replacement. Within twenty-four hours they had the good fortune to obtain Carol Wilson, another outstanding American Strauss soprano, who, at the time, was doing the role at Theatre Aachen in Germany, alternating performances with another singer. She and Wright were able to negotiate her release from her one remaining stint, and she was flown to Vancouver to finish what Voigt had begun. Wright recounted the incident: "That's when I earn my money . . . You use your experience, your network, the people you trust . . . You don't panic, you just remind yourself that while you don't know right now, . . . there will be somebody out there, and it will work . . . And everybody wants to help you . . . your colleagues . . . When we had to replace Voigt, Speight Jenkins [general director of Seattle Opera] called me four or five times . . . Nothing's a bad idea until you check it out [and] money doesn't matter—if you're flying in

▲ In this scene from Vancouver Opera's 2003 production of *Elektra*, Judith Forst as the demon-ridden Klytemnestra demonstrates her formidable dramatic talent. Mary Jane Johnson is an equally powerful Elektra.
TIM MATHESON PHOTOGRAPH

▲ *The Threepenny Opera*, staged by Vancouver Opera in 2004, was a departure from the usual repertoire of the company. In this scene, John Mann as Macheath (Mack the Knife) and Patricia O'Callaghan as Polly Peachum demonstrate a provocative sexuality.
TIM MATHESON PHOTOGRAPH

BravO!

somebody from Germany, you're flying in somebody from Germany."[14] In the press release, Wright's announcement of the bad and the good news was very generous: "We are, of course, extremely disappointed. Ms. Voigt is a wonderful artist, and could have made a great contribution to this production . . . However, we are delighted to welcome Carol Wilson to join [the ensemble] in bringing this magnificent work to life." Things went smoothly from then on to opening night, except in the costume department, where workers were feverishly taking apart Voigt's costumes, recutting them and reassembling them to fit Wilson—Voigt's very large frame precluding simple alteration as an option. Although Wilson could not fill Voigt's costumes, she could and did fill her metaphorical shoes. Wilson has a beautiful voice and is a fine actress, which was reflected in ticket sales. Doug Tuck confirmed: "*Rosenkavalier* did very well. I'm looking at dollars now, and single ticket sales. [It] was an opera that a lot of people were waiting to see . . . and, of course, there was the prospect of hearing Deborah Voigt for the first time in the role. That did not happen, but I don't think there was a single person who decided not to come as a result—even people who were flying in from out of town—and they were rewarded. Carol Wilson was wonderful. Tracy Dahl [in the role of Sophie] was great . . . It was gorgeous."

After hearing Darlington conduct *Macbeth* in Bordeaux in 2001, Wright

liked it so much, he thought of doing it in Vancouver in the future. When Darlington became music director, the two talked about making it happen and decided to schedule it as the first production of the 2006–07 season, when Darlington and the cast that Wright wanted would be available. It was to be a triple premiere: it was the first time it had ever been staged by VO, and it was both English soprano Jane Eaglen's VO debut and her role debut as Lady Macbeth.[15] American bass-baritone Greer Grimsley as Macbeth, Canadian tenor Luc Robert as Malcolm, Turkish bass Burak Bilgili as Banquo and American tenor John Bellemer as Macduff comprised the rest of the international cast. Grimsley's superb acting and singing were several notches above the fine performances of the others, but it was the orchestra, led by Darlington, and the chorus, led by chorus director and assistant conductor Leslie Dala who were singled out for providing the high-quality musical elements that the rest of the show occasionally lacked. Reviewer J.H. Stape (*reviewVancouver*, November 2006) had this to say: "If the production doesn't quite live up to the hype as 'edge of your seat opera' . . . all the other elements make for a night in the theatre that won't soon be forgotten. No little role in creating this magic is owed to Jonathan Darlington's vivid and detailed reading of the score, the fine orchestral playing, and the superb achievement of the chorus, which is put to hard work during this opera and comes off

gloriously . . . Stars and big names draw in the public, but the basis of consistently fine opera remains a visionary chief at the helm and a reliable core of artists who play and perform in opera after opera." One of the "other elements" was the set, a minimalist composition of great faux-stone columns and slabs, meant to be Macbeth's castle, behind which designer Jerome Sirlin, using computer technology and powerful projectors, created various backdrops that deepened the intensity of the onstage emotions or otherwise advanced the plot. Used increasingly in modern opera productions, it is a theatrical technique about which more will be said in the following chapter.[16] Despite inclement weather and the reticence of some to experience what they anticipated would be a demanding musical evening, attendance exceeded the company's expectations, indicating that a degree of trust was building between the company and its audiences.

J.H. Stape uses the popular word "hype" in the review mentioned above, and the same choice can be used to describe the publicity leading up to *The Magic Flute*. The concerted effort to publicize the process of planning and executing a production was like that of no other production in VO's history. James Wright and Randy Smith, then VO's director of artistic planning, both deeply believed that an opera company must reflect its location. In 2004, they saw in *The Magic Flute* a way to demonstrate this belief by bringing the deep spirituality of the historical beliefs and myths of the First Nations people to the innate spiritual elements of the opera. Wright went first to the First Peoples' Heritage, Language and Culture Council in Victoria and gained its commitment to support and guide the project to completion. The Council's help was invaluable: "Through the work of the advisory council, VO determined that it would be important to engage creative teams of theatre professionals and First Nations artists and educators to develop each element of the project . . . Invitations were made to the Aboriginal arts community, seeking participation in

▲ John Cheek as the lascivious Baron Ochs, is handed a letter by the duplicitous Annina, played by Nancy Hermiston, inviting him to an assignation with Mariendel, who has aroused his lust. The comic scene is from act 2 of *Der Rosenkavalier*, presented in 2004 on the Vancouver Opera stage. TIM MATHESON PHOTOGRAPH

Bravo!

costume and scenery design, dance and choreography, and performance."[17] The next three years occupied the creative energies of VO staff and the First Nations people involved in the project in the most intense period of cross-cultural artistic collaboration ever attempted in North America. It was not only the most ambitious venture ever undertaken by VO, but also the most costly: the budget was $1.4 million, 40 percent higher than any previous undertaking.[18] It was also a very rewarding experience for VO staff, as Doug Tuck, who was responsible for much of the "hype," confirmed: "We embarked on a three-year process with First Nations people not knowing where it would lead and what would be the result, and in that

respect it was very successful . . . It was very important as far as internal artistic growth of the company and in opening our minds to other ways of looking at classic works, and in working with people whom we don't normally work with—having to adjust to their ways of thinking, to their desires, to their ways of doing things, to their world view. That was hugely valuable to us."[19] Director Robert McQueen and conductor Derrick Inouye recounted what being a part of the production meant to each. McQueen: "What a wondrous gift it has been to be part of this team of extraordinary British Columbian artists brought together by Vancouver Opera to create a production that illuminates its own marriage between the glorious music

▲ Ute Selbig as Fiordiligi, and Kimberly Barber as Dorabella, hatch their silly scheme to deceive their respective lovers in act 2 of *Così Fan Tutti*, a Vancouver Opera 2005 presentation. TIM MATHESON PHOTOGRAPH

of Mozart and the beauty and profound spirit of the West Coast First Peoples' art, language and dance." Inouye: "It's Mozart's ability to make us feel his characters' longing for children, despair over losing a loved one, or genuine compassion and forgiveness that enables us to respond to the story whether it is set in a mythical Egypt or in the forests of Coast Salish territory. With that in mind, not a note of Mozart's music has been changed for our First Nations' reimagining of *The Magic Flute* story. With the stunning costumes and powerful artistry of the West Coast First Peoples' cultures, we feel privileged to be able to combine such rich elements to present you with a uniquely West Coast *Magic Flute*."[20]

Those who saw the show will likely never forget it. Many of us took family members—children or grandchildren who had worn out their beloved recording— who, to our great pleasure, were enchanted with hearing the familiar music played by a live orchestra and seeing the familiar characters transformed from their imaginations into visible incarnations. Most of the young people could readily relate to the First Nations elements, many having schoolmates and friends from within that culture. Did First Nations people attend? "Absolutely, absolutely," said Tuck. "For one thing, we provided a lot of tickets to that community, either discounted or free, and a lot of them took advantage of that . . . I think for many of

▲ Pamina, sung by Nathalie Paulin, and Tamino, sung by Philippe Castagner, appear before Sarastro, King of the Sun, played by Kevin Short, in act 2 of Vancouver Opera's production of *The Magic Flute*, 2007.
TIM MATHESON PHOTOGRAPH

Bravo!

them it was a very exciting validation in some way, or an accomplishment to be seen by a larger non-Aboriginal audience, to have their work on display in such splendid surroundings, and in such a splendid context."

The obvious question about the outcome of *The Magic Flute* is, was it worth the time, effort and money that went into it? Doug Tuck talked about the money: "It was risky and new, [and] certainly from the company's perspective, it was more successful than we could have imagined . . . It came very close to meeting its very ambitious revenue goals. It was a very expensive production, therefore it had a high ticket-sales goal. It came within a hair's breadth of meeting that." According to Tuck, the show averaged 92 percent capacity houses. He also said the production still exists, and he expects it will be remounted in the future. James Wright recounted what he heard from people after the show closed: "I got a few emails [telling me] 'We don't get it,' but overall, very strong response, and a

lot of response that I heard personally, even removed from the response to the performance itself, was how proud they were, how good they felt about us tackling it, about us attempting to do something that had never been done before." He also generously shared his own opinion of the artistic merits of the show: "There were things that I wish were different about it, better about it, and there were parts about it that I didn't think came through the way we wanted . . . Did we achieve everything we had hoped for, musically? No. But we accomplished what we wanted to accomplish, and I think the vast majority of the people in the house on the six nights thought that we did, too."

Tosca brought down the curtain on the 2006–07 season, and a grand finale it was. The first chords that came crashing out of the pit at triple-forte volume as the curtain rose put everyone, even those unfamiliar with the piece, on notice that the story was going to end badly. These chords become associated with Scarpia, the arch-villain, and contribute to the buildup of suspense

▲ Christine Reimer's wonderful sketch for the Queen of the Night's stunning costume for *The Magic Flute*, staged by Vancouver Opera in 2007.
CHRISTINE REIMER ILLUSTRATION

▲ Christine Reimer's drawing of the design for the costumes worn by the three ladies in *The Magic Flute*, Vancouver Opera's 2007 production.
CHRISTINE REIMER ILLUSTRATION

as the plot unfolds. Relief from the tension is afforded when Tosca murders Scarpia at the end of the second act, but it is short-lived. Tosca's beloved, Cavaradossi, is the victim of Scarpia's amoral duplicity in the third act, when he is killed by a firing squad using real bullets, not the blanks Scarpia had assured Tosca would be used. Horrified and grief-stricken, Tosca throws herself from the ramparts. Tosca usually jumps from the ramparts facing the back of the stage, but in this production she fell backward off the ramparts, facing the audience, making for a very effective finale. When the curtain came down, there were moments of stunned silence out front before the audience roared its approval and gave the entire ensemble a standing ovation.

Of course, without firm control by the director and the conductor and skilled acting and singing by the performers, the staging of such a plot could easily degenerate into melodrama. There was never any danger of that in this VO production. The orchestra, led by Canadian-born Robert Tweten, making his first appearance on the VO podium, played magnificently. Stanley M. Garner, a well-known American actor before becoming a director, kept the production moving with a sure hand, aided by the considerable talents of the cast and the stunning period set designed and constructed in the famous studio Scenografie Sormani-Cardaropoli in Milan, Italy. The principal roles of Floria Tosca, Baron Scarpia and Mario Cavaradossi were played by American soprano Cynthia Lawrence, American baritone Yalun Zhang and Italian-born tenor Renzo Zulian, respectively. Lawrence and Zhang had previously

▲ Hwang Sin Nyung plays a vengeful Queen of the Night in this act 2 scene from Vancouver Opera's 2007 production of *The Magic Flute*. The Three Ladies are behind her and Monostatos, played by Michel Corbeil, is off to her left. TIM MATHESON PHOTOGRAPH

performed their roles at the Metropolitan, and their debut performances on the VO stage reflected their deep understanding of their fictional characters. Lawrence was flawless, vocally and theatrically, as a woman whose world was spinning out of control. Zhang skilfully portrayed an utterly loathsome, pathologically evil villain, whose personality permeated the entire opera, even though he never appeared onstage again after act 2. Zulian's ringing tenor voice was equal to the demands of the music, and his acting skills matched those of his colleagues. The supporting cast and the chorus threw themselves wholeheartedly into making the production a truly exceptional one.

To bring this discussion to a close without mentioning the November 2008 production of *Eugene Onegin* would be to pass over the VO debut of soprano Rhoslyn Jones in the role of Tatyana. Jones, who lives in Aldergrove, BC, and is a graduate of UBC's School of Music, was a semi-finalist in the Metropolitan Opera National Council Auditions in New York in early 2008. She is at the beginning of what promises to be a fine career. In addition to her beautiful voice, she possesses fine theatrical skills that can only improve with experience. Keep your eye on her.

Vancouver Opera posted its seventh consecutive operating surplus in eight years at the end of the 2006–07 season. James Wright provided insight into this remarkable achievement:

Well, it's a lot of factors . . . It's a board that understands its role as governance body, as a setter of broad policy, its role in strategic planning and its responsibility to ensure that the income's there to cover the expenses . . . They take all those things very seriously . . . We have rolling budgets four years out, sometimes three, sometimes five . . . When I got here the planning horizon was extremely short. That doesn't help you get good deals, book singers . . . before they're at a higher rate, find other opera companies that you want to co-produce with . . . so you're spending a fraction of what it would cost if you were producing it by yourself . . . You have to have a team of people all of whom recognize the importance of . . . fiscal responsibility, and while that may seem like a given, it isn't always. Speaking internally, you're never going to be able to do everything you want, there are always compromises to be made, and you try to inculcate in the rest of the staff, especially in the production and artistic departments, the discipline of figuring out what not to compromise on and what to compromise on . . . It's also [increased] revenue. Our individual giving has increased in the last seven years from $600,000 to $1.3 million.

Since Wright's interview, VO posted another operating surplus for the year ending June 30, 2008. Wright and his board understand very well that individual

and corporate sponsors do not want to see their dollars applied to debt or deficit reduction; VO's surplus positions are ones of strength with which to approach people for financial support.

Another position of strength that the company enjoys is the stability of a dedicated group of artists, employees and volunteers, many of whom have been with VO for a long time. For example, stage manager Sheila Munn has just completed her fourteenth season at VO; Leslie Dala has been assistant conductor since 1995 and took over as chorus director from Leslie Uyeda, who filled that position for fourteen years; Doug Tuck joined VO in 1997; Bette Cosar and Doug Devillier are among the longest-standing members of the VO Chorus, dating from the early 1970s; thirteen musicians, including Sharman King, have played in the VO

Orchestra since it was first formed; and Susan LePage, Micki Partridge and Pat Hancock are volunteers whose service spans decades, not just years. James Wright signed a new ten-year contract in 2005 that extends his position as general director until 2015, and in November 2008, Jonathan Darlington, music director since May 2005, accepted a new contract through the 2011–12 season.

▲ In act 1 of *Eugene Onegin*, Brett Polegato, playing Onegin, a newcomer to the area, meets a neighbour, Tatyana, played by Rhoslyn Jones. In this scene from Vancouver Opera's 2008 production, Onegin and Tatyana discuss her novel-reading pastime.
TIM MATHESON PHOTOGRAPH

Bravo!

Finale
CELEBRATING OPERA
IN BRITISH COLUMBIA

SOME MARVEL THAT AN ART FORM DATING BACK TO THE LATE SIXTEENTH century continues to fill opera houses around the world. Yet, there is little difference between attending the opera, the symphony or the ballet and going to an art gallery or reading the classics. The accepted gold standard for art, whether it be performing, visual or literary, is that it has stood the test of time. Opera companies work hard at staying current by performing a mix of classic and modern works, yet the most popular operas remain those composed in the eighteenth and nineteenth centuries.

Opera companies aim for age diversity in their audiences. Although an increase in season ticket purchasers is always welcome, the real target at Vancouver Opera is the single ticket buyer, who, according to statistics provided by Doug Tuck, director of marketing and community programs, accounts for almost 50 percent of a sold-out house. Tuck described what tools VO employs today, and what it sees as the future challenges:

> It used to be that people would read a preview and then go down to the
> box office and buy a paper ticket. That's not how people decide to go
> to the opera anymore. They go online, they research, they look at your
> website, they want a lot of experience before they decide . . . and they want
> to make their purchase electronically. They want to tell each other about it,
> so there's this evolution of social networking, what we call "touch points."
> So that's the way we have to be thinking—how, within our means, we can
> . . . help people see, feel, hear how exciting opera can be.

Since Pacific Opera Victoria is in the enviable position of filling the Royal Theatre for most of its productions, the focus in Victoria is less on audience-building and more on ensuring that everyone enjoys being at the opera, especially when going for the first time. David Shefsiek, executive

◄   This ensemble scene featuring Michael Douglas Jones as the Marquis is from the Modern
    Baroque Opera world premiere production of *120 Songs for the Marquis de Sade*, staged at the
    Vancouver East Cultural Centre in 2002. YUKIKO ONLEY PHOTOGRAPH

director of POV, described the age diversity of the company's audiences in relation to the demographics of the city:

> Opera audiences are late thirties plus; . . . the basic makeup of Victoria, being a little bit older, [means] it's not unusual that it's probably a few years past that, but we still see a lot of young people here at the opera house. I think that's because there's been more and more arts education . . . We've been doing student dress rehearsals for years and years . . . The other thing, too, is that we always have this large influx of people in their fifties and sixties, so there's always hundreds, if not thousands, of people coming to the opera house for the first time here, but certainly not their first time anywhere . . . We have to make sure that the theatre feels welcoming to everybody at every age.[1]

To this end, POV volunteers mingle in the front of the house before the performances and during intermissions, on the lookout for possible newcomers or the ill-at-ease, and engage them in conversation to make them feel welcome and comfortable. The volunteers and the company are also aware of, and try to combat, another concern: "No matter what happens, no matter how much opera changes . . . there still seems to be this idea that [it] is elitist," said Shefsiek, adding, "I want to make sure that everyone in Victoria has access to [us]."

The Opera in the Schools program that both POV and VO have operated for many years is thought to lay the foundation for future attendance, but Tuck has his doubts: "We hear a lot of anecdotal evidence to that effect that, yes, people who want to start coming to the opera saw a show in their school when they were kids. Sometimes it takes them twenty years to remember that. For the most part, people who come to the opera for the first time are introduced to it by a friend . . . So [they] might not respond to a survey by saying the reason they came was because we took [the children's opera] *The Barber of Barkerville* to their school, but they're more likely to say, 'my friend brought me.'" On the same note, the excellent community and education programs offered by BC's two major opera companies are viewed primarily as community service and audience enhancement, not audience-building initiatives.

Building on the popularity of their international radio and television broadcasts, the Metropolitan Opera now broadcasts live performances worldwide to movie theatres equipped with satellite-based digital high-definition projection systems. At present there are more than twenty such venues throughout the province. Admission is about $20, and audiences are large. Newcomers to this format may well become curious and willing to spend more to see what a truly live performance is like—VO and POV single tickets start at around just $30.

Taking opera to a broader audience

through this and other methods, such as the free, outdoor live simulcasts done by the Metropolitan, Washington National Opera and others in the US and Canada, has had a noticeable effect on singers and opera companies. Today's young singers learn that they must not only sing and act for a theatre audience, but also look good on camera. For example, opera companies are passing over grossly overweight singers for the more svelte, especially for romantic roles. Deborah Voigt is a case in point: since being told several years ago by the Royal Opera House, Covent Garden, that she was too overweight to be hired, she has slimmed down considerably. Heather Thomson-Price, speaking as a singer and voice teacher at the UBC School of Music's Voice and Opera Division, confirmed that this fact of life will continue for opera singers, even at the pre-professional level:

> Companies will hire people for their looks rather than their voice . . . They'll go for a wisp of a soprano because she looks good in their costumes and their productions . . . or [because] she can do the athleticism that's required . . . and not necessarily take the voice that's best suited to that role. Once you're established and singing at the Met you can put on some pounds . . . like a [Luciano] Pavarotti or a Jessye Norman [American soprano]. But young people starting out have got to look good as well as act well and have colour in their voices, not just sing the notes.

James Wright, general director of Vancouver Opera, spoke from the company point of view: "I would never knowingly hire a 300-pound [136 kg] Mimi or Traviata or Susanna, because I don't need to any more, and that includes males as well. However, there are certain roles, certain operas [where size] takes a real back seat to . . . vocal fulfillment— most of the Wagner, lots of the Strauss, the heavy Verdi . . . It's a decision that an individual producer has to make."

David Shefsiek expressed his thoughts on the issue: "People aren't as willing to suspend their disbelief as they once were, so you see beautiful couples like [Russian soprano] Anna Netrebko and [Mexican

▲ The slave girl, Aida, sung by Susan Neves, is trapped by her jealous mistress, Amneris, sung by Jean Stilwell, into revealing her love for Radames, whom Amneris also loves. The scene occurs in act 2, scene 1 of *Aida*, Vancouver Opera's 2002 production.
TIM MATHESON PHOTOGRAPH

Bravo!

tenor] Rolando Villazón, . . . and a cult of singer stardom that is emerging again . . . that definitely drew people to the theatre in the sixties. But, if we make too many concessions on voice, we will start seeing an erosion of the form." Referring to the hackneyed phrase, "It's not over 'til the fat lady sings," Thomson-Price debunked the belief that opera stars need to be fat: "You have to be healthy. It has to do with the formation, the length, of the vocal chords . . . I've heard voices as big or bigger than Jane Eaglen, who is a very large lady, coming out of much smaller bodies."

The production side of opera is also attracting new and younger audiences. Opera staging has changed, slowly but surely, in part with the rise to prominence of the stage director during the mid-twentieth century. Believing that mainstream operas can be made more relevant to modern audiences through new interpretations, directors have tinkered with plot details, locales, costumes, sets, even libretti. Some renderings work; others do not. In previous chapters several POV and VO productions were mentioned that had a distinct director's stamp on them, with varying results. Directors are most often theatre or film people, and they have imposed their experience in those art forms on the drama component of opera. As a result, singers—not just the leads but everyone onstage, including members of the chorus—have become much better actors and, consequently, productions

▲ In act 1 of the Vancouver Opera 2005 production of *Turandot*, the three imperial ministers, Ping, Pang and Pong warn Calaf not to declare his love for Turandot. Pictured here from left to right are Peter Blanchet as Pang, Michel Corbeil as Pong and Gregory Dahl as Ping. Renzo Julian as Calaf stands in the foreground.
TIM MATHESON PHOTOGRAPH

have become much more dynamic and enjoyable.[2]

The need for acting skills has filtered down to the pre-professional level. Any young singer who seeks to enter the professional world without considerable acting, as well as singing, experience is at a distinct disadvantage, as Nancy Hermiston, head of the UBC School of Music's Voice and Opera Division, confirmed:

> You can be an outstanding singer in the studio, but if you don't have the performance experience . . . you'll be a big disappointment, because when you get onstage and have no stage technique, well, there's no mercy . . . It's hard to tell a young person, "Spend two more years getting your technique, and don't ignore your stage technique." We have our own acting classes here in theatre technique, and there's a lot of acting that is given in the opera workshop course as well— those are compulsory courses. If I was to be critical of our program, I would say that we need those acting courses to start in first year and have them every year.

Students at UBC get valuable acting experience through participation in the Opera Ensemble. Other schools have similar performing components in their voice programs. After graduation, the most promising are invited to enter the resident artist or young artist programs associated with professional companies, like those sponsored by VO and POV,

where they receive advanced coaching and the valuable experience of being onstage with seasoned performers under a variety of conductors and directors.

Advances in technology have profoundly influenced all aspects of production, from international databases like Operabase assisting in casting to programmed lighting design and special effects. Surtitles are fast being replaced by less intrusive technology that displays translations and programming notes on small LCD screens on the backs of seats— and can be controlled by the operagoer.[3]

These developments only scratch the surface of what can be expected in opera production in the future. One far-sighted enthusiast is promoting the creation of a digital centre for the arts in Vancouver and foresees a virtual opera set created using digital technology. Many companies already use minimal sets in some productions, enhancing them by video projections and other digital techniques. It might be assumed, mistakenly, that companies realize considerable savings in

▲ Randall Jakobsh as the ludicrous Mustafà, Bey of Algiers, takes an onstage bath with his yellow rubber duckie in one of many over-the-top scenes from Vancouver Opera's 2008 production of *The Italian Girl in Algiers*, exuberantly directed by Michael Cavanagh.
TIM MATHESON PHOTOGRAPH

BravO!

There's the jersey that she knitted,
with the anchor that she patterned.

production costs as a result. When asked about the impact this trend will have on POV's recently acquired 10,000-square-foot (929 m²) set facility, David Shefsiek said: "Minimal sets are [not necessarily] less expensive than the ornate sets, because you are paying for technology. [The set] may not use as much wood, but it requires a lot of thought, a lot of ingenuity, and the set facility is not going to go by the wayside because of that. In fact, it will probably become more essential, but we are going to have to make sure that the technological aspects of it continue to grow." Shefsiek is referring to the technical specialists now involved in modern stage production in addition to the standard three—the set designer, the

costume designer and the lighting designer. He explains that for some shows, the production team includes a video designer or a digital image designer. "Sometimes you need a sound designer for soundscape atmosphere, not amplification."[4]

Iain Scott, the opera expert and former VO Board member, has an interesting theory that applies, by extension, to the effect of film and digital technology on opera attendance: "Opera seems to be one of the two fastest-growing art forms amongst eighteen- to thirty-five-year-olds (the other is visiting museums). We might speculate that opera is catching the interest of this group, in comparison to symphonies or ballet companies, because the inherent multimedia experience of

▲ This scene from Vancouver Opera's 1995 production of *Peter Grimes* shows Ben Heppner as Peter Grimes in his cottage, with the text of the words he is singing visible in the surtitle projected above the set. Vancouver Opera began using the technology in 1990.
DAVID COOPER PHOTOGRAPH

opera mirrors their tastes and experience of Hollywood movies and video and computer games."[5]

David Shefsiek offered his thoughts on trends in opera repertoire:

> There's going to be more attention to late twentieth- and twenty-first-century works. I think we're going to be losing some late nineteenth-century works from the repertoire temporarily, if not permanently. Some of the big verismo pieces you just don't see done any more. You see the classics. You see early twentieth century popping into place. You're seeing a return to Baroque opera in innovative productions. Mozart's never going anywhere. You see *Lucias* [*Lucia di Lammermoor*] . . . not too much [bel canto] beyond that, except in specialty companies . . . Right now I think it's going to be a focus on clarity—I don't want to say minimalism—pieces that are clear; that's what people are liking. That goes for singing, that goes for the look. There's a crystalline approach that people want as opposed to bold primary colours."

DEVELOPING NEW WORKS

We look beyond the present to the future of opera in our province by drawing attention to new composers, new works and new ways of looking at how opera composition and presentation might evolve. Colin Miles, the regional director of the Canadian Music Centre (CMC)

and a charter member of the Vancouver Opera Orchestra, believes that the best way to pay homage to opera composers of the past is to encourage and embrace those of the present and the future. He and the CMC are dedicated to providing the knowledge and resources for people to do just that. In an interview, Miles described the centre as "an amazing place . . . we're a window for people in BC to find out what's happening both here in BC and also across the country . . . We have over 700 composers who are associate composers of the Canadian Music Centre . . . and in BC, about 110. This means they are acknowledged nationally and internationally as professional composers in the concert music field, which is the field in which operas are created."[6] The centre is not only a place to learn about who is composing and in what format, it also provides a free lending music library and library services. For example, the score for Vancouver composer Jean Coulthard's opera *The Return of the Native* (the largest work in the collection at 550 pages), is in bound, catalogued form on the shelves, available to be examined.[7] Although little of the collection is as yet available for loan in the form of recordings or DVDs, the national office of the CMC is embarking on a project that will make its thousands of archival recordings available in streaming audio on its website.

Miles spoke with enthusiasm and admiration for the composers currently working in BC and their music:

Bravo!

▲ For its 1988 production of *The Turn of the Screw* Vancouver Opera chose to advance the time frame of the opera by using sets more consistent with modern time than with its traditional nineteenth-century setting. Miles's bedroom, shown here, is an example. Jane Leslie MacKenzie as the Governess is with Alex Morin, who plays Miles. DAVID COOPER PHOTOGRAPH

▲ Nine years after Vancouver Opera's production of *The Turn of the Screw*, Pacific Opera Victoria's 1997 staging of the same work showed the influence of the trend in set design toward minimalism. An antique bed stands alone onstage as a representation of Miles's nineteenth-century bedroom. Alexander Miller plays Miles in this production. DAVID COOPER PHOTOGRAPH

There are little operas; there are comic operas; there are operas that deal with quite incredible schemes; there are operas that expand the boundaries of what opera is; there are operas that speak very clearly to issues we care about, to universal issues, and there are composers who are creating things that we can't even imagine . . . Lloyd Burritt, for instance, has written an opera [*The Dream Healer*] based on a novel by Timothy Findley, and Christopher Butterfield has done interactive kinds of works . . . Someone like Neil Weisensel . . . all his work is in opera; he writes these little comic gems. Theo Goldberg has some electronic operas. Peter Hannan has written two or three operas. Rudolf Komorous has written some operas, including a one-person opera that was done in Carnegie Hall. Ramona Luengen was the one who was chosen to write *Naomi's Road* for Vancouver Opera, and she's done [other] operatic works. David MacIntyre . . . pushed the boundaries in all kinds of ways. He has a cute little piece called *Humulus the Mute*, which is just so much fun—every schoolchild in BC ought to know [it] . . . He did *The Architect*. John Oliver composed an opera for the Canadian Opera Company [*Guacamayo's Old Song and Dance*, 1991]. He was commissioned by Montreal's Chants Libres lyric opera to create a bilingual version of his second opera, *Alternate Visions*, about love in the age of the internet, which was originally presented with other new works in a workshop at Con'temp'aria [festival of new opera] in Victoria. It was done in Montreal in 2007, with a simultaneous video feed to the Western Front [a multidisciplinary arts centre in East Vancouver] so people here could hear it. Sylvia Rickard has an opera called *Fletcher's Challenge* about environmental issues . . . Rodney Sharman has a number of operas that have been done here and around the world. Tobin Stokes had a very successful opera done at the Belfry Theatre in Victoria [*The Vinedressers*, in 2002] . . . Barry Truax has written operas that incorporate computerized sound. He's a world-renowned composer in the electroacoustic field. He's far better known in Venice and in Belgium and in Germany than he is here in Vancouver, but that's all right. It just means there's a secret we can get to know. Robert Turner has written a number of operas, and he's in his late eighties now. He has some major works that speak to the experience of being here—his operas are actually set in Victoria . . . Owen Underhill has done some quite amazing things and collaborative works. Leslie Uyeda is someone who really knows opera. First of all, she was chorus master at Vancouver Opera. She knows voices . . . her operas are really worth listening to. Charles Wilson has about ten different operas, small operas which have been

BravO!

done, and many of them could be redone
. . . A great number of works deserve a
second, third or fourth look. Somebody
said, "If you get a lot out of listening
to Bach and listening to Mozart, and
you get a great deal out of playing
and listening to the Beethoven string
quartets, you can't really thank those
composers for what a difference they've
made in your life, but what you *can* do
is support the composers of our time."
It completes the circle, because they are
in the same stream, they have the same
creative spirit.

Getting wholehearted support for
new works is never easy. Producers and
programmers must always pay attention
to the bottom line, and contemporary
works are risky propositions. Nevertheless,
if more opera fans accepted that there
is much to gain by being open to new
work, producers would take risks more
frequently, and the art form would
benefit from an infusion of contemporary
repertoire that would keep it from
becoming stale. Calgary Opera recognizes
the importance of new works and recently
commissioned two new Canadian operas.
Calgarians are also doing their part, as
demonstrated by the sold-out houses
for the world premiere of *Frobisher*, the
full-length work by John Estacio and
John Murrell that the company co-
commissioned and co-produced with the
Banff Centre during the 2006–07 season.
In British Columbia there have been

many initiatives in contemporary opera.
Canadian composers have found support
with commissions and performances, some
already mentioned: VO's *The Architect* by
David MacIntrye and Tom Cone in 1994;
VNM's six Canadian works presented
between 1975 and 1999; POV's *Erewhon*
by Louis Applebaum and Mavor Moore
in 2000; MBO's *120 Songs for the Marquis de
Sade* by Peter Hannan and Peter Hinton
in 2002. In 1986 POV presented a Guelph
Spring Festival production of English
composer Peter Maxwell Davies's chamber
opera *The Lighthouse* in the McPherson
Playhouse, demonstrating its intention
to pursue new works. And in 1995, from
June 1 to 4, the company presented
Con'temp'aria, Canada's first festival of
contemporary opera, during which the
completed works or works-in-progress of
seven young Canadian composers were
staged at three venues in Victoria: the
McPherson Playhouse, the Belfry Arts
Centre and the Planet Theatre. POV also
hosted several annual week-long composer-
librettist workshops for Canadian artists
between 2002 and 2006; the events, called
Lib-Lab, were modelled on Tapestry
New Opera Works Composer-Librettist
Laboratories, offered annually since 1995 in
Toronto to provide professional composers
and writers with an intensive week-long
opportunity to collaborate in an atmosphere
thought most conducive to creativity.[8]
POV's Lib-Labs have concluded to make
way for a new and exciting venture for the
company: the commission of a new opera.

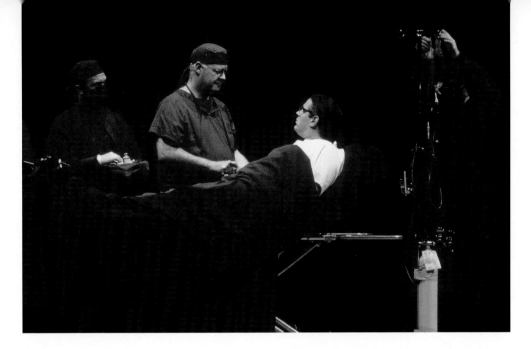

POV adopted a five-year strategic plan in 2007, and although its artistic goal is to present a varied repertoire, the commission of a Canadian opera was not as yet in the works. The conditions needed to bring that to pass were explained by David Shefsiek: "We are in the process of trying to identify a subject for commission . . . Our feeling here is that we want an idea to well up that *has* to be written, as opposed to 'in year four we're going to do a commission' . . . We want that idea to be so passionate that everybody wants it." Mindful of the fate of many Canadian works after their premieres, POV seeks a theme with the power and universality to become the foundation for a piece that will appeal to audiences everywhere, one that has the potential to become an enduring part of the opera repertoire in the twenty-first century. Shefsiek pointed out that whereas finding a Canadian voice has worked well in literature, and in the theatre and symphony orchestras, where Canadian writers and composers can be accommodated within a broader repertoire

or longer season, the same does not apply to the opera: "When you do three shows a year, maybe four, you're talking about 33 to 25 percent of your stuff—brand-new, untried, risk-taking work. You're being asked to do something bolder than any of those other art forms by the very nature of the art form, so you have to be very, very, careful about the context in which you do it." Two years later, in April 2009, it was announced that POV had commissioned composer Paul MacDonald and librettist Stephen Massicotte to create a new opera, to be called *Mary's Wedding*.

The Vinedressers by Tobin Stokes, mentioned above by Colin Miles, was taken on as a project by a visionary theatre company in Victoria, The Other Guys, whose director, Ross Desprez, had great confidence in Stokes's abilities. Stokes wrote the music and libretto at the same time, an unusual way to go about opera composition, but it worked. After its premiere, Asterisk Productions made it the subject of a half-hour documentary that aired on CBC TV. The work received

▲ Vancouver Opera's commissioned opera, *The Architect*, had its world premiere in 1994. In this scene, André Clouthier, who plays Even, is about to undergo an operation from which his surgeons do not intend that he shall recover. PHOTO COURTESY VANCOUVER OPERA

Bravo!

another staging when the Opera Academy of the Pacific in Powell River, BC, presented it as a student production on June 30 and July 1, 2006.

During the first week of December 2007, Vancouver New Music presented what is arguably the most innovative new work ever seen in Vancouver: *Fig Trees*, a contemporary video opera by composer David Wall, with words and images by John Greyson. The show's format gives veracity to Colin Miles's contention that opera is what the composer says it is. First of all, it is an installation, not a staged work. Second, it requires active participation by the viewers, who physically move, libretto in hand, following an instinctive path, through the scenes, which are not scenes in the traditional sense, but projections on the wall and on the floor. A few red velvet theatre seats are the only suggestion that the viewer is in an opera house. Gradually, an intelligible order becomes apparent to the participant as he or she mentally rearranges the disparate elements of the piece. It deals with historical figures—for example, Gertrude Stein and Saint Teresa—who are collaborating on a new opera based on actual events in South Africa involving Zackie Achmat, a man with AIDS, who refuses to take medication until it is made available to all in the country who suffer from the disease. Giorgio Magnanensi, the artistic director of VNM, described how he learned about the piece, and the public's reaction to it:

We had a good opening on World AIDS Day with a panel discussion about art and activism, and in spite of the snow we had a good audience . . . I knew about this project because it was in the Kitchener Open Ears Festival [Kitchener, Ontario] four years ago, and I was there when they were presenting one little installation . . . and I liked it very much, so I started by contacting John Greyson . . . Our version is not the full version . . . The modularity of the project allows us to present scenes and different parts and not the whole . . . For example, there was one scene I wanted to do [with] a van, but we couldn't really bring a van into the venue . . . The response we had from all the other

◀ Sandra Graham plays the Queen, shown in this shot with John Higgs as Stuart Howe from Pacific Opera Victoria's world premiere production of *Erewhon*, 2000.
TIM MATHESON PHOTOGRAPH

▲ The Marquis de Sade and his mother, sung by Michael Douglas Jones and Christine Duncan respectively, are pictured here in a tender scene from *120 Songs of the Marquis de Sade*, 2002. YUKIKO ONLEY PHOTOGRAPH

organizations, AIDS Vancouver, the [Scotiabank Dance] Centre, was great . . . definitely a work worth presenting again.[9]

To provide insight into this complex work, the program notes for act 2, scene 5, titled "The Fig Orchard," are reproduced here:

Bowing to pressure, the government reverses its AIDS policy and promises to distribute AIDS treatment drugs. In turn, Zackie decides to end his treatment strike and goes to a fig orchard to take his first dose. Gertrude [Stein] is dismayed: how can she meaningfully immortalize a tragic martyr if he refuses to die? Zackie cheerfully withdraws from her opera and takes his pills. Gertrude departs in a huff. Inspired by the tranquility of the sunlit orchard, St. Teresa remembers a time on a dusty road when she fainted and was revived by a stranger who offered her figs. The curtain falls.

Vancouver New Music's future presentations, if and when they occur, are not likely to bear any resemblance to the traditional art form, in view of Magnanensi's comments:

I make the distinction between opera and music theatre, because I see that the composers in Canada still work with an idea of opera that is pretty much harking back to that nineteenth-century thing, but for me that's over. As much as I like Puccini, I don't want to hear Puccini. I want to avoid using that word [opera], which refers so much to a specific idea of what opera is, so I use music theatre, because it's more open . . . I don't want to go in a space where there is this very strong, very assertive stage. The idea of a stage is a very old dynamic between a passive and an active group of people. I'd like to see a more engaging project. This installation, *Fig Trees*, was something in which people can be more actively engaged if they want. At least there is the option. And so something

▲ Michael Douglas Jones, playing Marquis de Sade, "moons" the audience in this scene from the award winning *120 Songs for Marquis de Sade*, commisioned and given its world premiere by Modern Baroque Opera in 2002. YUKIKO ONLEY PHOTOGRAPH

that fosters that idea is more appealing to me at this particular time . . . We are searching always for something that represents that path in the integration of new sound and new theatre . . . but we've stopped calling it opera.

Moving on to VO's initiatives in promoting new composers and their works, after the commission and staging of *The Architect*, the company organized a composers' workshop in conjunction with the Canadian Music Centre in the summer of 2003. Similar in format to POV's Lib-Lab, it afforded an opportunity for four well-known Vancouver composers—Janet Danielson, David MacIntyre, Neil Weisensel and Ramona Luengen—to workshop existing compositions over a ten-day period. After this event, VO

commissioned Ramona Luengen to write a new opera for schoolchildren called *Naomi's Road*, with a libretto by well-known Canadian director Ann Hodges based on Joy Kogawa's powerful novel, *Obasan*. Kogawa's work deals with a sensitive subject: the forced evacuation of Japanese Canadians from coastal areas to the BC interior and farms in Alberta during the aftermath of the Japanese attack on Pearl Harbor in 1941. The opera was completed in 2005 and, before touring schools and other centres throughout BC, southern Alberta and Washington State, it had its world premiere in Vancouver and sold out on four successive evenings at the Norman Rothstein Theatre in the Jewish Community Centre. Those evenings proved that, although intended for children in the upper elementary grades, the work has

▲ An ensemble scene of drunkenness and debauchery from Pacific Opera Victoria's 2003 staging of Berg's *Wozzeck*. DAVID COOPER PHOTOGRAPH

Bravo!

the power to move adults deeply as well, especially those old enough to have been onlookers to that painful episode in BC's history. Fittingly, *Naomi's Road* with its original cast was taken to Ottawa, where they gave twenty performances at the Canadian War Museum in November 2006.

Earlier in 2006, VO announced that it had commissioned a new full-length opera to be staged in 2010 during the celebrations planned around the fiftieth anniversary of the founding of the company. Chosen to write the work was the team of John Estacio and John Murrell, who had a successful track record as collaborators on two previous works, *Filumena* and *Frobisher*, as well as individual triumphs in their respective

fields of composer and playwright. The title of the new opera, *Lillian Alling*, refers to the colourful central character, a historical figure of the same name who travelled on foot from New York City to the Yukon, and thence through the frozen north to the Bering Sea to reach her Russian homeland. In a news release, James Wright said the following about the commission: "I believe that new operas are extremely important for the continued vibrancy of the art form and that it is imperative for an opera company of the size and capability of Vancouver Opera to aim to produce new work . . . With measured growth over a number of years, which will see the company almost double its investment in programming during the

▲ Sharing a rare bit of levity in this scene from *Regina*, staged by Pacific Opera Victoria in 2008, are left to right Benjamin Hubbard (Doug MacNaughton), Oscar Hubbard (Gregory Dahl) and their sister, Regina Giddens (Kimberly Barber).
PINK MONKEY STUDIOS PHOTOGRAPH

decade from 2000 to 2010, we have the artistic and financial capacity to take on a challenge like this."[10]

Nancy Hermiston believes that the UBC School of Music has an important role to play in fostering new works:

> We have a very difficult balance. We have to give our students an extended repertoire . . . but we also have to instill in them the love for new works, because we don't want our art form to die out. I think the university should be attuned to that. My problem with new works is purely a financial one, because I have to be as sensitive to that as an opera company. Now, I shouldn't have to be, because that limits what I can do, but every time I do a new work, I risk the income for the next year. When the [renovation of the] Old Aud is done, we'll be able to at least workshop a lot of new works for composers, and I hope we'll produce some of the new works there.[11]

Hermiston has found that one way to minimize the risk of producing new works is to form associations with other faculties within the university. For example, in 2006 the School of Music and the School of Nursing collaborated to produce Timothy Sullivan's 1992 opera, *Florence, the Lady with the Lamp*, as part of the Nurse Education International Conference in Vancouver that year. The UBC Opera Ensemble staged two performances in the Old Aud on May 12 and 13, just before the conference

began. Hermiston did the same thing with the Department of Psychiatry and the Institute for Mental Health in March 2008 when the world premiere of Lloyd Burritt's new opera, *The Dream Healer*, was presented as a three-way collaboration featuring four stage performances and a series of lectures on mental health topics.[12] The event celebrated UBC's centenary and the tenth anniversary of the opening of the Chan Centre for the Performing Arts. Staging of the piece deviated from the normal UBC Opera Ensemble production by engaging three high-profile professional artists—Judith Forst, John Avey and Dutch-born Canadian tenor Roelof Oostwoud—to take the leads. Singing the role of Emma Jung on alternate nights were Hermiston's students, soprano Simone Osborne, fresh from her triumph at the 2008 Metropolitan Auditions in New York, and soprano Gina McLellan. Ensemble singers had plenty of exposure in the ten other main roles and the forty-eight-member chorus, which was onstage during the entire performance. In addition, ensemble singers were understudies for the three principals. The UBC Symphony Orchestra, comprising fifty-two players from the School of Music, was led by internationally renowned conductor David Agler, a staunch supporter of the school.[13] Hermiston directed the production, and Robert Gardiner, professor of design in the Theatre Program at UBC, designed the sets. Hermiston described the students' excitement a month before the

BravO!

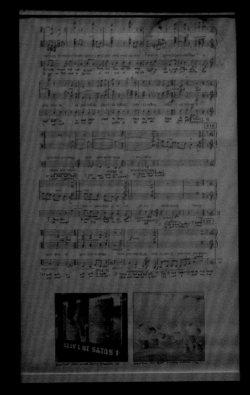

performance: "They were interested in *Florence*, but that opera had been performed once before. This one [*The Dream Healer*] is brand new. They're developing the parts and will be the first ones to sing those parts, so they're quite thrilled with it."

About ten years ago June Goldsmith, a Vancouver musician and impresario, expanded the usual format of Music in the Morning, her popular recital series, to include the world of opera. After hearing music by Janet Danielson, a talented associate composer at the Canadian Music Centre and teacher, living and working in Vancouver, Goldsmith commissioned her to write an opera, with the intention of supporting contemporary Canadian work by giving public exposure to a local composer whose work she admired. Danielson based her libretto on a medieval Dutch morality play about a young girl

liberated from the influence of Satan. The play and the opera have the same title: *The Marvelous History of Mariken of Nimmigen*.[14] In succeeding Septembers between 2002 and 2004, Goldsmith, employing professional singers and musicians, presented each of the opera's three acts in semi-staged format in the Koerner Recital Hall of the Vancouver Academy of Music as part of Music in the Morning's educational Composers and Coffee series. Danielson was onstage before the performances to explain the creative process, and afterward the audience provided her with valuable feedback.

NURTURING NEW TALENT

The opera scene in BC can be assured of one thing for the foreseeable future: a talent pool of well-trained musicians and singers coming out of the music

▲ A visitor to Vancouver New Music's 2007 innovative opera installation, *Fig Trees*, pauses before a wall projection of a video component of the work.
JARED RAAB PHOTOGRAPH

programs of the province's universities, colleges, academies and conservatories. Sharman King described the effect of this development from the point of view of a veteran musician of forty years' experience:

> Even though the music world has diminished—there's less and less work all the time—the standards have gone up and up . . . More and more players are formally educated at universities . . . There just aren't that many jobs, so they end up doing many different things . . . From the point of view of the arts organizations, it's wonderful, because for not that much money, especially in a city like Vancouver, they get a fantastic professional orchestra . . . As musicians we benefit, because you have to keep up with that constantly rising standard; . . . the new blood makes it better.

The competition is also stiff for singers, especially women singers, entering the professional opera world, but well-prepared graduates of a good music school can expect more employment opportunities than their instrumental musician colleagues. The importance of being well prepared cannot be underestimated, for rarely does a singer come out of nowhere today.

Under the capable and energetic leadership of Nancy Hermiston, UBC's opera program in the Voice and Opera Division of the School of Music enjoys a reputation in Canada second only to the University of Toronto's. Hermiston came to UBC in 1995 from a teaching position at the University of Toronto, and described how she incorporated her ideas and extensive experience as a renowned performing artist on the operatic stages of Europe and North America into the UBC program:

> The basic academic program remained the same . . . What I changed was the weight within the Voice and Opera Division between people who are interested in performance and people who are interested in general music studies. Before I came, there were about eighty-six singers, and there were only seven opera majors and maybe four voice performance students . . . I just started to give the kids more opportunities to perform and get them onstage, and then the balance flipped . . . [When] I started, I did two full productions a year with orchestra . . . and a concert of operatic excerpts, and before there was only one [production] every other year, I believe, and excerpts.

▲ This scene from Vancouver Opera's world premiere production, *The Architect*, was shot at the beach on English Bay in Vancouver. In it Gloria Parker, the successful architect Sandra, meets André Clouthier as Even, the beach bum, whose simple life begins to appeal to her. PHOTO COURTESY VANCOUVER OPERA

There are three streams in the Voice and Opera Division, all of which require an audition: general studies for those who have not chosen a specific field; voice performance, which prepares students for the concert and recital stage and concentrates on the art song; and opera, which is the opera performance option. Hermiston pointed out that although a high percentage of students in the opera program go on to a full-time career in opera, not all do so: "Some of them combine performing with teaching, or performing opera with some other kind of business within the profession, like arts management." The requirements for first-year students in the Bachelor of

Music, Voice and Opera Division include introductory courses in French, Italian, German and English, as well as courses in the history of music, musicianship, diatonic harmony and voice leading, lyric diction, vocal techniques and opera repertoire, and private vocal instruction. The requirements for second-year students are similar: chromatic harmony and voice leading, musicianship, music history, opera repertoire, sight-reading and private vocal instruction. By third and fourth year, students in the opera stream are heavily into courses that focus exclusively on theatre and vocal techniques, opera repertoire and coaching, and opera production.

Hermiston established the UBC Opera Ensemble in 1995 during her first year on the job. The opera ensemble shows are prepared in the third- and fourth-year opera workshop, which involves sixteen to twenty hours of the students' time, not including final rehearsals with the orchestra and conductor. Hermiston chooses the works to be produced and, after consultation with the voice teachers on the faculty, selects the students to sing the leads and smaller roles. She described the process:

One of the things that's been very important to me is that I produce operas that [the students] can use outside the university when they start their careers, so I try to balance between traditional and non-traditional repertoire, and do some contemporary work within their

▲ Members of the UBC Opera Ensemble onstage in an ensemble scene with professional singers John Avey (Carl Jung), Roelof Oostwoud (Pilgrim) and Judith Forst (Lady Sybil Quartermaine), who appeared courtesy of the Canadian Actors' Equity Association, in the 2008 production of *The Dream Healer.* TIM MATHESON PHOTOGRAPH COURTESY UBC SCHOOL OF MUSIC, VOICE AND OPERA DIVISION

▲ Simone Osborne, a member of the UBC Opera
Ensemble, sang the soprano role of Emma Jung in the
ensemble's 2008 production of *The Dream Healer*.
TIM MATHESON PHOTOGRAPH COURTESY UBC SCHOOL OF
MUSIC, VOICE AND OPERA DIVISION

Bravo!

undergraduate time . . . I do everything in the original language . . . This is important for my singers because . . . they must have experience with that before they leave school. We're one of the very few schools in Canada that does that. A lot of them might do French, Italian and German, but not very many of them do Czech and Russian, but those two languages are now standard operatic languages, and you *must* do that. Some of [the students] won't be ready to do as much performance as others, but I get them involved in chorus or small parts, or find things that they can perform at the level they are at . . . They're all at different levels, and you can't rush that. You have to keep your eye on them very carefully and make sure you're not giving them too much or too little.

Students also get experience in other aspects of the production side of opera by building sets, making props, sewing costumes and becoming involved in the publicity for their performances.

Hermiston has an extensive parallel career as a stage director. She directs the opera ensemble productions herself but always brings in a seasoned guest conductor so her singers experience what an opera conductor expects of them: "It's no use . . . giving them a . . . symphony conductor [who] has never conducted opera. That does them no good. A symphony conductor will not know what

▲ Sookhyung Park, in the title role of Daphne, is chided by Rebecca Haas as her mother, Gaea, for her reluctance to take part in the evening's fertility rights. Pacific Opera Victoria staged the Canadian premiere of *Daphne* in 2007. TIM MATHESON PHOTOGRAPH

an opera conductor knows," she said.

Hermiston has broadened the exposure UBC students receive for performance in the school's productions and concerts by getting them out into the local, provincial, national and international scene:

> I take them to Ontario to a festival there. I take them to different community music associations, to seniors' homes, to schools, to cultural organizations that have formed and give little concerts, and I take them throughout the Lower Mainland, throughout the province. We've done school tours in Alberta, Saskatchewan and Ontario. I take them to Europe in the summer to [Germany and to] the Czech Republic . . . We work with the Vancouver Symphony . . . We have a very strong bond with Bard on the Beach [Shakespeare Festival] . . . As a result, I think our students are much more confident than most university students at that level when they graduate, because they have had so much performance experience, and they know the theatre.

She is justifiably proud of her students:

> We have won many competitions . . . Our singers are getting employment in Young Artist Ensembles in the US and Canada and in Europe . . . We have four people in the Canadian Opera Company Ensemble in Toronto—two bass-baritones, one soprano and one mezzo—and that's something![15]

Simon Fraser University offers two options in music: a Bachelor of Fine Arts (BFA) with either a major or an extended minor in music. SFU's program concentrates on acoustic and electroacoustic composition for a wide range of musical formats, such as dance, theatre, film, video and opera. Many of BC's university colleges, formerly called community colleges, offer music programs for instrument and vocal training in locations such as Dawson Creek, Nelson, Nanaimo, Victoria, North Vancouver and New Westminster. Other institutions provide performance experience as well: at the Opera Academy of the Pacific, part of the Powell River Academy of Music, young professionals and advanced students perform in the academy's symphony orchestra and provide the music for the semi-staged productions of the Opera Academy; the Prince George Conservatory of Music is particularly known for the Borealis Chamber Choir, its award-winning choral ensemble, and the Sinfonia! Prince George orchestra, comprising faculty, students and musicians from the community. However, because the major educational institutions are located in the southwestern part of the province, any serious aspirant to a career in opera who wishes to remain in BC must apply to one of these.

The Vancouver Academy of Music offers a Bachelor of Music degree through Thompson Rivers University–Open Learning (TRU-OL). Students take all

their music courses at the academy and make up their academic credits by distance education from TRU-OL or by part-time attendance at one of the post-secondary academic institutions in the Lower Mainland. The Voice/Opera Division is under the direction of David Meek, who described the program during an interview:

> The goal of the program is, and always has been, to audition people [and] if we think they've got the vocal equipment to go into the profession, we take them in and work with them. We give them all the stage experience that we can; we give them all the vocal training that we can; they get coaching; we work with them on all the languages . . . and they get experience singing in front of their own colleagues in weekly master classes with

▲ Student singers Christine Turingia (Meg Page), Rachel Fenlon (Alice Ford), Heny Janawati (Mistress Quickly) and Lauren Patton (Nannetta) in the UBC Ensemble's 2009 production of *Falstaff*. NEIL CRAIGHEAD PHOTOGRAPH, COURTESY UBC SCHOOL OF MUSIC, VOICE AND OPERA DIVISION

me and occasional visiting professionals. Our program is thirty-two weeks a year, so they get thirty-two lessons and thirty-two master classes a year. We do two full sets of scene studies and a full opera once a year. We also do concert programs in the community.[16]

The scene studies are presented as four semi-staged public performances in the fall and winter terms, and the summer opera is a fully staged production directed by Meek. The orchestral ensemble is conducted by Frank Klassen, a Vancouver conductor of many years' experience in operatic work in Europe and locally. The summer 2008 opera was *Albert Herring* by Benjamin Britten, performed at the Metro Theatre in Vancouver.

Students studying with Meek are either working toward a bachelor's degree or are registered in the Artist Diploma Program, a two-year post-graduate course, or they may be Meek's private students. Diploma students are required to do two full recitals and participate in the opera program but have no outside academic requirements. Private students have access to master classes and the opera program. Many fine musicians and singers have gone on to professional careers after their studies at the academy, including soprano Tamara Hummel, a Metropolitan Opera Auditions winner, and Lambroula Maria Pappas and counter-tenor David D.Q. Lee, both runners-up in Metropolitan Auditions. Two young former students currently doing well are sopranos Robyn Driedger-Klassen, who sang the role of Marzelline in VO's 2008 production of *Fidelio*, and Melody Mercredi, a member of the VO Chorus who understudied the role of Queen of the Night for VO's 2007 production of *The Magic Flute*. Another, Tyler Duncan, a baritone from Prince George, now makes his home in New York and is in demand all over North America and Europe, singing lieder, opera and oratorio.

The School of Music at the University of Victoria offers a performance major, admitting students by audition. Successful candidates spend much of their undergraduate time in practice, weekly master classes and performance in large and small ensembles. In addition to taking part in student recitals throughout their four years of study, all fourth-year performance majors are required to present a full evening recital. The school expects most of its performance majors to go on to further studies, either in graduate schools or other organizations, such as a young artist program. The head of the Voice Department is distinguished tenor Benjamin Butterfield, who also maintains an active performance career.[17]

The Victoria Conservatory of Music was established in 1964. Its student productions date from the mid-1970s, when the Opera Workshop was initiated under the direction of Selena James, a prominent voice teacher in the city. In 1992, it became the Opera Studio, adding Robert Holliston, featured in Act II as the chorus master of Pacific Opera Victoria, as music director.[18] Opera Studio is open by audition to advanced conservatory voice students, as well as to other talented singers from the larger community. The content of the program has expanded considerably to include instruction in musical and vocal interpretation, acting, improvisation, character and score analysis, stage technique and audition skills, along with annual productions of standard operas.

Joanne Hounsell, a faculty member at the conservatory and a performing singer, is the founder of the Summer Vocal Academy, an intensive two-week program "dedicated to the advancement of young artists through a comprehensive and innovative training program built around close collaboration with established artists, teachers and coaches . . . The core of our program is close one-on-one work with the faculty in lessons, coaching and master classes, all of which culminates in a series of public performances."[19] Hounsell conducts live auditions in Montreal, Toronto, Vancouver and Victoria, but interested students may also audition by tape, video or sound file.

A similar program, the annual Okanagan Vocal Arts Festival, began in 2003 in Vernon, and takes place for two weeks during July. Singers audition for a place in the Young Artist Opera Program and receive instruction from some of Canada's best-known singers and teachers. Performance experience is gained by participation in various festival events, culminating in the production of two semi-staged versions of opera and musical comedy. In 2006, the ensemble performed *The Mikado* (Gilbert and Sullivan) and *The Marriage of Figaro* under the tutelage of artistic director Paul Moore and a distinguished faculty, which included Heather Thomson-Price, American tenor Perry Price, Bernard Turgeon, American soprano Theresa Santiago, Randall Jakobsh, BC mezzo-soprano Lynne McMurtry, BC baritone Andrew Greenwood and Maestro Frank Klassen.

Once singers have completed their education and training and are looking for employment opportunities, they are faced with a dilemma: either try to get a foot in the door on the local scene, or head immediately for the large urban centres, like Toronto and New York, where their chances of being heard by a representative of one of the many North American professional opera companies seeking new talent are considerably greater. Fortunately for those who decide to start out in BC, more opportunities are becoming available on the professional and semi-professional level.

A rapidly growing category, the semi-professional company, includes those that have been established for some years and others that are new arrivals on the scene. Burnaby Lyric Opera (BLO), based at the Shadbolt Centre for the Arts in Burnaby, started out in the early 1980s as a student company named Shoestring Opera, later grew into a professional company known as NorthWest Opera and, in 1997, when it found a permanent home, it was renamed Burnaby Lyric Opera. The BLO website states that it "continues its original vision to be an intermediate opera company that gives emerging professional and semi-professional opera singers in British Columbia the opportunity to sing leading roles in fully staged operas. These young singers . . . are often on the threshold of major careers . . . The company also gives student performers the chance to sing in the chorus and acquire the experience of the operatic stage."[20]

Vancouver Island Opera, known as Opera OLÉ until 2001, is a semi-professional company that operates much the same way. Professional singers, auditioned for the leads, and professional musicians work alongside emerging singers and amateurs in the company's twice-yearly productions, which comprise one mainstream opera and one chosen from the lighter repertoire. Both are fully staged and are popular with audiences from the mid-Island communities of Qualicum Beach, Nanaimo, Duncan, Port Alberni, Comox and Courtenay.[21]

Opera Breve has been performing one-act chamber operas in concert format since 1997 in a variety of venues, such as the Listel Vancouver Hotel ballroom, O'Doul's restaurant, private clubs, after-hours in a bank in the Downtown Eastside, and in private homes. Christ Church Cathedral became a favourite performance space after 2000 because of its fine acoustics and

▶ The principals in the cast of the Vancouver Academy of Music's Opera Studio presentation of *Albert Herring* in 2008 pose before the opening of the show. The singers are from left to right (standing): Douglas Millar as Mr. Gedge, the vicar; Katheryn Garden as Miss Wordsworth; Martin Sadd as Mr. Upfold, the mayor; and Heidi Lynn Peters as Lady Billows; seated is Andrzej Jeziorski in the title role. LYNNE SPENCER PHOTOGRAPH

musicians it auditions and hires on an ad hoc basis. The singers also audition, but perform without pay for the opportunity of stage experience and exposure, which sometimes brings welcome results: one of Klassen's singers was recently hired by Calgary Opera. The 2008–09 season included three concerts—one in a mattress gallery—and one opera, *Cavalleria Rusticana*, at the Wellbrook Winery, a heritage barn in Delta.[22]

The Opera Project (TOP) began in Winnipeg in 1997. When its founder and director, Heidi Klassen, a singer of international repute, moved to Vancouver in 2004, she introduced the company to local audiences through concerts and operas. TOP's mission was to give emerging young professional Canadian singers an opportunity to perform in principal roles and to invite established artists to work alongside them as mentors. However, after two active seasons in Vancouver, Klassen suspended TOP for a period to give herself a respite from ten years of directing; she intends to resume activities in the future.

Some of these relative newcomers may not have a high profile in the community because it is difficult to attract media attention and they cannot afford to advertise commercially. Nevertheless, they are known to young singers as avenues to explore for performance experience on their path to a professional career.

Opera Pro Cantanti is a new group of opera singers that has been more fortunate

convenient location. Opera Breve exists to provide pre-professional performance experience to its roster of rising young singers and to make "the experience of going to the opera accessible, unusual and unforgettable."

Opera Appassionata, a young, semi-professional company headed by artistic director and conductor Frank Klassen, is providing interesting performance alternatives at the semi-professional level for young singers. In the past three years, the company has presented fully staged operas in unconventional venues, including a winery, a greenhouse and an art gallery. Dependent on ticket sales and donations, the company can afford to pay only the

▲ Photographed in costume before the opening of the Vancouver Academy of Music's Opera Studio production of *Die Fledermaus* are, from left to right: Andrzej Jeziorski as Alfred, Katheryn Garden as Rosalinde and Dave Gibbons as Baron von Eisenstein. The 2009 production was directed by David Meek.
LYNNE SPENCER PHOTOGRAPH

in getting some recent publicity.[23] It is an independent repertory company, and was described by its owner and artistic director, Richard Williams, as "matchbox-opera on a shoestring," referring to the venue for the company's productions at the time, the small stage of the Denman Theatre in Vancouver's West End. Since then, the company has moved to a new location, the Cambrian Hall in East Vancouver. The singers themselves contribute to the costs of production in exchange for an opportunity to get performance experience. The company's roster of singers is surprisingly large, attesting to the demand for exposure. The focus of the group is on the singers: professional singers develop personal interpretations of their roles, and they and the director mentor those in the cast striving to become professionals. All work together to present four mainstream nineteenth-century operas during their season from November to June, with performances every Sunday evening. The singers make their costumes and props, and a pianist provides the instrumental accompaniment.

A bold new professional venture is City Opera Vancouver, which will devote itself to producing chamber operas from both traditional and contemporary repertoire. The company is the brainchild of Charles Barber, conductor and artistic director, and his friend and colleague, Tom Durrie.[24] Almost from the beginning of their collaboration in 2005, they envisioned the Pantages Theatre, a once grand but now dilapidated theatre at 152 East Hastings Street, as the perfect home for City Opera because of its size and superb acoustics. At the time, a vigorous campaign to restore the theatre was launched, spearheaded by the Pantages Theatre Arts Society, but three years of negotiations between the owner of the property and the City of Vancouver collapsed when City Council voted against the project in October 2008. The following words, spoken by Barber in an interview in February 2008, have even more relevancy today, in view of the likely fate of the Pantages:

> There are very few theatres appropriate for our kind of work, . . . a house that allows chamber opera to speak its own name, which is that eloquent intimacy of expression, of which chamber opera is uniquely gifted. Our first major opera may well turn out to be our first major commission . . .We're looking now at other works . . . and we hope there will be a [co-production] with a much smaller venue in Vancouver . . . These things are complicated to put together. It will make an extraordinary difference to this company, its life, its identity, and its prospects to have . . . its own opera house. Until that day, we are orphans, and that means we don't get to choose where we can perform, nor in what acoustical environment, nor at what expense. But we persist, and we are characters who never give up.

City Opera formally introduced itself to the community on October 26, 2007, in St. Andrew's-Wesley United Church with a well-attended singalong performance of Carl Orff's cantata *Carmina Burana*, featuring prominent local professional artists: soprano Phoebe MacRae, tenor William George and baritone Andrew Greenwood. On March 11, 2008, the company announced the commission of a new Canadian chamber opera, *Pauline*, based on the last days of the poet Pauline Johnson and designed as a showcase for the renowned and beloved singer, Judith Forst. The piece was originally planned to debut in early 2010 but has been put forward to 2011 to allow the company to find a suitable theatre. The choice of Canadian composer Christos Hatzis to write the music to Margaret Atwood's libretto, and Judith Forst in the title role will surely go a long way to getting financial support and ensuring the success of the project. Much to the company's delight, it has recently been awarded a Canada Council commissioning grant for *Pauline*.

Keeping its name before the public in the meantime, City Opera and its co-presenter, the Vancouver Holocaust Education Centre, staged *The Emperor of Atlantis (Der Kaiser von Atlantis)* in February 2009 in the Norman Rothstein Theatre, for five sold-out performances. The piece is a powerful chamber opera written in 1944 in a concentration

▲ Stephen Aberle (Loudspeaker) holds a microphone toward Vancouver baritone Andrew Greenwood (Emperor) and William George (Harlekin) observes from his high perch in this ensemble scene from *The Emperor of Atlantis*, City Opera Vancouver's 2009 presentation. MILAN RADOVANOVIC PHOTOGRAPH, COURTESY CITY OPERA VANCOUVER

camp by inmates Viktor Ullmann, the composer, and Petr Kien, the librettist. Miraculously, the music survived after both men were killed by the Nazis, and their work was turned into a stunning success for City Opera by stage director Peter Jorgensen and lead singers Andrew Greenwood, bass John Minagro and Robyn Driedger-Klassen.

Opera is on a roll in British Columbia, and the proliferation of performing groups is an indication of this. There are now three companies producing opera on a professional level and a remarkable number of semi-professional companies. And it's apparent that everyone involved wants everyone else to succeed. Charles Barber put it well: "Our view is that theatre begets theatre, music begets music, opera begets opera. There is no rivalry here at all—quite the contrary." Speaking specifically of semi-professional groups, he said: "To me, one of the most significant contributions that such companies make . . . is to allow the most practical of apprenticeships you could ever hope for as a young, rising professional entering the business, or as someone who has been singing for forty years, and wants a chance to do it again. From whatever vantage point one comes, it's an opportunity to make music with people of like mind and good heart in the best possible way." Established vocal and instrumental musicians, even those at the peak of fame, give as freely of their time as their schedules allow to mentor those

▲ In City Opera Vancouver's production, *The Emperor of Atlantis*, 2009, John Minagro as Death points his finger at William George, who plays Harlekin.
MILAN RADOVANOVIC PHOTOGRAPH, COURTESY
CITY OPERA VANCOUVER

Bravo!

who aspire to a career in music by giving master classes, teaching, coaching and performing with them, passing on their experience and giving them confidence. Opera companies on all levels have a dual mission: to bring the art form to as many people as possible, and in so doing, give emerging conductors, directors, musicians, singers and all the others associated with the production of this complex art form, a chance to showcase their abilities.

CELEBRATING THE FUTURE

The celebration of the fiftieth anniversary of Vancouver Opera and the thirtieth of Pacific Opera Victoria in 2010 will also be an occasion to recognize them for their undeniable influence on the development of opera in all its manifestations throughout British Columbia. If the VO and POV 2009–10 seasons, and the anticipated new operas, *Lillian Alling* and *Mary's Wedding*, are an indication of the rich offerings our opera companies have in store for us, we can have no doubts about the future of this art form. To the pioneers in this province who set opera on its path to its glorious present, and to those who will use their talents to ensure its continued excellence, we say a heartfelt "thank you."

Jane Heffelfinger, the redoubtable doyenne of POV, has the last word on the pleasure all these people bring to those of us who participate vicariously in this wonderful world of opera: "Opera is often referred to as the most sublime of the art forms. It combines the dramatic, vocal, orchestral and choral arts and, in the magic of its lighting, costumes and scenery, the visual arts as well. With its ravishing vocal risk-taking, opera is like a vocal Olympics . . . Its power and beauty will reach into your hearts and touch you in places you didn't know were there . . . Opera has the ability to transform the audience and envelop it in a shared experience reminding us of our common humanity."

APPENDIX A
VANCOUVER OPERA
PRODUCTIONS, SPRING 1960
TO 2009–10

*Canadian premiere
**North American premiere
***World premiere

BY SEASON:

Spring 1960
Carmen (Bizet)
April 2, 5, 7, 9, 1960

1960–61
La Bohème (Puccini)
November 5, 8, 10, 11, 1960

La Traviata (Verdi)
May 4, 6, 9, 11, 13, 1961

1961–62
The Tales of Hoffmann (Offenbach)
October 12, 14, 17, 19, 21, 1961

Rigoletto (Verdi)
March 8, 10, 13, 15, 17, 1962

1962–63
Tosca (Puccini)
October 18, 20, 23, 25, 27, 1962

Faust (Gounod)
March 7, 9, 12, 14, 16, 1963

Aida (Verdi)
April 27; May 1, 4, 7, 9, 11, 1963

1963–64
Norma (Bellini)
October 17, 19, 22, 24, 26, 1963

The Barber of Seville (Rossini)
February 20, 22, 25, 27, 29, 1964

La Bohème (Puccini)
May 1, 5, 9, 1964

The Consul (Menotti)
May 2, 6, 8, 1964

1964–65
The Marriage of Figaro (Mozart)
November 19, 21, 24, 26, 27, 1964

The Italian Girl in Algiers (Rossini)
February 20, 23, 25, 27; March
2, 1965

Carmen (Bizet)
April 24, 28; May 1, 4, 6, 8, 1965

1965–66
Madama Butterfly (Puccini)
October 28, 30; November 2, 4,
6, 1965

Il Trovatore (Verdi)
February 17, 19, 22, 24, 26, 1966

1966–67
Cavalleria Rusticana (Mascagni)
and *Pagliacci* (Leoncavallo)
October 13, 15, 18, 20, 22, 1966

Lucia di Lammermoor (Donizetti)
March 11, 15, 18, 22, 25, 29, 1967

La Traviata (Verdi)
May 4, 6, 9, 11, 13, 1967

1967–68
Rigoletto (Verdi)
October 21, 25, 28; November 1,
4, 1967

The Flying Dutchman (Wagner)
February 3, 7, 10, 13, 1968

Tosca (Puccini)
May 1, 4, 7, 9, 11, 1968

1968–69
The Barber of Seville (Rossini)
November 14, 16, 20, 23, 27, 1968

Faust (Gounod)
February 20, 22, 25, 27; March
1, 1969

Manon (Massenet)
May 1, 3, 6, 8, 10, 1969

1969–70
Salome (R. Strauss)
October 2, 4, 8, 10, 1969

The Elixir of Love (Donizetti)
November 20, 22, 25, 27, 29, 1969

La Bohème (Puccini)
February 21, 24, 26, 28, 1970

Un Ballo in Maschera (Verdi)
April 30; May 2, 6, 9, 1970

1970–71
Aida (Verdi)
October 1, 3, 6, 8, 10, 1970

Madama Butterfly (Puccini)
February 18, 20, 23 (matinee), 25,
27, 1971

The Tales of Hoffmann (Offenbach)
April 29; May 1, 5, 8, 1971

1971–72
Il Trovatore (Verdi)
September 30; October 2, 6, 9, 1971

Cavalleria Rusticana (Mascagni)
and *Pagliacci* (Leoncavallo)
February 17, 19, 24, 26; March 2
(children's matinee), 1972

Turandot (Puccini)
April 27, 29; May 3, 6, 1972

1972–73
Lucrezia Borgia (Donizetti)
October 26, 28; November 1, 4, 8,
11, 1972

The Marriage of Figaro (Mozart)
February 15, 17, 22, 24, 1973

Tosca (Puccini)
April 26, 28; May 1, 3, 5, 1973

1973–74
Don Carlo (Verdi)
October 25, 27, 31; November 3,
1973

Carmen (Bizet)
February 14, 16, 21, 23, 26, 1974

La Traviata (Verdi)
April 25, 27, 30; May 2, 4, 1974

1974–75
Lucia di Lammermoor (Donizetti)
October 24, 26, 30; November 2,
1974

Rigoletto (Verdi)
January 30; February 1, 4
(children's matinee), 6, 8, 1975

La Buona Figliuola (Piccinni)
February 16, 23, 1975; Resident
Artists' production in the
Playhouse Theatre

Die Walküre (Wagner)
March 13, 15, 19, 22, 1975

The Gondoliers (Gilbert and
Sullivan)
April 24, 26, 30; May 3, 1975

1975–76
Semiramide (Rossini)
October 23, 25, 29; November 1,
1975

The Queen of Spades (Tchaikovsky)
January 29, 31; February 5, 7, 1976

Faust (Gounod)
March 11, 13, 16, 18, 20, 1976

The Merry Widow (Lehár)
April 22, 24, 27, 29; May 1, 4, 1976

1976–77
  La Bohème (Puccini)
  October 21, 23, 26, 28, 30, 1976

  Mignon (Thomas)
  January 27, 29; February 3, 5, 1977

  Die Fledermaus (J. Strauss II)
  March 10, 12, 17, 19, 1977

  Un Ballo in Maschera (Verdi)
  April 21, 23, 28, 30, 1977

1977 Fall Repertory Season
  Le Roi de Lahore (Massenet)
  September 23, 25, 28; October 1, 9
  (matinee), 1977

  La Fille du Régiment (Donizetti)
  September 30; October 2, 5, 8, 15
  (matinee), 1977

  Don Giovanni (Mozart)
  October 7, 12, 14, 16 (matinee),
  22, 1977

1978 Spring Repertory Season
  Madama Butterfly (Puccini)
  March 29; April 1, 6, 1978

  The Magic Flute (Mozart)
  March 31; April 2, 5, 8, 1978

  The Barber of Seville (Rossini)
  April 12, 14, 15, 1978

1978–79
  Aïda (Verdi)
  October 7, 12, 14, 1978

  Carmen (Bizet)
  February 2, 8, 10, 1979

  La Traviata (Verdi)
  March 31; April 3, 5, 7, 1979

1979–80
  Cavalleria Rusticana (Mascagni)
  and *Pagliacci* (Leoncavallo)
  October 13, 16, 18, 20, 1979

  The Bartered Bride (Smetana)
  January 26, 29, 31; February 2,
  1980

  Il Trovatore (Verdi)
  March 15, 18, 20, 22, 1980

1980–81
  Tosca (Puccini)
  October 25, 28, 30; November 1,
  1980

  Rigoletto (Verdi)
  January 24, 27, 29, 31, 1981

  Otello (Verdi)
  August 1, 4, 6, 8, 1981

1981–82
  Turandot (Puccini)
  October 24, 27, 29, 31, 1981

  La Cenerentola (Rossini)
  December 5, 8, 10, 12, 1981

  Lucia di Lammermoor (Donizetti)
  January 23, 26, 28, 30, 1982

  Roméo et Juliette (Gounod)
  March 13, 16, 18, 20, 1982

  Man of La Mancha (Wasserman,
  Leigh and Darion)
  April 23, 24, 25 (matinee), 27; May
  1 (matinee), 1982

1982–83
  La Bohème (Puccini)
  December 4, 7, 9, 11, 1982

  La Traviata (Verdi)
  January 22, 25, 27, 29, 1983

  Carmen (Bizet)
  March 12, 15, 17, 19, 1983

1983–84
  Nabucco (Verdi)
  October 22, 25, 27, 29, 1983

  Madama Butterfly (Puccini)
  January 21, 24, 26, 28, 1984

  The Tales of Hoffmann (Offenbach)
  March 10, 13, 15, 17, 1984

  Norma (Bellini)
  May 5, 8, 10, 12, 1984

1984–85
  Un Ballo in Maschera (Verdi)
  October 20, 23, 25, 27, 1984

  I Puritani (Bellini)
  January 19, 22, 24, 26, 1985

  Eugene Onegin (Tchaikovsky)
  March 9, 12, 14, 16, 1985

  Così Fan Tutte (Mozart)
  May 18, 21, 23, 25, 1985

1985–86
  Fidelio (Beethoven)
  October 19, 22, 24, 26, 1985

  The Barber of Seville (Rossini)
  January 18, 21, 23, 25, 1986

  The Magic Flute (Mozart)
  March 8, 11, 13, 15, 1986

  Carmen (Bizet)
  May 3, 6, 8, 10, 12, 1986

1986–87
  From the House of the Dead°°
  (Janáček)
  October 4, 7, 9, 11, 1986

  The Marriage of Figaro (Mozart)
  January 24, 27, 29, 31, 1987

  Madama Butterfly (Puccini)
  March 7, 10, 12, 14, 1987

  Lucia di Lammermoor (Donizetti)
  May 2, 5, 7, 9, 1987

1987–88
  La Bohème (Puccini)
  October 24, 27, 29, 31, 1987

  The Cunning Little Vixen°
  (Janáček)
  January 30; February 2, 4, 6, 1988

  The Turn of the Screw (Britten)
  March 12, 15, 17, 19, 1988

  Die Fledermaus (J. Strauss II)
  April 30; May 3, 5, 7, 1988

1988–89
  Don Giovanni (Mozart)
  October 22, 25, 27, 29, 1988

  Ariadne auf Naxos (R. Strauss)
  January 21, 24, 26, 28, 1989

  Rigoletto (Verdi)
  February 25, 28; March 2, 4, 1989

  La Traviata (Verdi)
  April 22, 25, 27, 29, 1989

1989–90
  The Rake's Progress (Stravinsky)
  October 21, 24, 26, 28, 1989

  Norma (Bellini)
  January 27, 30; February 1, 3, 1990

  Werther (Massenet)
  March 10, 13, 15, 17, 1990

  The Merry Widow (Lehár)
  April 28; May 1, 2, 5, 7, 9, 1990

1990–91
  Alcina° (Handel)
  October 27, 29; November 1, 3,
  1990

  The Barber of Seville (Rossini)
  January 26, 29, 31; February 2,
  4, 1991

  Salome (R. Strauss)
  March 16, 19, 21, 23, 1991

  Madama Butterfly (Puccini)
  April 27, 30; May 2, 4, 6, 8, 1991

1991–92

Carmen (Bizet)
November 2, 5, 7, 9, 11, 1991

Tosca (Puccini)
January 25, 28, 30; February 1, 1992

The Marriage of Figaro (Mozart)
March 21, 24, 26, 28, 30, 1992

Don Pasquale (Donizetti)
May 2, 5, 7, 9, 1992

1992–93

Rigoletto (Verdi)
October 17, 20, 22, 24, 26, 1992

The Magic Flute (Mozart)
January 30; February 2, 4, 6, 8, 1993

Dialogues of the Carmelites (Poulenc)
March 13, 16, 18, 20, 1993

La Bohème (Puccini)
April 24, 27, 29; May 1, 2, 3, 1993

1993–94

La Traviata (Verdi)
October 23, 26, 28, 30; November 1, 1993

Jenůfa (Janáček)
January 29; February 1, 3, 5, 1994

Don Giovanni (Mozart)
March 19, 22, 24, 26, 28, 1994

Die Fledermaus (J. Strauss II)
April 23, 26, 28, 30; May 1 (matinee), 2, 1994

The Architect°°° (MacIntyre and Cone)
June 11, 13, 14, 15, 17, 18, 20, 22, 1994

1994–95

Nabucco (Verdi)
October 15, 18, 20, 22, 24, 1994

The Pearl Fishers (Bizet)
November 19, 22, 24, 26, 28, 1994

Peter Grimes (Britten)
January 28, 31; February 2, 4, 6, 1995

The Pirates of Penzance (Gilbert and Sullivan)
March 18, 21, 23, 25, 26 (matinee), 27, 1995

Madama Butterfly (Puccini)
April 29; May 2, 4, 6, 8, 11, 13, 1995

1995–96

Faust (Gounod)
October 21, 24, 26, 28, 30, 1995

Così Fan Tutte (Mozart)
November 25, 28, 30; December 2, 4, 1995

Carmen (Bizet)
February 3, 6, 8, 10, 12, 15, 17, 1996

The Makropulos Case (Janáček)
March 16, 19, 21, 23, 25, 1996

Candide (Bernstein)
June 8–29, 1996; eighteen performances, Vancouver Playhouse

Hansel and Gretel (Humperdinck)
June 29, 1996; part of Vancouver International Festival

1996–97

The Marriage of Figaro (Mozart)
October 19, 22, 24, 26, 28, 1996

Jenůfa (Janáček)
November 23, 26, 28, 30; December 2, 1996

Susannah° (Floyd)
February 1, 4, 6, 8, 10, 1997

Shenyang Peking Opera
February 21, 22, 23, 1997

Turandot (Puccini)
March 15, 18, 20, 22, 24, 27, 29, 1997

The Mikado (Gilbert and Sullivan)
May 10, 13, 15, 17, 19, 22, 24, 25 (matinee), 1997

1997–98

Il Trovatore (Verdi)
October 18, 21, 23, 25, 27, 1997

Salome (R. Strauss)
November 22, 25, 27, 29; December 1, 1997

X-treme Opera
January 31; February 3, 5, 7, 9, 1998

La Bohème (Puccini)
March 21, 24, 26, 28, 30; April 2, 4, 1998

The Barber of Seville (Rossini)
May 2, 5, 7, 9, 11, 14, 1998

1998–99

Tosca (Puccini)
November 21, 24, 26, 28, 30, 1998

Roméo et Juliette (Gounod)
January 30; February 2, 4, 6, 8, 1999

La Traviata (Verdi)
March 13, 16, 18, 20, 22, 1999

Bluebeard's Castle (Bartók) and **Erwartung** (Schoenberg)
May 1, 4, 6, 8, 10, 1999

1999–2000

Rigoletto (Verdi)
October 16, 19, 21, 23, 25, 1999

The Elixir of Love (Donizetti)
November 20, 23, 25, 27, 29, 1999

Don Giovanni (Mozart)
March 25, 28, 30; April 1, 3, 2000

Madama Butterfly (Puccini)
April 29; May 2, 4, 6, 8, 2000

2000–01

Lucia di Lammermoor (Donizetti)
October 14, 17, 19, 21, 2000

The Rake's Progress (Stravinsky)
November 18, 21, 23, 25, 2000

The Flying Dutchman (Wagner)
March 24, 27, 29, 31, 2001

The Magic Flute (Mozart)
April 28; May 1, 3, 5, 7, 2001

2001–02

The Marriage of Figaro (Mozart)
October 13, 16, 18, 20, 22, 2001

Die Fledermaus (J. Strauss II)
November 17, 20, 22, 24, 2001

Of Mice and Men (Floyd)
March 23, 26, 28, 30, 2002

Carmen (Bizet)
April 27; May 2, 4, 6, 8, 10, 2002

2002–03

Aida (Verdi)
October 12, 15, 17, 19, 21, 23, 2002

La Fille du Régiment (Donizetti)
November 23, 26, 28, 30, 2002

Elektra (R. Strauss)
March 22, 25, 27, 29, 2003

La Bohème (Puccini)
May 3, 6, 8, 10, 12, 14, 2003

2003–04

The Girl of the Golden West (Puccini)
October 11, 14, 16, 18, 2003

2003–04 *cont.*

The Barber of Seville (Rossini)
November 22, 25, 27, 29; December
1, 2003

The Threepenny Opera (Weill and
Brecht)
March 20, 23, 25, 27, 2004

La Traviata (Verdi)
May 1, 4, 6, 8, 10, 12, 2004

2004–05
Der Rosenkavalier (R. Strauss)
October 16, 19, 21, 23, 2004

Madama Butterfly (Puccini)
November 27, 30; December 2, 4, 7,
9, 11, 2004

Così Fan Tutte (Mozart)
March 12, 15, 17, 19, 2005

Un Ballo in Maschera (Verdi)
April 30; May 3, 5, 7, 2005

2005–06
Turandot (Puccini)
October 22, 25, 27, 29; November
1, 3, 2005

Dialogues of the Carmelites
(Poulenc)
November 26, 29; December 1,
3, 2005

Don Giovanni (Mozart)
March 4, 7, 9, 11, 13, 2006

Faust (Gounod)
April 22, 25, 27, 29; May 2, 2006

2006–07
Macbeth (Verdi)
November 25, 28, 30; December
2, 2006

The Magic Flute (Mozart)
January 27, 30; February 1, 3, 6,
8, 2007

Ariadne auf Naxos (R. Strauss)
March 3, 6, 8, 10, 2007

Tosca (Puccini)
April 21, 24, 26, 28; May 1, 2007

2007–08
Cavalleria Rusticana (Mascagni)
and **Pagliacci** (Leoncavallo)
November 10, 13, 15, 17, 2007

The Italian Girl in Algiers (Rossini)
January 26, 29, 31; February 2,
2008

Fidelio (Beethoven)
March 22, 25, 27, 29, 2008

La Bòheme (Puccini)
April 27, 29; May 1, 3, 6, 8, 2008

2008–09
Eugene Onegin (Tchaikovsky)
November 22, 25, 27, 29, 2008

Carmen (Bizet)
January 24, 27, 29, 31; February
3, 5, 2009

Rigoletto (Verdi)
March 7, 10, 12, 14, 17, 2009

Salome (R. Strauss)
May 2, 5, 7, 9, 2009

2009–10
Norma (Bellini)
November 28; December 1, 3, 5,
2009

Nixon in China° (Adams)
March 13, 16, 18, 20, 2010

The Marriage of Figaro (Mozart)
April 24, 27, 29; May 1, 4, 2010

Madama Butterfly (Puccini)
May 29; June 1, 3, 5, 8, 10, 2010

BY TITLE:

Aida (Verdi)
1962–63; 1970–71; 1978–79;
2002–03

Alcina° (Handel)
1990–91

The Architect°°° (MacIntyre and
Cone)
1993–94

Ariadne auf Naxos (R. Strauss)
1988–89; 2006–07

Un Ballo in Maschera (Verdi)
1969–70; 1976–77; 1984–85;
2004–05

The Barber of Seville (Rossini)
1963–64; 1968–69; 1977–78; 1985–
86; 1990–91; 1997–98; 2003–04

The Bartered Bride (Smetana)
1979–80

Bluebeard's Castle (Bartók) and
Erwartung (Schoenberg)
1998–99

La Bohème (Puccini)
1960–61; 1963–64; 1969–70; 1976–
77; 1982–83; 1987–88; 1992–93;
1997–98; 2002–03; 2007–08

La Buona Figliuola (Piccinni)
1974–75

Candide (Bernstein)
1995–96

Carmen (Bizet)
Spring 1960; 1964–65; 1973–74;
1978–79; 1982–83; 1985–86;
1991–92; 1995–96; 2001–02;
2008–09

Cavalleria Rusticana (Mascagni) and
Pagliacci (Leoncavallo)
1966–67; 1971–72; 1979–80;
2007–08

La Cenerentola (Rossini)
1981–82

The Consul (Menotti)
1963–64

Così Fan Tutte (Mozart)
1984–85; 1995–96; 2004–05

The Cunning Little Vixen° (Janáček)
1987–88

Dialogues of the Carmelites (Poulenc)
1992–93; 2005–06

Don Carlo (Verdi)
1973–74

Don Giovanni (Mozart)
1977–78; 1988–89; 1993–94; 1999–
2000; 2005–06

Don Pasquale (Donizetti)
1991–92

Elektra (R. Strauss)
2002–03

The Elixir of Love (Donizetti)
1969–70; 1999–2000

Eugene Onegin (Tchaikovsky)
1984–85; 2008–09

Faust (Gounod)
1962–63; 1968–69; 1975–76; 1995–
96; 2005–06

Fidelio (Beethoven)
1985–86; 2007–08

La Fille du Régiment (Donizetti)
1977–78; 2002–03

Die Fledermaus (J. Strauss II)
1976–77; 1987–88; 1993–94;
2001–02

The Flying Dutchman (Wagner)
1967–68; 2000–01

From the House of the Dead** (Janáček)
1986–87

The Girl of the Golden West (Puccini)
2003–04

The Gondoliers (Gilbert and Sullivan)
1974–75

Hansel and Gretel (Humperdinck)
1995–96

The Italian Girl in Algiers (Rossini)
1964–65; 2007–08

Jenůfa (Janáček)
1993–94; 1996–97

Lucia di Lammermoor (Donizetti)
1966–67; 1974–75; 1981–82; 1986–87; 2000–01

Lucrezia Borgia (Donizetti)
1972–73

Macbeth (Verdi)
2006–07

Madama Butterfly (Puccini)
1965–66; 1970–71; 1977–78; 1983–84; 1986–87; 1990–91; 1994–95; 1999–2000; 2004–05; 2009–10

The Magic Flute (Mozart)
1977–78; 1985–86; 1992–93; 2000–01; 2006–07

The Makropulos Case (Janáček)
1995–96

Man of La Mancha (Wasserman, Leigh and Darion)
1981–82

Manon (Massenet)
1968–69

The Marriage of Figaro (Mozart)
1964–65; 1972–73; 1986–87; 1991–92; 1996–97; 2001–02; 2009–10

The Merry Widow (Lehár)
1975–76; 1989–90

Mignon (Thomas)
1976–77

The Mikado (Gilbert and Sullivan)
1996–97

Nabucco (Verdi)
1983–84; 1994–95

Nixon in China* (Adams)
2009–10

Norma (Bellini)
1963–64; 1983–84; 1989–90; 2009–10

Of Mice and Men (Floyd)
2001–02

Otello (Verdi)
1980–81

The Pearl Fishers (Bizet)
1994–95

Peter Grimes (Britten)
1994–95

The Pirates of Penzance (Gilbert and Sullivan)
1994–95

I Puritani (Bellini)
1984–85

The Queen of Spades (Tchaikovsky)
1975–76

The Rake's Progress (Stravinsky)
1989–90; 2000–01

Rigoletto (Verdi)
1961–62; 1967–68; 1974–75; 1980–81; 1988–89; 1992–93; 1999–2000; 2008–09

Le Roi de Lahore (Massenet)
1977–78

Roméo et Juliette (Gounod)
1981–82; 1998–99

Der Rosenkavalier (R. Strauss)
2004–05

Salome (R. Strauss)
1969–70; 1990–91; 1997–98; 2008–09

Semiramide (Rossini)
1975–76

Shenyang Peking Opera
1996–97

Susannah* (Floyd)
1996–97

The Tales of Hoffmann (Offenbach)
1961–62; 1970–71; 1983–84

The Threepenny Opera (Weill and Brecht)
2003–04

Tosca (Puccini)
1962–63; 1967–68; 1972–73; 1980–81; 1991–92; 1998–99; 2006–07

La Traviata (Verdi)
1960–61; 1966–67; 1973–74; 1978–79; 1982–83; 1988–89; 1993–94; 1998–99; 2003–04

Il Trovatore (Verdi)
1965–66; 1971–72; 1979–80; 1997–98

Turandot (Puccini)
1971–72; 1981–82; 1996–97; 2005–06

The Turn of the Screw (Britten)
1987–88

Die Walküre (Wagner)
1974–75

Werther (Massenet)
1989–90

X-treme Opera
1997–98

APPENDIX B
PACIFIC OPERA VICTORIA PRODUCTIONS, 1980–81 TO 2009–10

*Canadian premiere
**World premiere

BY SEASON:

1980–81
The Barber of Seville (Rossini) – McPherson Playhouse
September 17, 19, 20, 22, 1980

Madama Butterfly (Puccini) – McPherson Playhouse
February 18, 20, 21, 23, 1981

1981–82
The Abduction from the Seraglio (Mozart) – McPherson Playhouse
September 16, 18, 19, 21, 1981

La Traviata (Verdi) – McPherson Playhouse
February 17, 19, 20, 22, 24, 1982

1982–83
Die Fledermaus (J. Strauss II) – McPherson Playhouse
September 16, 18, 21, 23, 25, 1982

Cinderella in Salerno (Walker and Beaumont; adapted from Rossini's *La Cenerentola* with original dialogue by Peter Wylde) – McPherson Playhouse
December 17, 18, 1982

Tosca (Puccini) – McPherson Playhouse
February 17, 19, 21, 24, 26, 1983

1983–84

The Elixir of Love (Donizetti) – McPherson Playhouse
September 15, 17, 20, 22, 24, 1983

Amahl and the Night Visitors (Menotti) – Christ Church Cathedral
December 19, 20, 21, 22, 23, 1983

Carmen (Bizet) – McPherson Playhouse
February 16, 18, 20, 23, 25, 1984

1984–85

Rigoletto (Verdi) – McPherson Playhouse
September 15, 18, 20, 22, 1984

Faust (Gounod) – McPherson Playhouse
February 14, 16, 18, 21, 23, 1985

1985–86

Don Giovanni (Mozart) – McPherson Playhouse
September 19, 21, 24, 26, 28, 1985

La Bohème (Puccini) – McPherson Playhouse
February 13, 15, 17, 20, 22, 1986

1986–87

Il Trovatore (Verdi) – McPherson Playhouse
September 25, 27, 29; October 2, 4, 1986

The Magic Flute (Mozart) – McPherson Playhouse
February 12, 14, 16, 19, 21, 1987

1987–88

Lucia di Lammermoor (Donizetti) – McPherson Playhouse
September 24, 26, 28; October 1, 3, 1987

Fidelio (Beethoven) – McPherson Playhouse
February 11, 13, 16, 18, 20, 1988

1988–89

The Barber of Seville (Rossini) – McPherson Playhouse
September 22, 24, 27, 29; October 1, 1988

The Tales of Hoffmann (Offenbach) – McPherson Playhouse, Canadian Opera Company Ensemble production sponsored by POV
November 18, 19, 1988

The Flying Dutchman (Wagner) – McPherson Playhouse
February 16, 18, 21, 23, 25, 1989

1989–90

La Cenerentola (Rossini) – McPherson Playhouse
September 21, 23, 26, 28, 30, 1989

Eugene Onegin (Tchaikovsky) – McPherson Playhouse
February 15, 17, 20, 22, 24, 1990

The Pirates of Penzance (Gilbert and Sullivan) – McPherson Playhouse
April 19, 21, 24, 26, 28, 1990

1990–91

The Marriage of Figaro (Mozart) – McPherson Playhouse
September 20, 22, 25, 27, 29, 1990

Roméo et Juliette (Gounod) – McPherson Playhouse
February 14, 16, 19, 21, 23, 1991

Madama Butterfly (Puccini) – McPherson Playhouse
April 11, 13, 16, 18, 20, 1991

1991–92

Così Fan Tutte (Mozart) – McPherson Playhouse
October 17, 19, 22, 24, 26, 1991

Un Ballo in Maschera (Verdi) – McPherson Playhouse
February 13, 15, 18, 20, 22, 1992

Die Fledermaus (J. Strauss II) – Royal Theatre
April 9, 11, 14, 16, 18, 1992

1992–93

The Abduction from the Seraglio (Mozart) – McPherson Playhouse
October 15, 17, 20, 22, 24, 1992

A Midsummer Night's Dream (Britten) – McPherson Playhouse
February 11, 13, 16, 18, 20, 1993

The Merry Widow (Lehár) – Royal Theatre
April 15, 17, 20, 22, 24, 1993

1993–94

Don Pasquale (Donizetti) – McPherson Playhouse
September 23, 25, 28, 30; October 2, 1993

Der Freischütz ° (Weber) – McPherson Playhouse
February 10, 12, 15, 17, 19, 1994

La Traviata (Verdi) – Royal Theatre
April 28, 30; May 3, 5, 7, 1994

1994–95

La Fille du Régiment (Donizetti) – McPherson Playhouse
September 22, 24, 27, 29; October 1, 1994

Macbeth (Verdi) – McPherson Playhouse
February 16, 18, 21, 23, 25, 1995

La Bohème (Puccini) – Royal Theatre
April 27, 29; May 2, 4, 6, 1995

1995–96

The Elixir of Love (Donizetti) – McPherson Playhouse
September 21, 23, 26, 28, 30, 1995

The Love of Three Kings ° (Montemezzi) – McPherson Playhouse
February 15, 17, 20, 22, 24, 1996

Carmen (Bizet) – Royal Theatre
April 25, 27, 30; May 2, 4, 1996

1996–97

The Pearl Fishers (Bizet) – McPherson Playhouse
September 19, 21, 24, 26, 28, 1996

The Turn of the Screw (Britten) – McPherson Playhouse
February 13, 15, 18, 20, 22, 1997

Tosca (Puccini) – Royal Theatre
April 24, 26, 29; May 1, 3, 1997

1997–98

The Italian Girl in Algiers (Rossini) – McPherson Playhouse
September 18, 20, 23, 25, 27, 1997

Werther (Massenet) – McPherson Playhouse
February 12, 14, 17, 19, 21, 1998

Rigoletto (Verdi) – Royal Theatre
April 23, 25, 28, 30; May 2, 1998

1998–99

Un Ballo in Maschera (Verdi) – Royal Theatre
August 7, 9, 11, 13, 15, 1998

The Mikado (Gilbert and Sullivan) – Royal Theatre
September 12, 14, 16, 17, 19, 1998

Ariadne auf Naxos (R. Strauss) – McPherson Playhouse
February 18, 20, 23, 25, 27, 1999

Don Giovanni (Mozart) – Royal Theatre
April 22, 24, 27, 29; May 1, 1999

1999–2000
Madama Butterfly (Puccini) – Royal Theatre
October 14, 16, 19, 21, 23, 1999

Erewhon°° (Applebaum and Moore) – Royal Theatre
February 19, 24, 26, 2000

Il Trovatore (Verdi) – Royal Theatre
April 27, 29; May 2, 4, 6, 2000

2000–01
The Barber of Seville (Rossini) – Royal Theatre
October 12, 14, 17, 19, 21, 2000

The Taming of the Shrew° (Giannini) – McPherson Playhouse
February 15, 17, 20, 22, 24, 2001

Nabucco (Verdi) – Royal Theatre
April 19, 21, 24, 26, 28, 2001

2001–02
La Traviata (Verdi) – Royal Theatre
October 11, 13, 16, 18, 20, 2001

Julius Caesar (Handel) – Royal Theatre
February 16, 19, 21, 23, 2002

The Gypsy Baron (J. Strauss II) – Royal Theatre
April 25, 27, 30; May 2, 4, 2002

2002–03
La Bohème (Puccini) – Royal Theatre
October 10, 12, 15, 17, 19, 2002

Wozzeck (Berg) – Royal Theatre
February 13, 15, 20, 22, 2003

The Marriage of Figaro (Mozart) – Royal Theatre
April 24, 26, 29; May 1, 3, 2003

2003–04
Lucia di Lammermoor (Donizetti) – Royal Theatre
October 9, 11, 14, 16, 18, 2003

The Tempest° (Hoiby) – Royal Theatre
February 12, 14, 19, 21, 2004

Carmen (Bizet) – Royal Theatre
April 22, 24, 27, 29; May 1, 2004

2004–05
Norma (Bellini) – Royal Theatre
October 7, 9, 12, 14, 16, 2004

The Cunning Little Vixen (Janáček) – Royal Theatre
February 10, 12, 17, 19, 2005

Tosca (Puccini) – Royal Theatre
April 21, 23, 26, 28, 30, 2005

2005–06
Eugene Onegin (Tchaikovsky) – Royal Theatre
October 6, 8, 11, 13, 15, 2005

The Rape of Lucretia (Britten) – Royal Theatre
February 9, 11, 16, 18, 2006

Rigoletto (Verdi) – Royal Theatre
April 20, 22, 25, 27, 29, 2006

2006–07
Manon Lescaut (Puccini) – Royal Theatre
October 12, 14, 17, 19, 21, 2006

Daphne° (R. Strauss) – Royal Theatre
February 15, 17, 22, 24, 2007

Don Giovanni (Mozart) – Royal Theatre
April 19, 21, 24, 26, 28, 2007

2007–08
Idomeneo (Mozart) – Royal Theatre
October 11, 13, 16, 18, 20, 2007

Madama Butterfly (Puccini) – Royal Theatre
February 14, 16, 19, 21, 23, 2008

Regina° (Blitzstein) – Royal Theatre
April 17, 19, 22, 24, 26, 2008

2008–09
Thaïs (Massenet) – Royal Theatre
October 16, 18, 21, 23, 25, 2008

Semele (Handel) – Royal Theatre
February 14, 17, 19, 21, 2009

The Magic Flute (Mozart) – Royal Theatre
April 16, 18, 21, 23, 25, 2009

2009–10
La Traviata (Verdi) – Royal Theatre
October 1, 3 (matinee), 6, 8, 10, 2009

The Rake's Progress (Stravinsky) – Royal Theatre
November 12, 14 (matinee), 17, 19, 21, 2009

Capriccio (R. Strauss) – Royal Theatre
February 25, 27 (matinee); March 2, 4, 6, 2010

Così Fan Tutte (Mozart) – Royal Theatre
April 15, 17 (matinee), 20, 22, 24, 2010

BY TITLE:

The Abduction from the Seraglio (Mozart)
1981–82; 1992–93

Amahl and the Night Visitors (Menotti)
1983–84

Ariadne auf Naxos (R. Strauss)
1998–99

Un Ballo in Maschera (Verdi)
1991–92; 1998–99

The Barber of Seville (Rossini)
1980–81; 1988–89; 2000–01

La Bohème (Puccini)
1985–86; 1994–95; 2002–03

Capriccio (R. Strauss)
2009–10

Carmen (Bizet)
1983–84; 1995–96; 2003–04

La Cenerentola (Rossini)
1989–90

Cinderella in Salerno (Walker and Beaumont)
1982–83

Così Fan Tutte (Mozart)
1991–92; 2009–10

The Cunning Little Vixen (Janáček)
2004–05

Daphne° (R. Strauss)
2006–07

Don Giovanni (Mozart)
1985–86; 1998–99; 2006–07

Don Pasquale (Donizetti)
1993–94

The Elixir of Love (Donizetti)
1983–84; 1995–96

Erewhon°° (Moore and Applebaum)
1999–2000

Eugene Onegin (Tchaikovsky)
1989–90; 2005–06

Faust (Gounod)
1984–85

Fidelio (Beethoven)
1987–88

La Fille du Régiment (Donizetti)
1994–95

Die Fledermaus (J. Strauss II)
1982–83; 1991–92

The Flying Dutchman (Wagner)
1988–89

Der Freischütz* (Weber)
1993–94

The Gypsy Baron (J. Strauss II)
2001–02

Idomeneo (Mozart)
2007–08

The Italian Girl in Algiers (Rossini)
1997–98

Julius Caesar (Handel)
2001–02

The Love of Three Kings*
(Montemezzi)
1995–96

Lucia di Lammermoor (Donizetti)
1987–88; 2003–04

Macbeth (Verdi)
1994–95

Madama Butterfly (Puccini)
1980–81; 1990–91; 1999–2000;
2007–08

The Magic Flute (Mozart)
1986–87; 2008–09

Manon Lescaut (Puccini)
2006–07

The Marriage of Figaro (Mozart)
1990–91; 2002–03

The Merry Widow (Lehár)
1992–93

A Midsummer Night's Dream (Britten)
1992–93

The Mikado (Gilbert and Sullivan)
1998–99

Nabucco (Verdi)
2000–01

Norma (Bellini)
2004–05

The Pearl Fishers (Bizet)
1996–97

The Pirates of Penzance (Gilbert and
Sullivan)
1989–90

The Rake's Progress (Stravinsky)
2009–10

The Rape of Lucretia (Britten)
2005–06

Regina* (Blitzstein)
2007–08

Rigoletto (Verdi)
1984–85; 1997–98; 2005–06

Roméo et Juliette (Gounod)
1990–91

Semele (Handel)
2008–09

The Tales of Hoffmann (Offenbach)
1988–89

The Taming of the Shrew* (Giannini)
2000–01

The Tempest* (Hoiby)
2003–04

Thaïs (Massenet)
2008–09

Tosca (Puccini)
1982–83; 1996–97; 2004–05

La Traviata (Verdi)
1981–82; 1993–94; 2001–02;
2009–10

Il Trovatore (Verdi)
1986–87; 1999–2000

The Turn of the Screw (Britten)
1996–97

Werther (Massenet)
1997–98

Wozzeck (Berg)
2002–03

APPENDIX C
MODERN BAROQUE OPERA
PRODUCTIONS

Vancouver East Cultural Centre
(VECC)
*Canadian premiere
**North American premiere
***World premiere

1996
   Le Cinesi** (Gluck)
   May 26–June 8
   Seventeen performances at the
      Gastown Theatre
1997
   Orpheus and Eurydice (Gluck)
   February 5–15
   Seven performances at VECC

   The Music Master** (Paisiello)
   May 29–June 1
   Six performances at the Vancouver
      Children's Festival

   Le Cinesi (Gluck)
   October 28–November 8
   Eight performances at VECC
1998
   Scipione** (Handel)
   June 9–19
   Nine performances at VECC
1999
   Arcifanfano, King of Fools* (Von
      Dittersdorf)
   May 5–13; during the 29th Opera
      America Conference
   Six performances at VECC

   Venus and Adonis (Alessandro
      Scarlatti) and *The Amazement***
      (Domenico Scarlatti)
   December 2–11
   Six performances at VECC

2000

Angelica and Medoro** (Porpora)
May 31–June 3
Four performances at VECC

The Choice of Hercules* (Handel)
October 20, 21
Two performances at the Vancouver
    Playhouse

*The Child, the Book and the
    Broomstick**** (Burrich and
    Morris)
December 2–12
Nine performances at VECC

2002

*120 Songs for the Marquis de
    Sade**** (Hannan and Hinton)
March 2–16
Nine performances at VECC

2003

The Diana Cantata*** (Hannan
    and Hinton) and *Ino***
    (Telemann)
February 5–8
Four performances at VECC

Max & Moritz (Corness and
    Turner)
May/June
Five performances at the Vancouver
    Children's Festival

*The Garden (Il filosofo di
    campagna)*** (Galuppi)
September 30–October 4
Five performances at VECC

NOTES

PROLOGUE

1. Donald J. Grout, *A Short History
    of Opera*, 57–59. Including the
    bibliography and index, Grout's
    "short" history runs to 913 pages.
2. Ibid., 365.
3. Robert Dale McIntosh, *A
    Documentary History of Music
    in Victoria, Vol. 1*. Although
    the date of the opening of the
    Royal is often given as 1861,
    this newspaper item confirms
    that it must have opened in
    1860. Renaming the theatre
    was obviously done after the
    appearance of the article. The
    cited *Colonist* references in the text
    are all from McIntosh.
4. Quaintance Eaton, "Ladies on the
    Loose."
5. If "English" appeared in the name
    of the company, it usually meant
    that all productions were sung in
    that language.
6. See Darko Zubrinic's website,
    www.croatianhistory.net/etf/
    et12a.html. The website shows a
    photograph of De Murska on the
    London stage.
7. See the Juch history website,
    www.juch.net/ferlach.htm, for
    photographs of Emma Juch.
8. "Opera House Opened," *The
    World*. When the permanent seats
    were installed, the house seating
    capacity was 1,200.
9. Mary Jane Matz, *Opera: Grand and
    Not So Grand*, 60–61.
10. Robert Dale McIntosh, *A
    Documentary History of Music in
    Victoria, Vol. 2*, 461–78.

OVERTURE

1. For an excellent treatise
    on amateur musical groups
    throughout the province, see
    McIntosh, *The History of Music in
    British Columbia, 1850–1950*.
2. Ray Chatelin, "Opera," in *The
    Greater Vancouver Book*.
3. Among the first who accepted
    were Mrs. B.T. Rogers, Mrs.
    Ronald Graham, Messrs. Walter
    Koerner and Harold Foley.

ACT I

1. David Watmough, *The Unlikely
    Pioneer*, 46.

2. A member of the VOA Guild had
    provided Andrew with her toy
    poodle to carry around on stage.
    Unfortunately the animal was not
    used to the situation, and when
    Andrew began to sing, it nipped
    her on the lip. This anecdote was
    contributed by singer Heather
    Thomson-Price in an interview.
3. Don Obe, "Opera Off. So's
    Everything Else." For a different
    version of this anecdote, see
    Watmough, *The Unlikely Pioneer*,
    48–49.
4. Grist is an American coloratura
    who, in 1960, made her European
    debut in Cologne. She was the
    first black American woman to
    appear in the opera houses of
    Europe. Her parents were from
    the West Indies, but she was born
    and brought up in New York City.
5. Thomson's performance resulted
    in an offer from Sadler's Wells
    Opera, now called the English
    National Opera, to join the
    company in London, which she
    accepted.
6. Although the preference for
    hearing opera sung in the original
    language preceded the era of
    surtitles, readers should bear in
    mind that the VOA offered libretti
    for sale in the theatre lobby prior
    to each performance.
7. Thomson made her New York
    debut in 1969 as Marguerite
    in *Faust* at the New York City
    Opera. In 1974 she made her
    European debut at the Augsburg
    opera house as Violetta in *La
    Traviata*. Over the years, she has
    appeared in leading roles for five
    Vancouver Opera and two Pacific
    Opera Victoria productions.
8. Matinee performances for adult
    patrons continued sporadically
    until May 1997. See Appendix A.
9. Three performances were to
    follow in Edmonton as part of
    the cost-sharing arrangements
    between VOA and Edmonton
    Opera.
10. After he left Vancouver Opera,
    Guttman's career reached
    international heights. For his
    role in the development of opera
    in Canada, he was inducted as a

Member into the Order of Canada in 1988 and was awarded the Order of British Columbia in 2002.

INTERLUDE

1. Ray Chatelin, "Sour note to Vancouver's opera brass."
2. Roy Shields, "Discordant notes at the Vancouver Opera."
3. Ibid.
4. John Becker, *Discord*, 61.
5. Ibid.
6. Dave Robbins was a renowned jazz and classical musician and teacher. His career is documented in *The Encyclopedia of Music in Canada*. King said the recording session referred to took place in April or May. He explained that the contractor is the musician who assembles the orchestra, informs the other musicians what they are going to play and organizes the logistics of the work. Zena Wagstaff continued as the VO Orchestra contractor for some time after the first production.

ACT II

1. Vernon studied conducting under Otto-Werner Mueller at the Victoria School of Music. He went to Vienna for further studies before returning to Canada in 1975 to take up a number of conducting and operatic posts.
2. The venue was not specified on *The Barber's* program, and no program is extant for *Butterfly*, but Erika Kurth confirms that both were staged in the McPherson Playhouse.
3. Timothy Vernon, "A message from the Artistic Director."
4. Christopher Dafoe, "The little opera house that grew." One year before this article was published, Ben Heppner was in Victoria, participating for no fee in a fundraising concert for POV. One wonders if it was a payback gesture on his part.
5. Beverly Morgan has since changed her name to Jessica Ryder.
6. Pacific Opera Victoria, "Message from the President." The other milestone was the 1997 production

of *The Turn of the Screw*, which will be discussed in a later chapter.
7. Russell Braun is the son of baritone Victor Braun, who had a distinguished operatic career. Victor Braun died in 2001.
8. Stuart Hamilton is best known as the quizmaster for the CBC Radio broadcast of the "Saturday Afternoon at the Opera Quiz." He was also the first Music Director of the Canadian Opera Company Ensemble.
9. A report written in 2001 indicated that POV's volunteer chorus was not unique. At that time, the chorus of Opéra de Québec (Quebec City) was also non-professional. Since then, however, it has become a professional group. Calgary, Edmonton and Manitoba opera companies also have volunteer choruses.

ACT III

1. Sharman King interview.
2. Maria Pellegrini emigrated to Canada in 1958, and became a naturalized Canadian in 1965. Some years after her performance in Vancouver, she was called the greatest Butterfly alive by Lord Harewood of Covent Garden. Siedentop later changed her name to Sieden.
3. King explained that VOA never used a prompter, and removing the box would not only make more room in the pit, but would greatly improve the visibility of the conductor for those seated at the rear and sides of the pit.
4. The proscenium opening of the QE Theatre was 70 feet wide (21.3 m) and 30 feet high (9.1 m); the curtain line to the rear wall measures 64 feet. When the current renovations are complete, the proscenium opening will be reduced to 56 feet in width (19.5 m).
5. Irena Welhasch's career began in Winnipeg with Manitoba Opera during the late 1970s and early 1980s. She made her debut in a major role with the Canadian Opera Company in 1983. Victor Braun sang the same role for L'Opéra de Montréal in 1983 and

1988. His son, Russell Braun, has achieved fame in his own right as a singer.
6. Readers are reminded of POV's 1983 production of *Carmen*, which was considered bold by having a ghetto blaster play the prelude music. Pintilie left the VO production a week before the opening because of disagreements with the conductor. He was replaced by the associate director, Ceri Sherlock, who wholeheartedly supported Pintilie's direction.
7. Jamie Portman, "Operatic tantrums out; Director seeks solid performance." Timothy Vernon of POV said that what these stage directors produce is called "Eurotrash" in opera-speak.
8. *La Traviata* may have been one of Järvefelt's last productions. His death at the age of forty-two was announced in London on November 30, 1989.
9. John Cox directed a new production of the work in 1975 at the Glyndebourne Festival Opera. The same production would be staged by VO. Capital funding for the surtitle introduction was supplied by the Martha Lou Henley Charitable Foundation, the City of Vancouver, the BC Lottery Fund and the Vancouver Foundation.
10. According to those close to the situation, Fyfe, then eighty years of age, was asked by Hallam to leave. He died in 1995.
11. Cosar, a singer and voice teacher, has been singing in the VO chorus since October 1973, except for a two-year period of study in England.
12. Yvonne Siemens, "How the set reflects the opera." Mr Big & Tall was a well-known Vancouver store. It is still in business.
13. David E. Gillanders, "Message from the President."
14. The venue was the Russian Hall, 600 Campbell Avenue in Vancouver's Downtown Eastside. At the time, Underhill was the Artistic Director of VNM, and continued in that position until 2006.

ACT IV

1. Baroque refers to a style of composition that flourished in Europe from 1600 to 1750. In contrast to the Renaissance style, which preceded it, Baroque music has more complex harmonics and contrasts. More emphasis was placed on the solo performer, who often improvised by elaborate vocal ornamentation, especially when the score was not fully written out, as was often the case.

2. Because it is a project grant, the Alcan Award recipient is identified the year before the actual presentation. As a condition of the award, the work must be premiered at The Vancouver East Cultural Centre. By giving MBO a matching amount, Vancouver New Music became the co-producer of *120 Songs for the Marquis de Sade*. Hutchinson was by that time MBO's full-time Artistic Director, having given up all her other work in 1999.

3. David Shefsiek, POV's Executive Director, questioned this figure. He believed a Metropolitan singer's highest fee per performance then was set at $15,000.

4. A lirico spinto voice possesses the power and edge required for dramatic climaxes. The term applies to both male and female voices.

5. When young, Livingston had dropped out of the voice program at the Conservatory to care for her diabetic mother for the next twenty years. During rehearsals for the opera, her mother became gravely ill. Livingston was able to fly to her bedside in Comox the day after the dress rehearsal to see her, thanks to Maestro Vernon's arrangements.

6. Burton L. Kurth was a singer, composer, choirmaster, and supervisor of the Vancouver schools music programs for many years, and Olive Kurth was Erika Kurth's first voice teacher.

7. Mrs. Faris became President in 1996–97. She is the current Chair of the Vancouver Opera Foundation.

8. Readers will recall the dismal financial record of the NDP provincial government of the 1990s. In addition to the economy, stiff competition from events at the new Ford Centre for Performing Arts and the Chan Centre for the Performing Arts were siphoning off entertainment dollars from VO. The New Year's Eve concert of the Three Tenors on December 31, 1997, is estimated alone to have removed $14 million from the revenue pool of local arts organizations.

9. VAST was an initiative of the Vancouver Foundation based on the model of the National Foundation for the Arts in the US. It was begun in 1995 in recognition that funding for the arts was not a priority for the NDP provincial government, which, together with increasing competition for the entertainment dollar, was putting a severe strain on the major arts organizations in the city. By rigorous involvement with management and Boards, VAST assisted them to develop a sustainable, long-term plan for a sound fiscal future. VO had to satisfy VAST that its business plan met the VAST criteria before it could qualify for the grants.

10. Rob Hallam went to Nebraska as President and CEO of the Omaha Symphony Orchestra. David Agler has been very much in-demand on the international scene as an opera and symphonic conductor since leaving VO, and has recently completed his second term as Artistic Director of Wexford Festival Opera in Wexford, Ireland.

11. The second thing Wright did that Tuck admired was honouring Irving Guttman.

12. The other two were *I Puritani* on August 8, 2006, and *Werther* (Massenet) on October 14, 2006.

13. Lotte Lenya, the darling of the cabaret scene in Berlin in the late 1920s and early 1930s, and Weill's wife, recorded her own version of "Mack the Knife" in 1956 on a CD titled *Kurt Weill: Berlin & American Theater Songs* (CBS MK42658), which many people in the audience would also have been familiar with.

14. The cooperation VO received is not at all unusual in the operatic world. Tim Vernon of Pacific Opera Victoria also speaks of being on the receiving end of such collegiality.

15. Eaglen, an international star from England, is best known as a Wagnerian soprano, although her repertoire is by no means limited to works by that composer. In addition to her demanding stage and recording commitments, she is Artist in Residence at the University of Washington in Seattle and Principal Voice Instructor for the Young Artists Program of Seattle Opera.

16. Sirlin used this technique to great effect in the Broadway production of *Kiss of the Spider Woman*.

17. Vancouver Opera, *Voices of The Magic Flute*. This publication was inserted in the program of the opera.

18. This figure includes the cost of the school version of the show.

19. Among other things, Tuck was responsible for the community programs "Where Cultures Meet" and "Opera Speaks" that were offered in the months before staging, and gave the pre-show talks in the theatre before every performance, as he has done since shortly after joining the company in 1997. Regrettably, Randy Smith, who had made such a valuable contribution to the project, did not live to see it through to production.

20. Robert McQueen, "Director's Notes" and Derrick Inouye, "Conductor's Notes" from the *Magic Flute* program.

FINALE

1. Victoria has two large post-secondary institutions in close proximity to the Royal Theatre, University of Victoria and Royal Roads University, with a

Bravo!

significant student population, many studying music.

2. As an aside, the film director Woody Allen was hired by Los Angeles Opera to direct a production of *Gianni Schicchi,* Puccini's comic one-act piece, which opened on September 6, 2008. Allen is new to directing opera, and the reviews of the show make for interesting reading.

3. Thanks to Emily Vroom, Development Manager, Donor Services at VO, for telling me about the demonstration of the Figaro Simultext® System she and other staff and Board members attended recently at the Queen Elizabeth Theatre. This system was developed by Santa Fe Opera.

4. Shefsiek also points out that the set facility is not entirely devoted to POV's needs. Other arts groups hire its expertise in set creation, and the company makes its opera sets available to other companies for rental.

5. Iain Scott, "Leading Questions on the Future of Opera in Canada."

6. The 700 associate composers of the CMC include those no longer living. Of the 110 listed as associate composers in BC, 90 are living and many are active in writing opera. See www.musiccentre.ca.

7. Coulthard's opera was begun in 1956 but not completed until 1979. It was performed in concert form in 1993 but has never been staged.

8. For an interesting article on artistic collaboration in opera composition, see Tim Christian's "Kindred Spirits," *Opera Canada,* Jan/Feb 2007, 26.

9. The installation venue was the Scotiabank Dance Centre at 677 Davie Street.

10. At the time of writing, *Lillian Alling* is in the workshop phase of development.

11. The Old Aud is the old auditorium, one of UBC's original buildings. It houses a 600-seat theatre, which Hermiston says will be a "little gem" when it is

done over. The building is being renovated under the UBC Renew program, an initiative jointly funded by UBC and the BC Ministry of Advanced Education and Labour Market Development. Construction began May 2008 and will be completed in 2010; the renovation will extend the life of the building by at least forty years.

12. Burritt's opera is based on Timothy Findley's book *Pilgrim,* a novel that delves into the world of schizophrenia. The original librettist was Christopher Allan; the revised libretto and additional material are by Don Mowatt.

13. Agler and Judith Forst were extremely helpful to Hermiston when she first arrived in Vancouver, knowing no one else.

14. The play is thought to be the first appearance of the Faust legend. For more information, see Janet Danielson's lecture, March 23, 2004, on the website of the Graduate and Faculty Christian Forum at UBC, gfcf-ubc.ca/archive_2003_2004.htm.

15. Third-year School of Music student, Simone Osborne, and UBC School of Music graduate, Rhoslyn Jones, were semifinalists in the Metropolitan Opera National Council Auditions in New York. Osborne was one of the five winners in the final competition on February 17, 2008.

16. Meek is a well-known tenor who has performed in Germany and with most of the opera companies in Canada. He left a teaching post at UBC's School of Music to join the Academy faculty in 2001.

17. Butterfield once attended the University of Victoria and the Victoria Conservatory of Music, before obtaining a scholarship to study voice performance at McGill University. After graduation, he become renowned on the international operatic and concert stages.

18. Holliston gave up that position in 2007. The new POV Chorus Master is Michael Drislane.

19. The Victoria Conservatory of Music's Summer Vocal Academy

website is www.vcm.bc.ca/sva.html. All components of the program take place at the Victoria Conservatory of Music.

20. Read about the evolution of Burnaby Lyric Opera at www.burnabylyricopera.org/evolution.html. David Boothroyd, a veteran coach and rehearsal pianist for over twenty-five years, is the Music Director of Burnaby Lyric Opera. The Stage Director of the company, Matthew Bissett, has more than twelve years experience to his credit.

21. VIO's website is www.vancouverislandopera.com. The Artistic Director of Vancouver Island Opera is Tatiana Vasilieva, a retired star of the operatic stage, a recording artist and former member of the Canadian Opera Company, who later became a successful director. The company's Music Director is Gerald van Wyck.

22. Opera Appassionata website: www.operaappassionata.org.

23. It was mentioned in Malcolm Parry's column in the *Vancouver Sun* on February 23, 2008, and was the subject of a feature article in the *Vancouver Province* on February 17, 2008. Opera Pro Cantanti website is www.operaprocantanti.com.

24. Barber was born, brought up and educated on Vancouver Island before getting a PhD at Stanford University in California. After a twenty-year career in music in the States, he returned to BC. Tom Durrie is the former manager of the Pacific Baroque Orchestra, and the founder of the Save the York Theatre Task Force.

SELECTED RESOURCES

INTERVIEWS

Barber, Dr. Charles, Conductor and Artistic Director, City Opera Vancouver; February 26, 2008, Vancouver. Tape recording.

Corrigan, Patrick, Director of Marketing and Development, Pacific Opera Victoria; February 26, 2007.

Cosar, Bette, chorus member, Vancouver Opera; October 4, 2006, Vancouver. Tape recording.

Danielson, Janet, composer; March 8, 2008, by telephone.

Goldsmith, June, Director, Music in the Morning; April 4, 2008, by telephone.

Guttman, Irving, Artistic Director Emeritus, Vancouver Opera; September 12, 2006, Vancouver. Tape recording. And July 28, 2007, by telephone.

Hareid, Bjorn, patron and former member, Vancouver Opera Board of Directors; October 17, 2006, West Vancouver. Tape recording.

Hareid, Lori, patron and volunteer, Vancouver Opera; October 17, 2006, West Vancouver. Tape recording.

Heffelfinger, Jane, founding Board member, patron and volunteer, Pacific Opera Victoria; February 26, 2007, Victoria. Tape recording.

Heller, Edwina, founding Board member, Vancouver Opera Association; August 18, 2006, Vancouver. Tape recording.

Hermiston, Nancy, singer and Head of Voice and Opera Division, UBC School of Music; February 8, 2008, Vancouver. Tape recording.

Hutchinson, Kate, Artistic Director, Modern Baroque Opera; October 2, 2007, Vancouver. Tape recording.

Kelly, Dr. Nora, President, Board of Directors, City Opera Vancouver; February 26, 2008, Vancouver. Tape recording.

King, Sharman, musician and founding member, Vancouver Opera Orchestra; August 30, 2007, Vancouver. Tape recording.

Klassen, Frank, Conductor and Artistic Director, Opera Appassionata; February 16, 2008, by telephone.

Kurth, Erika, founding Board member and patron, Pacific Opera Victoria; February 27, 2007, Victoria.

Lemon, David, former Board member, Vancouver Opera Association; June 7, 2007, Vancouver. Tape recording.

LePage, Susan, volunteer, Vancouver Opera; November 6, 2006.

Magnanensi, Giorgio, Artistic Director, Vancouver New Music; December 11, 2007, Vancouver. Tape recording.

Mahon, Kenneth, former Chairman, Board of Directors, Vancouver Opera; December 5, 2007, Vancouver. Tape recording.

Mathisen, Peggy, volunteer, former Board member and patron, Vancouver Opera Association; September 13, 2006, Vancouver. Tape recording.

McIntosh, Nicolette, former Board member, Vancouver Opera Association; March 22, 2007, Bowen Island. Tape recording.

Meek, David, Head of Voice/Opera Division, Vancouver Academy of Music; March 26, 2008. Tape recording.

Miles, Colin, musician and Regional Director, Canadian Music Centre; January 24, 2008, Vancouver. Tape recording.

Shefsiek, David, Executive Director, Pacific Opera Victoria; February 20, 2008, Victoria. Tape recording.

Thomson-Price, Heather, singer, teacher, Voice and Opera Division, UBC School of Music; September 17, 2007. Tape recording.

Tuck, Doug, Director, Marketing and Community Programs, Vancouver Opera; December 13, 2007, Vancouver. Tape recording.

Vasilieva, Tatiana, Artistic Director, Vancouver Island Opera; February 7, 2008, by telephone.

Vernon, Timothy, Conductor and Artistic Director, Pacific Opera Victoria; July 18, 2007, Victoria. Tape recording.

White, Mary, former Board member, Vancouver Opera Association; September 7, 2006.

Wright, James, General Director, Vancouver Opera; November 29, 2007, Vancouver. Tape recording.

PRIMARY SOURCES

Pacific Opera Victoria. Board of Directors. *Minutes,* August 15, 1966.
——— . *President's Report to the Annual General Meeting.* November 23, 1994.
——— . *President's Report to the Annual General Meeting.* November 28, 1996.
Special Collections, Vancouver Public Library.
Vancouver Opera Association. *Annual Report of the President.* 1961–79. Vancouver Public Library, 782.05 V22a.
——— . *Consolidated Financial Statements.* Vancouver Public Library, 782.05 V22c.
——— . Fonds. City of Vancouver Archives, Add. MSS 464.
——— . Vertical files. Fine Arts Division, Vancouver Public Library.
Vancouver Opera House. City of Vancouver Archives, PAM 1911-33.

SECONDARY SOURCES

André, Martin. "Notes from the Conductor." *La Traviata: A Special Edition of Playboard Magazine.* BC: Archway Publishers, 1983, 9.
Arthur, Desmond. "Carmen Survives Moment of Truth." *Vancouver Sun,* April 4, 1960.
Barber, James. "Operatic Magician Crafts One Hell of a Faust." *Georgia Straight,* October 26, 1995.
——— . "Heather Thomson was unbelievably perfect in the role." *Vancouver Province,* February 21, 1969.
Becker, John. *Discord: The Story of the Vancouver Symphony Orchestra.* Vancouver: Brighouse Press, 1989.
——— . "Finding Fear's Musical Language." *Georgia Straight,* March 18–25, 1988.
Bligh, Stanley. "Opera Guild in Triumph Again." *Vancouver Sun,* January 21, 1938.
——— . "Time Opportune Now to Start Grand Opera Here." *Vancouver Sun,* March 30, 1957.
——— . "La Traviata Production Best in Past Three Decades Here." *Vancouver Sun,* May 5, 1961.
Burnaby Lyric Opera. http://www.burnabylyricopera.org.
Calgary Opera. http://www.calgaryopera.com.
Canadian Music Centre, British Columbia. http://www.musiccentre.ca/bri.cfm.

Canadian Opera Company. http://www.coc.ca.

Chamberlain, Adrian. "Opera revival well worth the effort." *Times Colonist* (Victoria), sec. E, February 17, 1996.

Chatelin, Ray. "Aida is a Triumph." *Vancouver Province*, April 28, 1989.

———. "Ambitious new operas next season." *Vancouver Province*, December 13, 1974.

———. "Kopernikus boils with symbolism." *Vancouver Province*, sec. FA, September 30, 1990.

———. "Opera." In *The Greater Vancouver Book: An Urban Encyclopedia*, edited by Chuck Davis, 688–89. Surrey, BC: Linkman Press, 1977.

———. "A powerhouse of sensation." *Vancouver Province*, sec. FA, October 2, 1988.

———. "Sour note to Vancouver's opera brass." *Vancouver Province*, October 26, 1974.

Dafoe, Christopher. "Arcifanfano is an opera fool's paradise." *Vancouver Sun*, sec. D, May 7, 1999.

———. "The little opera house that grew." *Globe and Mail*, sec. C, February 19, 1994.

———. "Tenor plays Victoria for a song: Homecoming Richard Margison waives his fee to sing Verdi at the Pacific Opera this week." *Globe and Mail*, sec. C, August 7, 1998.

Docherty, Ian. "Sounds of a Century." *Vancouver Province*, October 4, 1971.

Down, Susan. "Opera Verismo!" *Times Colonist* (Victoria), sec. D, October 11, 2001.

Dykk, Lloyd. "They got the pain part right." *Vancouver Sun*, sec. 3, March 5, 2002.

———. "Timely opera necessarily naive—and naively necessary." *Vancouver Sun*, sec. C, June 25, 1994.

———. "Uzan and Damonte spit at Carmen's fire and put it out entirely." *Vancouver Sun*, sec. C, February 5, 1996.

Eaton, Quaintance. "Ladies on the Loose." *Opera News*, October 23, 1965, 32–34.

Encyclopedia of Music in Canada. Edited by Helmut Kallman, Gilles Polvin, and Kenneth Winters. Toronto: University of Toronto Press, 1992.

Evans, Chad. *Frontier Theatre*. Victoria: Sono Nis Press, 1983.

"First Opera House Opened, February 9, 1891." Unidentified publication, April 23, 1925. City of Vancouver Archives, MS 15.669-2.

Gillanders, David E. "Message from the President." *Faust: A special edition of Playboard Magazine*. Richmond, BC: Archway Publishers, 1995, 4.

Godfrey, Stephen. "Boos and bravos for shocking Carmen." *Globe and Mail*, sec. A, May 6, 1986.

———. "This Magic Flute is out of tune." *Globe and Mail*, sec. A, March 12, 1986.

———. "Vancouver Opera stages glorious Eugene Onegin." *Globe and Mail*, sec. FA, March 11, 1985.

Grout, Donald J. *A History of Western Music*. New York: W.W. Norton, 1960.

———. *A Short History of Opera*. New York: Columbia University Press, 1988.

Grout, Donald J., and Hermine Weigel Williams. *A Short History of Opera*. New York: Columbia University Press, 2003.

The Grove Book of Operas. Edited by Stanley Sadie. Oxford: Oxford University Press, 2006.

Guthrie, Tyrone. *Report to the Vancouver Festival Society, July 20, 1955*. Community Arts Council Fonds, City of Vancouver Archives, Add. MSS 301.

Hart's Opera House. Major Matthews Collection. City of Vancouver Archives, BU. P. 691 N585.

H.M.S. Pinafore program. Hart's Opera House. City of Vancouver Archives, PAM 1888-5.

Inouye, Derrick. "Conductor's Notes." *The Magic Flute: A special edition of Playboard Magazine*. BC: Archway Publishers 2007, 12.

Jordan, Robert. "Opera Explores Theme of Alienation." *Georgia Straight*, sec. FA, January 27, 1995.

———. "A Trovatore dull to behold but lovely to listen to." *Globe and Mail*, sec. R, May 1, 2000.

Juch history. http://www.juch.net/ferlach.htm.

Kana, Reet, ed. *25 Years: Vancouver Opera Guild*. Vancouver Opera Guild, 2005.

Kennedy, James. "Ominous and grand." *Monday Magazine*, September 20–26, 1984, 13–14.

———. "Smoke and Mirrors." *Monday Magazine*, October 2–8, 1986, 14.

———. "Voices and pits." *Monday Magazine*, October 1–7, 1987, 15.

Lascelles, George H.H. *Opera in Canada: A Report by the Earl of Harewood*. The Ontario Arts Council and the Canada Council, 1972.

Library and Archives Canada. "History of Opera Performance in Canada." http://www.collectionscanada.gc.ca/gramophone/m2-3020-e.html.

Macdonald, Marjorie. "Vancouver Opera Celebrates 30 Years!" *Westworld*, Spring 1990, 30.

Matthews, J.S. Notes, September 20, 1963. City of Vancouver Archives, Add. MSS 15.669-2.

Matz, Mary Jane. *Opera: Grand and Not So Grand*. New York: William Morrow, 1966.

McIntosh, Robert Dale. *A Documentary History of Music in Victoria, British Columbia, Vol. 1: 1850–1899*. Victoria: University of Victoria, 1981.

———. *A Documentary History of Music in Victoria, British Columbia, Vol. 2: 1900–1950*. Victoria: Beach Holme, 1994.

———. *History of Music in British Columbia, 1850–1950*. Victoria: Sono Nis Press, 1989.

McQueen, Robert. "Director's Notes." *The Magic Flute: A special edition of Playboard Magazine*. Richmond, BC: Archway Publishers, 2007, 11.

Miles, Colin, ed. *Canadian Operas: An Annotated Catalogue of Operas and Staged Vocal Works by Canadian Composers in the Canadian Music Centre*. Toronto: Canadian Music Centre, 1999.

Munro, Ivan. "A Storm of Applause." *Monday Magazine*, February 19–25, 2004, 16.

The New Kobbe's Opera Book. Edited by the Earl of Harewood and Antony Peattie. New York: G.P. Putnam's Sons, 1997.

Noteriety: News and Information for Pacific Opera Victoria Subscribers, n.d.

Obe, Don. "Opera Off. So's Everything Else." *Vancouver Sun*, October 18, 1961.

Opera Appassionata. http://www.operaappassionata.org.

Opera.ca. http://www.opera.ca.

"Opera House Opened." *The World*, February 10, 1891. City of Vancouver Archives, MS 15.669-1.

Opera Pro Cantanti. http://www.operaprocantanti.com.

Opera Today: www.operatoday.com/content/2004/10/deborah_voigt_w.php. Vancouver Opera *News Release*, March 24, 2006.

Pacific Opera Victoria. "Message from the President." *Tosca* program, April 2005.

Portman, Jamie. "Operatic tantrums out; Director seeks solid performance." *Edmonton Journal*, sec. E, October 6, 1989.

Powell River Academy of Music. http://www.powellriveracademy.org.

Prince George Conservatory of Music. http://www.pgconservatory.ca.

reviewVancouver. http://www.reviewvancouver.org.

Richards, Jerry. "Opera Buffa or Opera Ragtime?" *Times Colonist* (Victoria), October 20, 1995.

Rowe, Dan. "Loving Elektra." *Vancouver Sun*, sec. D, March 20, 2003.

San Carlo Opera Company. Programs. City of Vancouver Archives, PAM 1920-32; PAM 1934-83; Und. 322; PAM 1936-187; PAM 1938-151; PAM 1940-137; PAM 1944-122.

Scott, Iain. "Leading Questions on the Future of Opera in Canada." *Opera Canada*, October 2003, 6–7.

Scott, Michael. "Alcina production a triumph for Mostart." *Vancouver Sun*, sec. B, October 29, 1990.

——. "Heppner fishes for right approach to Peter Grimes: B.C. tenor takes title role in difficult Britten opera." *Vancouver Sun*, sec. C, January 26, 1995.

——. "New chamber opera a gem of inventiveness." *Vancouver Province*, sec. D, October 7, 1989.

——. "Star Catalogues form stunning musical constellation." *Vancouver Sun*, sec. C, October 24, 1994.

——. "Vancouver music lovers heard much to adore in 1994." *Vancouver Sun*, sec. C, December 29, 1994.

Shields, Roy. "Discordant notes at the Vancouver Opera." *Edmonton Journal*, November 23, 1974.

Siemens, Yvonne. "How the set reflects the opera." *Peter Grimes: A special edition of Playboard Magazine*. Richmond, BC: Archway Publishers, 1995, 38–39.

Simon Fraser University. http://www.sfu.ca.

Somerset-Ward, Richard. *The Story of Opera*. New York: Abrams, 2006.

Stape, J.H. "Pacific Opera Victoria, Rape of Lucretia." *reviewVancouver*, www.reviewvancouver.org, February 2006.

——. "Raking them in." *reviewVancouver*, www.reviewvancouver.org, November 2000.

——. "Verdi's *Macbeth*." *reviewVancouver*, www.reviewvancouver.org, November 2006.

Sudlow, Dina. "The mouse that roared: Erewhon, a sort of Alice in Wonderland meets The Magic Flute, is a lyrical comedy created by cultural giants Mavor Moore and Louis Appelbaum." *Vancouver Sun*, sec. E, February 19, 2000.

Symcox, Peter. "Midsummer Night's Dream." *Monday Magazine*, May 18–24, 1993, 13–14.

"Thirty years ago." Unidentified source, February 22, 1939. City of Vancouver Archives clippings, MS 15.669-1.

Times Colonist (Victoria). "Grand production, real forest." Sec. A, October 2, 2005.

Todd, Richard. "A great leap ahead for Pacific Opera." *Monday Magazine*, February 29–March 6, 1980, 22.

——. "Hair's breadth success." *Monday Magazine*, September 21–27, 1979, 30–31.

La Traviata: A special edition of Playboard Magazine, March/April 1989, 9.

University of Victoria School of Music. Performance Program. http://finearts.uvic.ca/music/programs_undergrad/perform/index.html.

Vancouver Community College School of Music. http://music.vcc.ca.

Vancouver Festival Society. *Vancouver Festival Souvenir Anniversary Book*. Edited by Julia Switzer. Vancouver: Vancouver Festival Society, 1967.

Vancouver Foundation. http://www.vancouverfoundation.bc.ca.

Vancouver Island Opera. http://www.vancouverislandopera.com.

Vancouver New Music. *Fig Trees* program, 2007.

Vancouver Opera. *Vancouver Opera eNews*.

——. *Voices of The Magic Flute: A Brief History of Vancouver Opera's New Production*. Vancouver: Vancouver Opera, 2007.

——. http://www.vancouveropera.ca.

"Vancouver Opera Celebrates 30 Years." *Westworld*, Spring 1990, 30.

Vancouver Province. "Opera group in red." August 29, 1964.

Vancouver Sun Magazine Supplement. October 1, 1955, 7. CVA clippings, MS 15. 669-2.

Varty, Alexander. "*Gang* Proves Fear Can Be Sexy." *Georgia Straight*, June 12–19, 1997, 53.

Vernon, Timothy. "A message from the Artistic Director." Pacific Opera Victoria *The Barber of Seville* program, 2001–02 season.

Victoria Conservatory of Music, Opera Studio. http://www.vcm.bc.ca/opera/index.html.

——. Summer Vocal Academy. http://www.vcm.bc.ca/summervocal/index.html.

VOA: Vancouver Opera Association, 1960–1975. Vancouver: Rothmans of Pall Mall Canada Limited, c. 1975.

Von Westerman, Gerhart. *Opera Guide*. Edited by Harold Rosenthal. Translated by Anne Ross. London: Sphere Books, 1968.

VO VOICE: A news magazine for Vancouver Opera subscribers and donors. Vancouver: Vancouver Opera.

Wasserman, Jack. "Tuney Types." *Vancouver Sun*, February 24, 1965.

Watmough, David. *The Unlikely Pioneer: Building Opera from the Pacific through the Prairies*. Oakville: Mosaic Press, 1986.

Weinman, Jaime J. "It's not over 'til the slim lady sings." *Maclean's*, November 12, 2007, 63.

Wyman, Max. "Light cast on the human comedy." *Vancouver Sun*, February 18, 1972.

——. "Traviata—a last, grand, glorious Guttman opera." *Vancouver Sun*, April 26, 1974.

——. "Richard Bonynge brooks no interference—none!" *Vancouver Sun*, May 9, 1975.

Zubrinic, Darko. "Croatian Classical Music." http://www.croatianhistory.net/etf/et12a.html.

Bravo!

INDEX